Dry Lands: Man and Plants

Robert Adams
Marina Adams
Alan Willens
Ann Willens

ST. MARTIN'S PRESS · NEW YORK

Acknowledgments

It is never possible to thank everyone who has been connected in some way with the preparation of a book: this book is no exception. But there are those who have considerably influenced us, and of the many people to whom we have spoken, Dr. John Hepworth, of the Institute of Geological Sciences, and Dr. Amos Richmond and Dr. D. Pasternak, of the Ben-Gurion University of the Negev, gave us, through their knowledge, a richer understanding of the desert environment. Sadly, it has proved quite impossible to use all the materials, references and contacts they kindly suggested to us.

We have consulted many books in the preparation of this work, and we would like to record our particular appreciation of *Deserts of the World*, edited by W. G. McGinnies, Bram J. Goldman and Patricia Paylore (University of Arizona Press, 1968). Apparently little known in Europe, this book has proved an invaluable source of information, ideas and references. We would like to thank Patricia Paylore individually for her kind interest and prompt despatch of information.

Especial mention must be made of Renée Kemp, Elizabeth Walters and John Randall: Renée Kemp for typing, reading and researching the various manuscripts countless times, offering so much sensible advice; Elizabeth Walters for help in setting up the filing system which subsequently guided the book onto new ground; and John Randall for acting as a sounding-board throughout. No recompense is possible for their 'behind the scenes' work, only our heartfelt thanks. Our thanks are similarly due to Minster Agriculture and its staff for their co-operation and support in typing and for the use of their library. We would like to give particular thanks to Dr. John Meadley of Minster for his helpful comments and advice. We are grateful also to the various individuals and organisations who kindly provided photographs for the book and who are named in the captions to the photographs concerned.

There are however many people whose ideas have been absorbed, and whose names now elude us. From these people, we ask forgiveness. There are too all those whose books we have browsed through and not remembered. To those authors too we apologise for failing to refer to their works in the bibliography.

We cannot end our acknowledgments without mentioning Godfrey Golzen, for without his clearheadedness this work would undoubtedly have stumbled. For this service we will remain forever appreciative.

Printed in Great Britain
Library of Congress Catalog Card Number 78-65219
ISBN 0-132-22042-1

First published in the United States of America in 1979

Contents

Preface

In 1977, several British newspapers carried a series of advertisements placed by the charitable organization OXFAM (Oxford Committee for Famine Relief) that called attention to the 'chilling statistic that 400 million people in the world are seriously undernourished . . .'.

Quite clearly, in the less well-developed countries, standards of nutrition must be established to ensure the survival of man and animals, before any expansion of consumer commodities can be considered.

Man has two priceless assets at his disposal: the earth, with its climate, vegetation, natural resources and multiplicity of ecosystems; and himself, to provide labour and technical skills. Difficulties only arise when the balance is upset by such disturbing elements as climate variation, soil erosion, people living where there is no work, natural resources being rapidly over-exploited, or where by-products that harm both man and land are generated.

It is so often forgotten that man, like plants, animals, birds and insects, is a member of the Earth's ecosystem, and is separated from the other members only by his powers of logic and reason. By using these abilities, he can force changes on his environment, although he seldom appreciates that he will, sooner or later, be affected by his activities. In future, man may well have to be prepared to change, or even to evolve and develop adaptation techniques, like other living things, in order to survive, otherwise he will have to use increasing volumes of non-renewable resources to support his standard of living.

During the course of this century, we have seen the disappearance of too many species of plants, animals, birds and insects, because of unequal competition—usually with man. Every year, more species become endangered, and it is rapidly becoming a question whether mankind will be next. Will the Australian Aborigines or the Kalahari bushmen be the next to vanish? Or perhaps it will be the people of the Sahel, or the East African Masai.

If action is taken now, and man is taught to become aware again of the earth and all its life-forces, he may yet learn to co-exist successfully with all the ecosystem members, and in this way lay the foundation for a richer future. If he ignores these essentials, the poorer people of the world may be condemned to sink without trace.

Realistically speaking, the Earth is man's only natural resource, and the only one he will ever have. If our activities eventually bring about our disappearance, the Earth will not care. Environmentally, we are at the crossroads: one way leads towards effective international co-operation in the conservation and proper management of the resources of this planet; the other leads to a break-up into protectionist, self-interested groups. We have the ability to exploit the Earth's resources sensibly for the general good of all mankind, and whether or not we take up this challenge and ensure that all peoples get a fair share of the cake, our decisions will be reflected in the quality of our future and that of our children and all the generations to follow. We still have some influence, fortunately, on the shape of things to come, and that influence is vital to the survival of so many presently endangered peoples, and ultimately to us all. Let it be beneficial.

1 Introduction

DRY LANDS AND THEIR ECOLOGY

The significance of the world's vast areas of dry land can only be appreciated when it is realized that over a quarter of the Earth's land surface is either arid or semi-arid. Although most deserts lie between 15° and 35° north and south latitudes, the dry lands, including the desert fringe lands, extend to lie predominantly between the tropics of Cancer and Capricorn.

These lands may vary in extent and character, but in essence, whether they are located in Africa, America, Asia or Australia will not affect man's chances of survival. Furthermore, plants, animals, birds and insects must coexist and face the same problems of survival, and at the same time, they must also tolerate man.

In recent years, the greatest advance in environmental understanding is the appreciation that coexistence between all members of an ecosystem is vital to the perpetuation of that ecosystem. The botanist and plant ecologist have long been aware that plants at every stage in their development are part of a living, dynamic system which extends far around them, down into the earth and up into the air above them. The character of the climate and the nature of the soil provide stimuli to which the plants react, for each stimulus affects the manner in which the plant establishes, grows, flowers and produces seed, and thus influences the way, and often the ease, by which the plant perpetuates itself.

Understanding these processes, and the way they affect plant life and plant relationships, is easier in the temperate lands of the world, where plants grow more rapidly than they do in dry lands. When the climate is relatively wet, the soils are rich because the balance is in favour of increasing

Monument Valley Arizona
A clear demonstration of the precarious balance between man and land in desert areas. Man's efforts are tuned to the return he expects from the land
PHOTO: US INFORMATION SERVICE, LONDON

soil fertility. The changes within an ecosystem are recognizable simply because growth is there to be seen. However, plants in drier lands grow at a slower tempo and react more slowly to the natural stimuli, and because the climate is harsher, the soils are poorer and the balance goes against fertility. In fact, when the conditions dry-land plants have to contend with are studied, it is all the more remarkable that they manage to survive. They have managed to do so only by evolving very special, and sometimes extraordinarily elaborate, adaptations which enable them to exist. Growth is slow, evolution still slower, and plant regeneration potential suffers as a result.

The usual image of the natural desert environment is of a stable, but rather sterile environment, whose animation is apparently virtually suspended. Nevertheless, in spite of their barren appearance, which was responsible for the misconceptions about their fertility, the deserts of the world are lively ecological communities. As a rule, they support some life, although there are exceptions like the Great Salt Desert in Iran. Marco Polo, writing of this desert in his thirteenth-century *Description of the World*[1] said:

'There are no dwellings, everything is desert and great drought . . . There are no wild animals either, they would find nothing to eat, the earth is so dry and hard that grass could not grow. . . .'

As a true picture of all deserts, this is no longer acceptable, yet there remains remarkably little knowledge of how much life deserts can support, and old superstitions die hard. Even though most deserts are stable in area, they tend to expand and contract as the climate varies from one year to another, and although these variations are minute by comparison with the scale of the deserts, they occur on the peripheries and can affect many people who eke out a living in these fringe lands.

Types of arid land and their characteristics
Four grades of land can be distinguished within the dry-land zone: the extremely arid desert interior, the arid

Matilla Oasis Atacama Desert
Here in the Atacama Desert a fertile oasis contrasts strongly against the poor and pulverized desert soils surrounding it
PHOTO: ANGLO-CHILEAN SOCIETY, LONDON, EDMUNDO STOCKINS SERIES

regions, the desert fringe and the semi-arid lands often surrounding all the others. Each is clearly defined, primarily by its climatic pattern, then by its soils, these two factors combining to set controls for vegetation establishment and subsequently for any life which exploits it.

The interiors are almost completely devoid of any life, because of the high degree of aridity, the very low rainfall, the extremes of temperature and solar radiation during the day, followed often by cool or cold nights giving a wide diurnal temperature range. There is a virtual absence of water, whether in the air or in the ground, as rain falls so seldom, even over a 12 month cycle. Soils are very primitive, loose rocks or sand, and are very susceptible to weathering and erosion. Cloud cover is almost nil and evaporation rates can exceed 3 metres in a year. It is no surprise that these areas are the most hostile in the world, and are of little immediate functional value to man.

The arid zones which surround the extremely arid habitat are distinguished by a marginal improvement in climate stimulating a richer soil and denser vegetation cover, which, though significantly greater than in the desert interiors, is still extremely sparse. Temperature and radiation extremes are still a common feature, and rainfall is low, coming usually as thunderstorms causing floods. The soils are poor, but in certain locations where sand collects or is protected from weathering and erosion, plants are found growing and completing their life cycles. The surface of the land is still loose and rocky, sometimes bare rock, but moisture levels in the soil are higher because evaporation extremes are less intense. Humidity in the air is higher and dew is a valuable addition to the total volume of water available.

The desert fringes, on the borders of the arid and semi-arid zones, have a similar improvement in climate, soils and

vegetation over the arid regions, but cannot be classified with either the arid or semi-arid zones, because they are subject to shifts in climate, varying between drier and wetter years. In good years, they support a vegetation cover similar to that carried by semi-arid lands, and during those periods have an important potential for grazing and for fuel timber. If these exploitative pressures continue during poor years, the vegetation cover is rapidly eliminated by man or beasts, plant roots no longer bind the soil surface, erosive forces increase, and the soil disintegrates and becomes arid in character. These lands are exceptionally vulnerable, and if climatic changes are not adequately appreciated, serious deterioration of the ecosystems will occur.

The semi-arid lands contain the only dry-land ecosystems where a regular, though still comparatively low, rainfall can be expected. Temperatures, radiation and evaporation rates are low enough to encourage a permanent flora, and therefore a sustained, but limited, economic potential can be achieved. Soils are well-structured, and provided the balance between man, animals and land remains undisturbed, they can be successfully exploited. The surface soil is held firmly by plant roots, making it less susceptible to erosion, and the plants shade the soil, thereby lowering surface temperatures and radiation. Humidity levels are higher, both in the ground and in the air. The soils, being better structured, hold greater volumes of water, thus enabling a wide range of vegetation to be established. More intensive exploitation can be supported, but, because rainfall is scanty and a hot climate prevails, these areas are still vulnerable to any activity which promotes over-use, with the consequent danger of stripping the land bare, and forcing a regression towards the arid-type ecosystem.

DESERT EXPANSION AND ITS CAUSES

There are two schools of thought about the mysteries of the expanding deserts: either the changes are due entirely to climatic variation, or man is the cause, independently of the

Top : **Death Valley California**
A hostile land
PHOTO : US INFORMATION SERVICE, LONDON
Below : **Iquique, Chile**
The very low rainfall is inadequate to support such large plants—it is clearly evident that dew forms a significant water resource
PHOTO : ANGLO-CHILEAN SOCIETY, LONDON, EDMUNDO STOCKINS SERIES

climate or in association with its variations. Accurate data from palaeoclimatology is still sparse, but fossil dunes have been found well beyond the present-day desert limits, for instance in Nigeria and Botswana, which must surely indicate major climatic fluctuations in the past. However, until these phenomena can be accurately linked to palaeoclimatic variations, it must be assumed that man is the most common cause, sometimes in combination with climatic variations but generally on his own.

The history of the origin, development and expansion of certain of the 'true' deserts, such as the Arabic-Sinai, the Central Sahara, the Libya–Egyptian, the Namib, the Atacama and the Western Australian, is known through records and archaeology. Their aridity has always been far too severe to have been significantly altered by man.

On the other hand, the development of other dry-land areas is less defined. Major fluctuations in climate over the last 20,000 years have played an important role, and the responses man has made to them can be seen in the different cultures and life-styles he adopted to suit his changing circumstances.

Pressure from climate

None of the climatic variations appears to have formed part of predictable cyclical trends, so far as we understand them

Top : **Turkmen, USSR**
Land denuded by the herding of Karakul sheep. Such tracks should be moved annually to allow the regeneration of vegetation so that erosion is prevented
PHOTO: NOVOSTI PRESS AGENCY, LONDON
Left : **Kalahari Desert**
Continuous grazing has left the land bereft of vegetation. The hoofprints of animals in the foreground prove the numbers trying to find grazing PHOTO: SATOUR, LONDON
Below : **Kalahari Desert, Botswana**
Fossil dunes seen from the air support the theory that the desert front has fluctuated in the past, caused more likely by climatic changes than by overgrazing PHOTO: DR. J. HEPWORTH

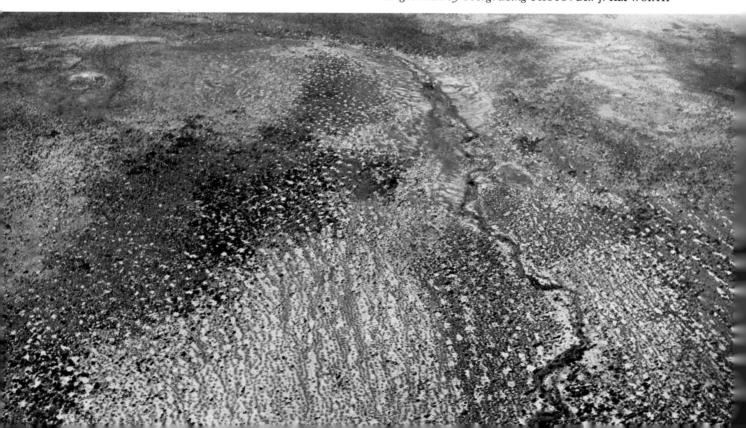

at present. The minor climatic shifts experienced in recent years have caused drought and famine, and have added to the consternation that the creeping deserts are further encroaching on cultivable land. Whether these shifts are temporary or represent a long-term change in climate is still debatable. The theory that these are temporary fluctuations is supported by studies of rainfall records, which show no systematic long-term patterns of rainfall variation.

The opposite opinion is held in particular by Bryson, and also Lamb, Leroux and Winstanley: they contend that an expansion of cold air from the poles causes a shift of the major high pressure belts towards the equator, thus limiting the extent to which the equatorial moist air can progress over the tropics. If the anti-cyclones do not move as far polewards as is usual in summer, the dry desert areas move closer to the equator as the monsoonal rains become less extensive and reliable. Temperature trends in Iceland and over the North Atlantic, the frequency of droughts in India and the patterns of monsoon rains and frosts are cited as evidence. Undoubtedly, there is a great need to extend and improve climatic theory, to test for example the latest ideas of correlating climatic variations with sun-spot activity.

A more precise prediction of long-term climatic trends will help to maintain the high-technology agriculture needed to support larger world populations. Should climatic change be thought inevitable, the creation of more flexible systems of food production, independent of complex inputs of energy and capital, would be very advantageous.

The progress of desert expansion is now being charted

Great Salt Desert, Iran
A small caravan skirting the Dasht-e-Kavir, one of the least known and most hostile environments in the world
PHOTO: C. V. MALCOLM

by satellite imagery and aerial photography. Although desert margins fluctuate, current thinking is that the recent droughts, particularly in the Kalahari and the Saharan Sahel, have only caused devastating losses of livestock and vegetation because over the preceding years of good rainfall, herds had been considerably enlarged as a result of the parallel increase in available vegetation for fodder.

Human pressures on productive land
Productive land, at whatever stage of efficiency, has always been under increasing pressure from man. The never-ending demand for food forces agriculture to expand further and further into those areas where man only managed to survive by keeping in precarious balance with nature. The size of the indigenous populations was regulated by a death rate, due to disease, starvation or tribal warfare, which balanced the birth rate, keeping the population size stable. The rapid expansion of improved medical services has decreased deaths from disease; international aid programmes have reduced the level of starvation artificially by supplying food from outside the areas's natural abilities to produce it, thus overriding the laws of supply and demand; and improved law enforcement and tribal settling programmes have reduced the numbers of deaths caused by feuding and warfare. These three factors combined have produced a population explosion, exerting further pressure on food production and demand.

Taking as an example the nomadic pastoralists of the Sahel region, south of the Sahara, it can be seen that in the favourable years of the late 1950s and early 1960s, the sizes of herds considerably increased. When the series of severe droughts of the late 1960s and early 1970s came, the ecosystem could no longer support the larger animal population, and consequently the people were put at great risk. In spite of well-intentioned aid programmes which provided funds for drilling large new wells to supply the

water vital for the herds, no-one anticipated that the wells would act as such magnets, attracting vast herds of cattle, which then proceeded to eat and trample all the existing vegetation for hundreds of square kilometres around the wells. Thousands of animals died, not of thirst but of starvation.[2]

Farmers of the more productive areas of the world are having to face similar problems. The continuing development and expansion of irrigation projects is putting increasing strains on the known water resources, as can be seen in various areas of the Kingdom of Saudi Arabia, the United Arab Emirates, Texas in the U.S.A., and in Libya. Such large volumes of water have been extracted that the water-tables are falling rapidly, by as much as a metre a year in some areas. As the water level drops, so the salt content rises, and then as the saltier water is reached it is less easily usable. Quite apart from this, a falling water-table indicates that underground water-storing rock aquifers are being depleted faster than they are able to recharge, a point of truly sinister significance.

Furthermore, even though the costs of irrigation system installation and maintenance are rising, not enough attention is being paid to the results of inaccurate supply methods, or the use of poorer quality water. Fertile soils, even desert sands, can become water-logged through inadequate attention to drainage, and the combination of high temperatures and low atmospheric humidity means that all water on or near the surface rapidly evaporates, leaving salt crystals on the surface of the soil. Eventually these become mixed with the soil, leaving it saline. It was this sort of lack of forethought and knowledge that eventually contributed to the disintegration of the great Mesopotamian Empire, which was based on artificial irrigation from the waters of the Tigris and Euphrates rivers.

However, many countries, like the Sudan, have begun to

Niger

The first stage in overgrazing is the elimination of the sub-vegetation which leads directly to the pulverization of the soil surface

PHOTO: D. OSTLE

appreciate the problems associated with expanding rural and subsequently urban populations and meeting the increasing food requirements. Nevertheless, it remains, sadly, the general rule that as populations grow so the landscape becomes progressively more impoverished through the depletion of resources caused by over-grazing and over-cropping. Thus, more and more land is gradually taken out of the food cycle, exposing yet more land to the risk of deterioration. It is still not sufficiently realized that conservation of the environment's natural resources is the only way of ensuring the survival of more people and larger herds.

The case for restoring and conserving resources

The following question must be answered: 'Is it sensible to put so much effort and money into the creation of new environments where the terrain, the climate and often the people are so hostile?' If it is remembered that it is over a quarter of the Earth's land surface, which, although arid and vulnerable, is at stake, and should be used to its fullest potential, the answer must be 'Yes'. Man dares not ignore these vast and basically untouched lands any longer. Their conservation and development can only be achieved with the application of new technologies, even though there may be difficulties in finding those that are in harmony with the limitations of the existing landscape.

Once this is agreed, all that is required is to identify the potential and then to establish the best method of achieving it. Although there are cases where this has been accomplished in the past, it has too often been at the expense of

Timimoun Oasis, Algeria

This old settlement has long been in balance with nature. The whale-back dune above the settlement is stable, otherwise the oasis would have been engulfed long ago

PHOTO: ALGERIAN INFORMATIVE SERVICE, LONDON

soil and plants, and when the climate has deteriorated, and the population of man and more particularly his animals has remained the same, the conditions are then ripe for desertification—the expansion of deserts—spreading into the fringe-lands and semi-arid regions.

Desertification can be seen in almost every desert region. The Kalahari Desert in southern Africa achieved its vast size through over-grazing activities, encouraged and promoted by man. Such man-made deserts are also known as 'false' deserts. Another is the Sahel region, especially in the Sudan, where over-grazing has permanently transformed hundreds of thousands of hectares of semi-desert to desert, in the zone between 14° and 16° north.[1] Further examples are seen in northern Kenya, Somalia and Ethiopia. In the Pakistan highlands, whole hillsides have been grazed bare, or overcropped for timber.[3]

It is because so many inhabitants of these impoverished lands are now at serious risk that desertification has attracted such close attention. The combination of erratic rainfall and poor soils, exacerbated by high temperatures, solar radiation and evaporation, forces people to persist in expanding their herds (i.e. their wealth) as best they can, with little or no thought as to what effects such a custom will have on their land or their community. Drought forces the herds to seek further afield for fodder. The palatable plant species are consumed and eventually eliminated, leaving only the extremely unpalatable species, which then multiply rapidly, in the absence of competition. In the meanwhile, spaces open up between the remaining plants, and under the impact of the sun, extreme temperatures and

wind, the surface soil disintegrates into particles of dust and sand. These are picked up by the wind and blown away, and the larger fragments left behind are not a fertile medium for plant colonization, so the land is left barren.

On the other hand, some countries have made notable progress in wresting valuable land from 'worthless' desert. In the United States of America, large-scale management of water resources and water distribution has enabled large areas of desert to be converted to productive land. China, Russia and India have likewise made substantial advances in reclaiming large areas, as have also Algeria, Iraq, Israel and Iran.

The secret of restoration and the conservation of resources lies in balancing the relationship between the availability of water and its efficiency of use by both man and plants. Rural communities understand this balance and constantly endeavour to preserve it. They settle around a source of water, wherever there is cultivable land, as for example around an oasis. The land is planted or sown with food crops, and the livestock herds simply eat what they can find on the outskirts. Such a system is self-regulating, depending solely on the natural balances. Man used the areas of differing intensities of aridity in different ways depending always on the amount of water and vegetation available. The deep desert interiors could support only a very few communities and these were small and nomadic in style, always following the rains or keeping to the trade routes. Their impact on the desert was always restricted.

However, whenever water is plentiful, as it sometimes is in the desert fringelands and the semi-arid areas, devastations to the arid ecosystem often occur, largely because of over-grazing, or over-extraction of water. The prestige of owning large herds, supported by aid in the form of boreholes to extract deep water, and the organisation of nomadic peoples into permanent settlements, all encourage an attitude which is completely out of balance with the natural carrying capacity of the land. The effects of such activities can be summarized as follows:[3]

1 The complete destruction of the indigenous flora, which is usually more pronounced on the desert fringes where annual crops are cultivated: the soil is left bare for part of the year, but should the rains fail, it can be barren for several years and erosion will start

2 The partial elimination of natural vegetation by cutting, grazing, etc: although this process is usually selective, it will cause a reduction of the total plant cover, a change in botanical composition, or a change in dominance

3 The influence of grazing on the total plant cover is intensified in the dry years, when many less palatable species, avoided as a rule in the normal years, are grazed

4 The selective destruction of the whole plant, or parts of the plant, will change plant population formations and inter-relationships: the removal of seeds, for example, will diminish the possibility of regeneration

5 Moderate grazing will partially thin out plants, stimulating any or all of the above results, and soil erosion is the usual consequence: once soil erosion has started, it is usually irreversible and it may eliminate the natural vegetation of an area forever

6 The instigation of uncontrolled or ill-advised activities can cause the expansion of deserts into regions that are not naturally deserts, and subsequently can often force a migration of people into less arid areas, and so the cycle is repeated continuously.

The drier the climate, the more difficult is the regeneration of plants, animals and soils, because reclamation techniques become increasingly more expensive. Large areas of alfalfa (lucerne) can support sheep in the depths of the Libyan Desert; in the U.S.A., Australia and Africa ranching provides food and a livelihood on the desert fringes. But Libya is using 'fossil water' laid down many thousands of years ago and not being replenished by the normal hydrological cycle. Ranching is now becoming beset by disease, loss of vegetation cover, and by shrinking water supplies.

MANAGEMENT OF RESOURCES AND RESTORATION

There are so many examples of the devastating effects of wasteful manipulation of natural resources and land, that new emphasis is being placed on examination of the patterns of survival and the qualities of self-regulating and self-sustaining rural communities. Instead of forcing the environment to accept major alterations that can only be sustained by continuous and costly maintenance, new methods are being sought, which will not be in conflict with the environment. Therefore, instead of submitting to the desert and ignoring its natural potential, the desert is being explored to see whether its resources can be exploited without long-term detriment to the ecosystems, and at the same time, efforts are being made to improve awareness and increase alertness to climatic fluctuations.

So far the emphasis has been on the development of rural areas, but it has not been restricted to them, or to

Komsomolabad State Farm, Uzbekistan Steppe
A new state farm in the USSR built to house people working on the newly-reclaimed virgin lands
PHOTO: NOVOSTI PRESS AGENCY, A. VORFOLOMEEV

agriculture. In the Middle East, Australia and Russia, new urban settlements are expanding, either in the desert or on its fringes. New landscapes, new parks and gardens are needed to enhance the environment. Many plants are required, and are often not available locally, especially in the Middle East. Formerly lack of knowledge of the native floras forced the importation of plants from the better-developed countries with similar climatic characteristics, rather than the more sensible technique of using plants that grow within the regional or parallel climatic zones. The comparatively recent science of phytogeography (plant geography) has identified such parallel regions, as well as the regions from which the plants originated. The recent shipment of 80,000 plants from Greece to Saudi Arabia should not have been allowed, as it is ecologically unsound practice, quite apart from the risk of an enormous failure rate. Surely practices of this kind demonstrate the need to expand research into indigenous flora?

If developments are planned to harmonize with the natural balances, the landscape will accept them. If for any reason the development intrudes and forces changes within the natural equilibrium, the environment will attempt to reject it, and return to its former state unless it is prevented from doing so by constant maintenance and supervision. Such 'suspension of ecological time' is extremely costly in terms of manpower and resources. It is not coincidental that examples of desertification come from some of the less rich countries, while those of conservation and restoration are from the 'super-powers', where most money, expertise and technology are available.

Means of identifying resources
The emphasis on the ways the environment is manipulated must change. Instead of forcing the environment to accept major alterations which can only be sustained by continuous and costly maintenance, new methods are being sought which the environment can intrinsically support. Instead of submitting to the desert and ignoring its natural resources, the attitude is to explore it to establish whether

its potential can be exploited, without long-term detriment to the ecosystem.

In order to do this, a great deal of research is still needed to classify deserts in detail, especially to identify plant communities and their ecology, and to recognize the stability of the various ecosystems. While many plants and their inter-relationships have been identified, there evidently are different approaches to deserts and their plant communities. Some authorities are efficient, others produce a minumum of useful information, in particular when dealing with the more valuable species. Land use planning eventually must cater for protected areas of indigenous vegetation, where plants can be studied under conditions as similar as possible to their place of origin, and which will eventually become the 'gene banks' of wild plants, so significant to the breeding of certain plants for desert and semi-arid conditions.

Many 'master plans' have been drawn up for urban development in arid lands, often concentrating only on human cultural and physical requirements, but as yet, few have registered the impact such developments will have on future land use and the natural potential of the area. New processes in learning and testing integrated approaches relating man's needs to site conditions and adapting them to the new situations that arise as a result are still being interpreted. Shortages in the supply of resources have promoted research into alternative energy sources, new settlement patterns and new cropping systems. Even religious and spiritual motivations are being taken into account. Although man has the ability to adapt to these new ideals, there will undoubtedly have to be a psychological revolution to bring people to the point of acceptance, for such ideals will deeply affect the structure of society and its aims for the future.

Conservation of resources

To bring about this psychological revolution will require profound changes in the methods of teaching, in particular an acceptance of environmental sciences, to create a better balance between sciences and arts throughout formal education. Above all, encouragement of flexible attitudes towards thought and practice, while allowing for spiritual attitudes, is essential so that alternative, simpler solutions can be applied to changing circumstances. Pilot studies can be set up quite inexpensively, to challenge planning concepts or faulty techniques and to produce flexible settlement or cropping programmes, which are essential if rapid changes in technology, ecology or even climate are to be absorbed.

There is a tendency to legislate ahead of social, economic or institutional practices which was further emphasized by the *United Nations Plan of Action to Combat Desertification* (1977), which lists laws, economics, demography and sociology, ahead of the development of expertise in natural resource planning. But this presupposes that rational environmental planning is easily accomplished. Where life itself is as precarious as it is in these parched and hostile territories, survival policies surely should be the first criterion—for what use are agreements where man cannot survive, or has great difficulty in doing so? The onus is now on the Governments of the world to ensure that there is an inter-dependence of all land uses, to maintain our planet's resources in the most healthy condition possible, for use by future generations. Land use planning is therefore essential and should include self-sufficient, self-regulating, ecologically-based land uses that exploit resources efficiently and simultaneously eliminate wastage. Although people are still attracted to the cities, this trend must be reversed by providing social planning and social incentives to persuade people to remain on the land.

Correct approach to land development

What is necessary is the identification of activities which will bring man, crops and animals back into harmony with their environment—an identification and an understanding of the ecological equilibrium which will permit man and his beasts to use the land and its resources without reducing its capacity for conservation. In other words, there must be an integrated approach to land development on both an international and a project basis, correlating man's aspirations with the ecology and climate of the land.

This approach embodies three main principles:

1 Development with plants should be based on a thorough knowledge and understanding of the site resources and man's needs, and of the interactions and interdependence of these two influences

i.e. *Match land use to site resources and match plants to land use and site ecology*

2 Development should, as far as is possible, be self-sustaining and be in balance with the natural resources of the area, without requiring large inputs of external resources to sustain them. Land uses must be fitted to land capabilities and each ecosystem treated appropriately and separately, though in perspective with its neighbours

i.e. *Developments should be ecologically-based*

3 Short-term benefits should never be exploited to the detriment of the long-term future of the area

i.e. '*Live as though there is no tomorrow, but farm as though you will live for ever*'—North African Bedouin proverb.

The means are available for man to identify the pressures on the ecosystem he inhabits (see also Appendix 4.9). Surveys by satellites, aerial photography and mapping techniques, meteorological and hydrological recording stations, and studies of historical records all assist in correlating and monitoring ecological changes with climate and land use. Data retrieval and analysis by computer of the results of experiments and trials are piecing the information together so that a more complete appraisal of the situation can be gained eventually. These techniques are still relatively new, and other systems are being developed to interpret and synthesize the valuable data resulting from the many studies carried out in arid lands, particularly over the last twenty years.

Strategies for the future

Man must realize that *he* is the greatest enemy of the arid lands, since he can, both directly and indirectly, cause changes to the structure of the environment and its ecosystems. The activities most difficult to rectify are those which result from traditional customs, like grazing patterns, fuel gathering and over-cropping. The ecological balance is continuously changing, by evolution and in response to stimuli, but man generally does not change; until the productivity of dry-land ecosystems is increased sufficiently to support increased populations, a low standard of living will prevail. A higher standard of living cannot be achieved by present methods, without the importation of an increasing volume of external resources.

To reach a higher standard of living in arid lands requires the acceptance of the principle of the integrated approach. There must be a complete interchange of ideas taking into account the inter-relationship of all the criteria resulting in a well-regulated environment, with which indigenous people will co-operate, and there must be a balance of disciplines. Since the survival of man and animals is directly related to the supply of suitable foodstuffs, attention should first be directed towards useful plants which can withstand prevailing local conditions.

In terms of plant material, useful and suitable plants may not be immediately available, and hybridisation may have to be researched. According to need, plant breeding stations should be set up to produce these new plants incorporating special features, for example: increased water efficiency, better heat tolerance, good wind resistance, a high salt tolerance, an increased forage yield by means of faster-growing varieties, improved palatability, and low management and maintenance requirements. Greater attention than has so far seemed necessary or been possible should also be paid to the examination of environmental changes that may occur when alien introductions (while proving only too successful) prove to be unsuitable. Such a risk is perhaps best typified by the *Opuntia ficus-indica* (prickly pear), introduced into Australia, amongst other areas, from South America in 1789. Even though biological control by the moth *Cactoblastis cactorum* was eventually effective, it did not prevent the invasion of 15 million hectares of Australia by 1920.

It is useless to despair at the ignorance shown in many less-developed areas, especially when wilful waste of

Above: **Satellite sensing, Gemini 4**
A view of the eastern tip of the Arabian peninsular showing the sief dunes of the Rub' al Kali in the south-west corner, the land forms, and the water drainage patterns of the east coast
PHOTO: US INFORMATION SERVICE, LONDON

Below: **Prickly pear colonization**
A new settlement in Saudi Arabia with a young colony of Opuntia ficus-indica. *This plant has very strong drought resistance and incredible regeneration ability*
PHOTO: J. MCMAHON MOORE

resources can be seen in the 'developed' world as well as everywhere else. Resources are there to be exploited, certainly, but only with respect. Their potential should be analysed and fully recorded before exploitation starts, which has apparently been impossible so far. The nature of the resource has seldom been fully appreciated: understanding can only come with serious examination of the way a resource was created, how it developed and under what conditions it exists, survives or regenerates. Regeneration of mineral resources can only be catalysed by vast geological activity, which would end the world as we know it, but plant and animal life has a remarkable ability to start again, and in combination with rejuvenated soils their vitality can mask man's understanding of the essential role plants, animals and soil play in his own survival.

The use to which land will be put should therefore be carefully selected so that the maximum productivity can be sustained. The successful choice will depend on the stability of the various land uses that are proposed. This will depend in turn on the ability of these lands to adapt to the following:

1 The climate and microclimate, including the amount and duration of rainfall, and its relationship to potential evaporation, temperature and exposure or aspect of the land
2 The maintenance of soil structure, texture and fertility
3 The prevention of water-logging and salinity, wherever irrigation is practised
4 Where soil moisture is limiting to productivity, using conservation methods and recycling where possible, to encourage efficient water usage
5 The natural processes in the hydrological cycles, in particular when water extraction must balance water recharge in the aquifers
6 The development and subsequent management of the plant ecosystem
7 The cultural and spiritual aspirations of mankind, which are probably the most difficult factors to quantify.

Strategies must therefore be compiled on an international or community basis, to regulate water use and mineral extraction and to improve land management and planting techniques, depending on land capability and land use plans. Socio-economic plans can be correlated with long-term resource management, with the communities themselves involved in the planning and the implementation of these strategies. This can be achieved through education in schools, institutes and universities, through books and publications, public discussion and on radio and television, as well as through extension services and action groups. It will be a slow process towards an understanding of how to use dry-land resources appropriately, requiring a major reconsideration of social, legal and demographic policies.

Time and discipline are now needed: time to reassess and evaluate research methods, time to educate local people, so that they can willingly extract benefit from foreign aid programmes and imported technologies, and time to monitor the effect any development has on the environment. Discipline is required in planning procedures and decisions, and to ensure that valuable resources are not exhausted by expediency. The exploitation of land and the extraction of water and minerals must be based on

discriminating procedures, geared not only to short-term needs but also and always to long-term requirements.

Any development likely to have any impact whatsoever on the environment must be analysed and its operation monitored so that it receives the attention it deserves in the future, and in consequence the environment will never again be subjected to such arbitrary and aggressive alterations as it has suffered in the past. At the very least, populations struggling in these hazardous lands will have a better chance for survival. At the best, man's hopes and aspirations will be achieved, and new and functional landscapes will emerge, heralding a rational and valuable exploitation of a major part of the Earth.

Top : **Yemen Arab Republic**
Terrace agriculture in the Yemen with the rougher terrain on the higher ground for grazing
PHOTO: R. HARRISON

Bottom : **Avdat Experimental Farm, Negev, Israel**
Note the fence in the foreground to prevent animals coming off the desert to feed on the crops
PHOTO: ISRAEL EMBASSY INFORMATION SERVICE, LONDON

NOTES

1 Le Houerou, H. 'The Nature and Causes of Desertification', *Arid Lands Newsletter No 3*. University of Arizona, USA, Arid/Semi-Arid Natural Resources Program: 1976
2 Oxby, C. *Pastoral Nomads and Development*. International Institute, London: 1975
3 Hills, E. S. Reprinted by kind permission of Unesco from *Arid Lands : A Geographical Appraisal* © Unesco/Methuen: London 1966

2 The desert environment

Richard Stone, writing on deserts in *The Encyclopaedia of Geomorphology*[1] described a desert as a 'region . . . capable of supporting only a few forms of life . . .' adding that '. . . most commonly the term is used to denote regions which are barren because they are dry . . . They have been colonized by special plants of low stature and open spacing . . .' and they often have 'saline soils and distinctive landforms, developed under the influence of the arid regime . . .'.

The desert landscape is very variable and includes all the common landscape elements: mountains, valleys, plateaux and plains. The mountains are usually bare and angular, rock outcrops are very common and it is rare to find smooth rounded surfaces. The plateaux and plains are almost completely flat, and their surfaces vary from pure sand to rough stone. Soils of varying thickness are found.[2] The economic potential of deserts is closely linked to their water retention abilities, for the volume of water held within the soil affects both the natural vegetation cover, and the way man and animals can exploit this vegetation. The mor-

phology of the land and the way it influences the behaviour of any water falling on it affect in turn the character and texture of the soils forming on its surface.

There are a number of other characteristics typical of the desert landscape. Vegetation is always scarce, sometimes completely absent, and a complete vegetation cover hardly ever develops, except after rain. Rainfall is invariably erratic and never dependable, but whenever rain does fall in adequate quantities, the scene is transformed, although the range of plants is limited by the amount of rain. Wind tends to be strong, because the open surface creates little friction. Dust and sandstorms are therefore common, with

Palm Valley, Central Australia
A rugged semi-arid landscape demonstrating the variable nature of desert land forms: rocky outcrops, both smooth and angular, and valleys with sandy soils. Water erosion in this instance predominates
PHOTO: AUSTRALIAN INFORMATION SERVICE, LONDON, J. BRIAN

dust storms being more frequent, because the smaller particles can be lifted by wind blowing at lower speeds, and as a result taken high up into the atmosphere. Cloud cover is scant, except where fogs are a characteristic climatic feature, or when thunderstorms occur. Temperatures are always high, except in the cold deserts, and cloud cover does not mitigate the temperatures. Humidity is low, sometimes as low as 5%, although much higher atmospheric moisture readings can be found near the sea. Open water surfaces are therefore very rare, because evaporation levels can exceed 3,000 mm a year. When such high evaporation rates occur, the soil becomes very saline, because the evaporation of the water leaves behind salts which then mix with the soil.

In order to understand the desert environment, it is essential to understand the inter-relationships of all the elements of the landscape and its climate. It is an oversimplification to assume that the problems of the desert can be solved by the provision of water. In temperate climates, no environmental solution can be found without reference to the full range of data, and the same holds true for the desert and its fringes. An inadequate assessment creates at least as severe a risk in the desert as in more moderate zones: the climatic, geological, edaphic (soil) and vegetative factors should all be appreciated, for work in the desert can pose problems never encountered in moister and cooler environments.

ARIDITY: ITS CAUSES AND CHARACTERISTICS

For man to function efficiently in the desert, he must understand the concept of aridity, and its causes. Aridity affects the relationships between the water that is naturally available and its exploitation by plants and man. It therefore decides the basic potential of any land surface, whether it be a rocky mountain face, or a deep alluvial soil, since it influences the ultimate behaviour of the soil and the ecosystems associated with it.

Causes of aridity
There are three distinct causes for arid regions:[2]
1 They can be caused by the separation of a region from an ocean, either by topographical barriers like mountain ranges, or by distance, as in mid-continental regions
2 They can develop where dry stable air masses form, and resist convective currents, whose turbulence normally promotes rain formation
3 They can occur where there is a lack of storm systems which must lift the air before rain can fall.
Each different cause of aridity can exist on its own, or in combination with one or both other causes. The deserts of the sub-tropical latitudes, for example the Thar Desert in India, are very prone to cyclonic weather movements. The Arabian, Australian and Saharan desert zones are found between major wind belts, with their associated storm systems. Parts of the Monte-Patagonian Desert of South America, and the desert zones of the United States of America are separated from the oceans by mountain ranges. The Eurasian deserts—the Takla-makan, the Turkestan and the Gobi—are separated by great distances from moisture sources.

Characteristics of aridity
In order to understand the processes influencing desert ecosystems, it is essential to appreciate aridity, and particularly its intensity. This can only happen if accurate climatic data is available. However, any measurements made are of detailed value only in the location where they originate, since microclimatic influences can significantly alter the overall shape of the data.

Because the availability of water, and consequently the volume of water held in the soil, is of prime concern, there are three elements which have to be considered in detail to establish the pattern or characteristics of aridity:[2]
1 The volume of rain, its frequency and rate of fall
2 The range of temperatures, with particular reference to its maximum values
3 The relative humidity of the atmosphere.
The sporadic nature of dry-land rainfall is more pronounced where extremely arid lands are found, and its regularity improves on the semi-desert fringes. As rainfall becomes more erratic, it comes characteristically in the form of thunderstorms, which can create 'flash floods'. The nature of the soil determines how much water runs off over the ground, to collect in wadis or streams. The more regular rainfall of the semi-arid areas is not so closely connected to cloudbursts, and in this case, the soil is not subjected to such great flood forces, and is able to absorb greater volumes of water as a consequence.

Evaporation rates in arid lands are commonly 15–20 times as much as the annual rainfall, and have been known to reach 30 times the volume of available water. Even such high rates can be exceeded, should exceptionally strong drying winds occur. No depression of evaporation rates can be expected from cloud cover, since this is usually extremely low, except perhaps in coastal deserts like the Namib in southern Africa, and the Atacama in Chile.

The soil texture will influence the rate of water movement within it, and therefore influences the upward movement of moisture attracted by the evaporative forces. The finer the texture, the greater the loss of water; where large soil air spaces are found, resistance to these forces is greater.

SCIENTIFIC METHODS FOR DETERMINING ARIDITY

The desert environment is principally determined by the intensity of its aridity values.[2] Many authorities have collated climatic data to produce empirical formulae for classifying various world types. Climatic regions with close similarities have been identified, based on the seasonal combination of the distribution of temperature and rainfall. Differences between climatic types develop through changes in response of the environment to the climate.

Köppen's classification system
In 1931, Köppen devised a classification system which distinguishes the world climatic patterns by relating vegetation differences to climatic types, a theory based on the belief that the natural vegetation is the best expression of the climate. Basing his classification on annual and

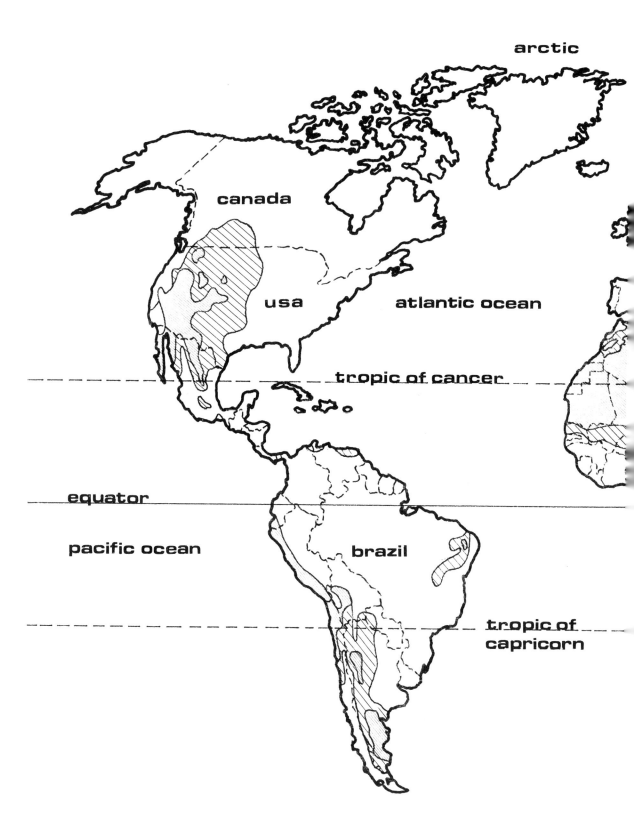

arctic

canada

usa

atlantic ocean

tropic of cancer

equator

pacific ocean

brazil

tropic of
capricorn

Fig 1 *The world's dry lands compiled from 'Deserts of the World' (ed McGinnies, Goldman and Paylore), University of Arizona Press 1968 (after Meigs)*

the world's dry lands

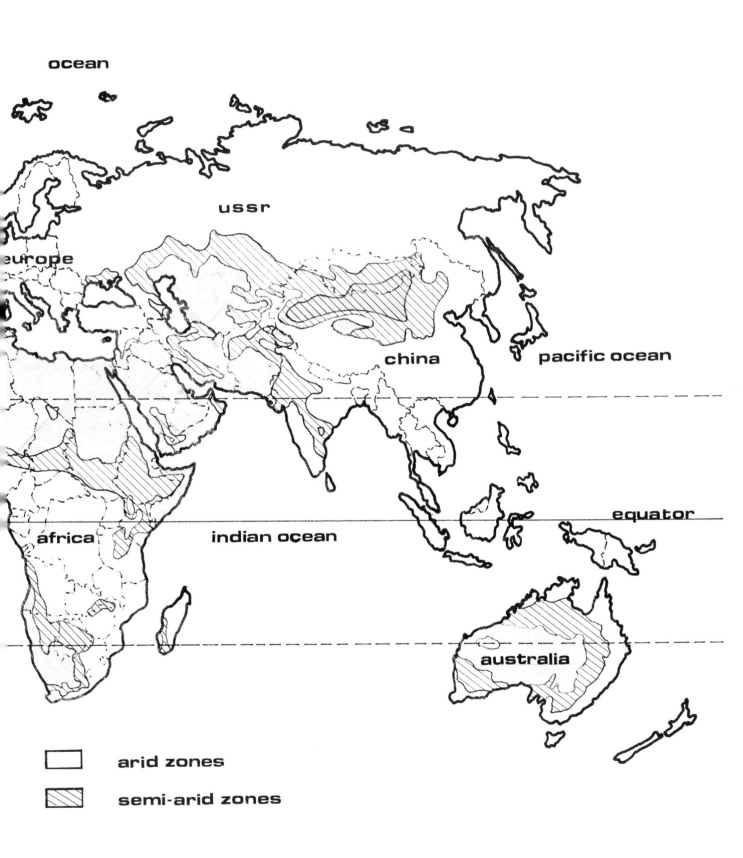

ocean

ussr

europe

china

pacific ocean

equator

africa

indian ocean

australia

☐ arid zones

▨ semi-arid zones

monthly means of temperature and precipitation, Köppen recognized that the effects of rainfall on plant growth depend not only on rainfall, but also on the dimensions of transpiration (evaporation of moisture from plants) and evaporation from open water surfaces. He identified five climatic groups and eleven principal climatic types, and together these form the basis of his understanding of the world's climatic patterns. His system consists of a simple formula, which uses a pair of letters, one symbolizing temperature and the other precipitation. For example, a dry climate is expressed by the combination 'BW': 'B' indicates that precipitation is exceeded by evaporation, and 'W' indicates that the greatest amount of rain is likely to fall in the winter. He added a number of sub-divisions, to classify the smaller details.

Thornthwaite's and Meigs' Indexes

Thornthwaite's index, devised in 1948, was the most popular for many years, and was revised (with Mather) in 1962 to consist of the following formula:

$$Im = [(s-d)/PE]100$$

where 's' = excess of monthly rainfall over potential evapo-transpiration and storage in the soil during wet months, 'd' = the deficit of rainfall plus available soil moisture below potential evapo-transpiration in dry months, and 'PE' = potential evapo-transpiration.

Meigs, in 1953, produced a system which used Thornthwaite's model of aridity. He selected specific values of Thornthwaite's index to identify different measurements of aridity so that he could identify differences within the arid zone, and he established that the term 'extremely arid' was insufficient to include areas where there were records of rain not falling for more than twelve months, giving them the classification of 'intense aridity'. His system uses not only the index of aridity, but also seasonal rainfall patterns and temperatures. Using letters and numerals, he can show the extent of aridity, when rain falls, the mean temperature of the coldest month and the mean temperature of the hottest month. His system is valuable because it describes areas throughout the world which have the same basic climate. This can be demonstrated through the following formula 'Ab23', where 'A' = Arid, 'b' = summer precipitation, '2' = mean temperature of between 10°C and 20°C for the coldest month, and '3' = mean temperature of between 20°C and 30°C for the hottest month.

This describes a zone south of the equator, in Australia or southern Africa, where the rainfall occurs during the summer, influenced by the tropical climatic system. It should be realized however that Meigs's system cannot appreciate local differences and influences, but it is valuable on a macro-scale.

Calculation of evapo-transpiration

There are a number of authorities: de Martonne, Preston, Budyko and Penman, to name but a few, who have developed calculation systems for measuring evapo-transpiration, usually involving extensive equipment and a lot of measuring. A comparatively recent improvement, which is being used increasingly in arid lands across the world, is the Class 'A' Pan evaporimeter, from which water loss can be accurately measured. The United States Weather Bureau originated this method. Dr A. W. Marsh, at the university of California, Riverside, U.S.A., has produced a formula, yet to be perfected, which converts the evaporation from the pan to an irrigation volume. The Piche evaporimeter is another method for measuring evapo-transpiration.

It is obvious that it is necessary to calculate the water needs of plants accurately; calculations are still needed to establish the increasing volumes of water required by plants in the years subsequent to planting. There is a further factor, pointed out by Dr Colin Leakey, and named the 'k' factor, which records the extent of the influences of areas outside the irrigated zone upon the irrigated area.

As might be expected, the introduction of water into a dry environment, particularly into an extremely arid one, changes the climate artificially to an arid or semi-arid type over the area being irrigated, provided that irrigation is continued for a minimum period to fix the change. However, it has little effect on the district's climate. While it has been found that the number of dew points has increased over the irrigated area, there is no change beyond it. Even open water surfaces have no effect on the climate beyond their immediate vicinity, and this form of water storage is very wasteful in arid lands, since evaporation levels are so high.

ARID AREAS: THEIR LOCATION AND NATURE

There are five major arid zones, two in the northern hemisphere and three in the southern, and each is separated from the others by either oceans or wet equatorial zones. The northern hemisphere contains deserts which are considerably larger in total area than those of the southern hemisphere: the zone stretching from West Africa to China is larger than all the southern deserts combined.

Since climate is the predominant element influencing the morphology of the land and therefore the soils, it will be considered simultaneously with the description of location. Discussion of the soils found in the various deserts will follow.

● Northern hemisphere desert zones

There are two major desert systems in the northern hemisphere: the North African–Eurasion zone, and the North American desert zone. Owing to their magnitude, their formation has been influenced by a number of climatic factors, as can be seen from their enormous spread.

The North African–Eurasian zone

This is the largest of all the desert zones, starting in northern Mauritania in western Africa, and stretching to China. The Sahara is the world's largest desert and stretches across North Africa, encompassing Mauritania, Morocco, Tunisia, Algeria, Libya and Egypt. The desert zone continues on the other side of the Red Sea into northern and central Arabia, to the northern Arabian States, as far as the Arabian (formerly the Persian) Gulf. Over the Gulf, the desert zone passes through Iran, including within its boundaries the Great Salt Desert, one of the world's least hospitable and least explored areas, on through Afghanistan and Pakistan and into northern India, with a minor branch going southwards to the Deccan Plateau. There are two main branches of this desert zone, the northern one being the most prominent. It is formed in the shadow of the Himalayan Mountain ranges, stretching into Turkestan in the U.S.S.R., and going eastwards into China through the Takla-makan desert into the Great Gobi. The second, minor branch spreads southwards from the Libyan Desert through Ethiopia, into Somalia, across the Red Sea into the Yemen and Muscat and Oman, influenced by the Hadramaut Mountains.

The climate of such an enormous zone is extremely complex, as would be expected. There are in all eight distinct climatic systems, although three of them are sub-divisions of one major climatic zone, the Mediterranean zone. The six major zones are described below.

1 The Mediterranean climate system
Principally, the Mediterranean climate influences the northern coast states of North Africa, and the eastern coast states of the Middle East. It can be sub-divided into three smaller zones:

THE NORTHERN SAHARA The region can be further divided into the area influenced by the maritime Mediterranean climate and the continental type, found in the interior. The Mediterranean climate gradually loses its influence as it goes southwards from the North African coast. The typical pattern of hot dry summers is replaced by extreme heat and very low winter rainfall. The zone extends from Morocco to Egypt, and Le Houérou[3] suggests that the limit of the northern Sahara coincides with the 100 mm rainfall isohyet (the mapping line linking areas of equal rainfall), stating that one quarter of the total area of the Sahara receives less than 20 mm of rain in a year. Even when the 50 mm isohyet is reached, plant cover is still very poor, especially in the north, north west and parts of western Sahara. Vegetation can be found in the centre of the Sahara, but is restricted to the wadi beds: the rocky outcrops and hillsides are barren.

NORTHERN ARABIA This zone is the eastern coastal zone of the Mediterranean and includes Syria, the Lebanon, Israel, Jordan, northern Saudi Arabia, Iraq and Kuwait. Its climate is typified by hot dry summers and winter cyclonic rains, coming off the Mediterranean. M. Zohary has distinguished three different types within this zone: the 'rain deserts', where the vegetation, though sparser than the northern Mediterranean flora with which it has affinities, is nevertheless supported by rainfall; the 'run-off' desert, where the rainfall can only support plants in

Below : **Northern Sahara–Bou Saada, Algeria**
Vegetation fringing a river bed while the surrounding uplands are devoid of plants
PHOTO: ALGERIAN INFORMATION SERVICE, LONDON

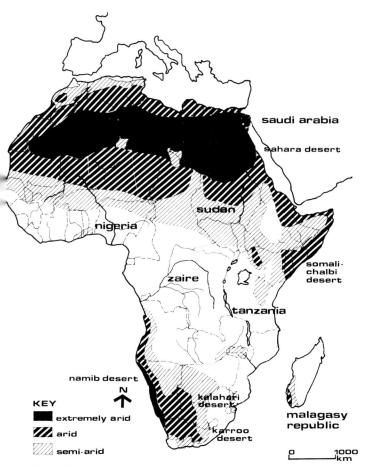

Fig 2 *Desert areas of Africa (after Meigs)*

depressions; and 'absolute deserts', where there is no rainfall.

North of the tropic of Cancer, the Mediterranean Sea strongly influences the flora of the Red Sea area including northern Saudi Arabia, Jordan and Israel, and even more so in Syria, where the total rainfall can reach a valuable 350 mm a year. In the northern and central Negev in Israel, the annual rainfall is between 75 mm and 100 mm, but further north the scanty rain is augmented by 100 mm of dew. In Iraq, the 150 mm isohyet appears to be the critical limit between desert and semi-desert, while in Jordan, the boundary seems to be 100 mm a year.

IRAN The Iranian desert zone is not restricted to the geographical boundaries of Iran itself, for it includes the desert area within Afghanistan. This area is affected mainly by the Mediterranean climatic system, which develops winter cyclonic rains, though of a more desertic character, as rain is predominantly from storms. The area is influenced in a minor way by the Indian monsoon system, which occasionally brings rain in April.

Although the monsoon plays a relatively small role in the Iranian climate, when it does enter the area, and meets the mid-latitude Mediterranean system, cataclysmic rains result, and these cause very severe damage.

The five Iranian deserts are the Dasht-e-Kavir, the Kavir-i-Namak, the Dasht-e-Lut, the Dasht-i-Naomid and the Dasht-i-Margo. The Dasht-e-Kavir (the Great Salt Desert) is the largest area in the world to support no vegetation whatsoever. Scanty rains are all that can be expected, and the summer temperature of 54°C and over is made even less comfortable by the frequent stormy winds that blow throughout the zone.

2 The Southern Sahara

This area is the desert zone south of the major central expanse of the Sahara. Tropical weather systems have the greatest influence and the mid-latitude systems are considered to be of peripheral significance only.

This zone stretches from southern Mauritania to the Sudan, and includes on its southern borders the states of Mali, Upper Volta, northern Nigeria, and the Cameroons. Its climate is part of the tropical system which defines the weather of the area by the shifts of the inter-tropical convergence zone.

Although meteorological figures are not available for all the countries involved, much valuable information has come from the Locust Control Programme funded by the United Nations. Rainfall can be expected in summer, and reaches 250 mm a year.

3 The Somali-Chalbi and Southern Arabian climate systems

This area includes the very variable geographical features of both Ethiopia and Somalia, with influences into Kenya and Tanzania, as well as southern Arabia, including the Yemens, Muscat and Oman, southern Saudi Arabia and the states of the United Arab Emirates. Its climate is complex, affected by topography, thermal low pressure and coastal upwellings, as well as the Indian monsoon. Its southern fringes come under the Tropical Climate systems, and there is a very rapid transition from pure desert to equatorial rain forest. A particularly interesting feature of the eastern Somali coastal area bordering the Red Sea is that this area was under the sea in recent geological history, and is of great academic value in the study of plant colonization and the process of erosion.

In 1955, Pichi-Sermolli made an excellent survey for the Arid Zone Research Unit of Unesco:[4] while appreciating the enormous complexities of the climate, he managed to distinguish eight principal arid zones, each characterized by different vegetation patterns depending on proximity to the sea, soil differences, topographical changes and temperature variations. Rainfall is not considered a major factor, for its volumes are generally low.

The interior of Saudi Arabia is dominated by the great sand deserts of the An-Nafud, the Ad Dahna', and the Rub'al Kali. Here vegetation differences are linked to differences in either soil temperature or sand colour.

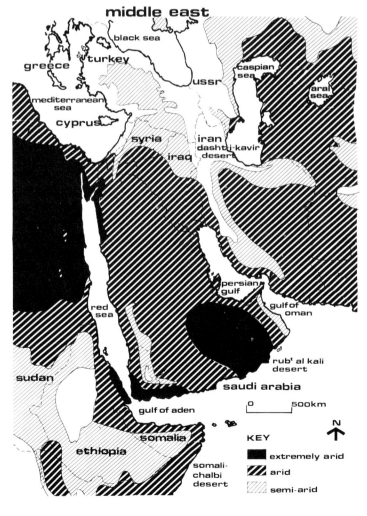

Top : **Iran**
Arid hills on the road from Tabriz to Ahar in north-west Iran
PHOTO: C. V. MALCOLM
Above : **Southern Sahara, Nigeria**
The fragility of the Sahel region is clearly seen, with sparse trees and extremely poor sub-shrub vegetation
PHOTO: R. HARRISON
Fig 3 (*right*) *Desert areas of the Middle East (after Meigs)*

Facing page : **Central Saudi Arabia**
PHOTO: J. MCMAHON MOORE

Southern Arabia: Oman Mountains, Fujaira, UAE
The southern Arabian coast is influenced by the monsoon.
Here lush palms flourish in a large wadi bed
PHOTO: DR. J. HEPWORTH

Rainfall appears to be higher on the mountain slopes facing the sea, but the area becomes drier to the east, further inland. Rainfall is more reliable in the winter than in the summer, showing the slight predominance of the northern mid-latitude climate system over the monsoon system.

4 The Thar Desert
The Thar desert is on the borders between Pakistan and north-west India. The north and west of the Thar region receives winter rainfall from the mid-latitude cyclones, and cold weather can be expected from these western climatic disturbances. The east of the area in India receives its rain during the summer monsoons, whose influence terminates in western India, although occasionally it stretches as far as west Iran. There seems to be a strong correlation between the behaviour of the monsoon and the high level winds over the area. There has been some difficulty in establishing precisely how much of this area is naturally arid and how much the aridity has resulted from the activities of man. For the purposes of defining the desert region, the 250 mm isohyet appears to be a suitable point (Barucha, 1955).

5 The Turkestan Desert
This area in the U.S.S.R. is an enormous undrained basin, with large areas below sea-level. The southern part of the area is influenced by the Mediterranean climate, while the north is more continental and severe, with extremes of both heat and cold. The region is bordered on the west by the Caspian Sea, on the south by the mountains between Iran and Afghanistan, on the east by the Western Sinkiang mountains, and on the north by the Kirghiz Step Mountains.

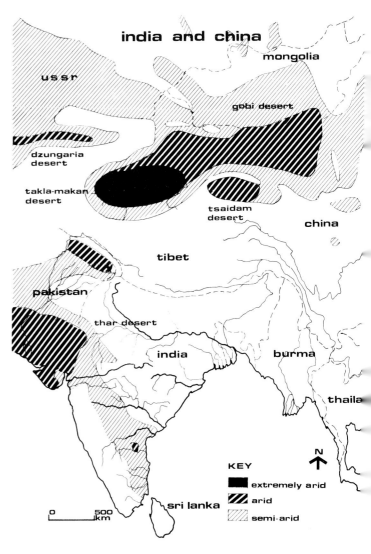

Fig 4 *Desert areas of India and China (after Meigs)*

Above: **South Punjab Desert, Pakistan**
A small settlement almost completely surrounded by sand dunes
PHOTO: PAKISTAN INFORMATION DIVISION, LONDON

Right: **Turkmen, USSR**
The Kara–Kum canal passing through the Kara–Kum desert. What is surprising is what little influence the canal has on its neighbouring vegetation. (Its concrete sides prevent seepage.) However, it would be interesting to see the same stretch in five to ten years time, for the humidity increase associated with the canal may well influence the canalside vegetation
PHOTO: NOVOSTI PRESS AGENCY, LONDON

Below right: **Kazakhstan, USSR**
There can be little doubt that the USSR is heavily committed to a vast and rapid expansion of her agriculture. Main and side canals are seen here under construction. The vegetation indicates that the land is on the fringe of the desert proper. The natural water resources are poor and the hummocky vegetation indicates a windy, and (in this instance) a cold climate
PHOTO: NOVOSTI PRESS AGENCY, LONDON

Two other deserts of note are the Kara-Kum and the Kyzyl-Kum, which are crossed by the Amu Dar'ya and Syr-Dar'ya rivers. The rainfall averages between 90 mm and 370 mm.

The Turkestan desert has a rainfall of between 75 mm and 200 mm, usually occurring in late spring and early autumn. The summer and winter months have no rain, particularly in the northern sector. Temperatures vary widely between 40°C and minus 57°C. Strong winds are also typical.

6 The Takla-makan and Gobi Deserts

This desert region is separated from maritime moisture sources both by topographical barriers and by enormous distances. The Tibetan Plateau, with its average altitude of 3,600 metres, is a major interruptive structure, preventing any moist air from moving northwards from the Indian Ocean. Its height affects both the formation and movement of cyclones which modify the high level air flows.

north america

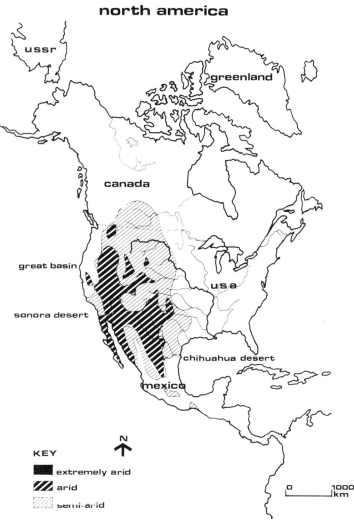

KEY

█ extremely arid

▨ arid

▨ semi-arid

Fig 5 *Desert areas of North America (after Meigs)*

The Gobi is to the north-east of the Takla-makan Desert, and is located in outer Mongolia and inner and Chinese Mongolia. South of the Gobi and east of the Takla-makan Desert, are the Tsaidam, Alashan and Ordos Deserts. These deserts have no external drainage, receive very little rain, seldom more than 100 mm and averaging around 50 mm. The range of temperatures is between minus 6°C and minus 19°C in January, to between 24°C and 26°C in July.

West of the Gobi is the Dzungaro-Kazakhstan Desert. Its climate is moderately continental, and rain arrives with the cyclones off the Pacific in spring and summer.

The North American desert zone

The arid zone of North America spans 20° latitude from south-western Mexico to southern California and Arizona. Both topographical barriers and separation from the sea are major influences in desert formation, as are dry stable air masses, found because of a lack of storm systems which are required to lift air before rain can fall. All these are factors contributing to the formation of the American desert zone.

On the northern boundaries, the topographical barriers are the Rocky Mountains: these are the most important as they affect winter rainfall. During the summer the Pacific region is influenced by the stable eastern portion of the sub-tropical high pressure cell as cyclone frequency ceases when the cyclone tracks shift to the north. The southern portion, including the Sonora and Chihuahua Deserts, has summer rainfall while the northern and western sections have winter rainfall. Arizona, north of the Sonora Desert, receives some rain in summer and winter, and has therefore a transitional character, falling between the two main climatic influences.

● Southern hemisphere desert zones

There are three major desert systems in the southern hemisphere, again with differing characteristics. They are the desert areas of southern Africa, with three distinct zones, South America, with two distinct zones, and Australia.

The South African desert zone

The Kalahari inland, and the Namib on the western coast are the two main deserts. South of the Kalahari lies the Great Karroo and further south, the Little Karroo, which extends eastwards towards Port Elizabeth.

1 The Namib Desert

This desert is a transitional zone, with summer rains on its equatorial boundary, and winter cyclonic rains on its southern boundaries. The rain in the summer months is related to the equatorial westerlies.

The Namib desert has two distinct climatic districts. The extremely arid zone stretches 50–70 miles (80–100 km) inland from the Atlantic Coast. Although this area has less than 50 mm of rain in a year, extra water reaches the area in the form of fogs and dews, augmenting the annual volumes of available moisture. The cold Benguela current, sweeping northwards up the coast, meeting the hot air blowing off the desert, forms clouds which then hug the coastline and form the most important feature of the area.

Further inland, the Great Western Escarpment is found 100 miles (160 km) away from the coast. The climate here is less arid. Moving further east, before reaching the western boundaries of the Kalahari, the climate improves and semi-arid conditions prevail.

2 The Kalahari Desert

The climatic patterns of the Kalahari Desert mirror those of the Namib, with equatorial summer rains in the north, and winter rains in the south. The southern sector of the desert as far as the Orange River, from approximately 22°S latitude, has land which is more typically desert, but the north, although desertic in appearance, does not have true desert vegetation. This area is known locally as 'thirstland', and is a 'false desert' created by the overgrazing of man's herds of cattle.

One area of particular interest is the Okavango Swamp, in the northern area. This swamp was formerly a rich delta, but is now a salt swamp, into which drains all the water

Above right : **Namib Desert, Namibia**
The sandy desert coastal strip supports virtually no vegetation whatsoever. When plants are found they have tapped the dew and coastal mists for moisture
PHOTO: SOUTH AFRICAN EMBASSY, SOUTH AFRICAN RAILWAYS
Below right : **Kalahari Desert, Botswana**
The 'thirst-land' of the northern Kalahari desert—a typical savannah-like scene with Acacia-like scrub, small trees and short tough grasses capable of surviving through the hot dry seasons. But, if overgrazed, it rapidly degenerates into desert
PHOTO: A. SOBOTT
Facing page : **Yuma Sands, California**
The hottest and driest zone in the USA
PHOTO: US INFORMATION SERVICE, LONDON

from the Okavango River. The enormous potential of this river has not been exploited for many years. The catchment of the delta is 600 miles away in Angola, with two main river branches: the Cubango and the Cuito. The delta itself is 100 miles (160 km) wide, on a north-east–south-west axis.

3 The Karroo Desert

The southern equatorial climate is no longer dominant and the main climatic pattern is of winter rains, resulting in arid to semi-arid conditions.

The Australian deserts

Although the centre of Australia is covered more or less continuously by desert, five separate desert areas have been identified: the Gibson Desert and the Great Sandy Desert to the west, the Great Victoria Desert in the south, the Simpson Desert in the Northern Territory to the east of Alice Springs, and the Sturt Desert, west of the Grey Range, on the borders of Queensland and South Australia.

The climate depends on two systems: the tropical on the equatorial side and mid-latitude cyclonic rain both north and south. They are therefore similar to the Kalahari and Namib systems.

Over half of Australia is arid, with less than 250 mm of rain a year, and 20% of the continent has less than 65 mm per year. Because there are no records of past meteorological observations, it is not known how dry the centre of Australia is. In Northern Australia, although rainfall reaches 600 mm or more a year, vegetation is not as lush as might be expected from the figure alone, because the rain falls in summer, when temperatures are at their highest and evaporation loss is considerable.

Karroo Desert, South Africa

The Karroo Desert in South Africa stretches flatly for hundreds of miles : inhospitable to say the least for humans, but the source of an enormous range of unique succulent plants
PHOTO: SATOUR, LONDON

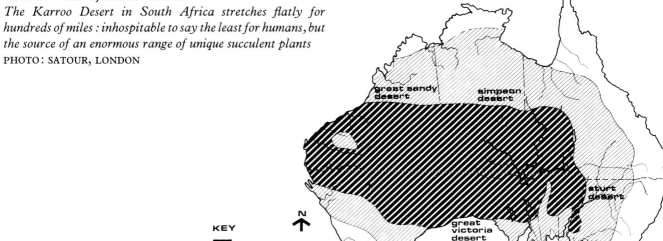

KEY

N↑

■ extremely arid
▨ arid
▨ semi-arid

0   500km

australia

Fig 6 *Desert areas of Australia (after Meigs)*

The winter rain of 250 mm in the south is considered equivalent to the 600 mm isohyet in the north, and is therefore two and a half times more effective. The southern deserts, the Great Victoria and the Sturt, are considered by Emberger to be Mediterranean in character, and the Central Gibson and Simpson Deserts form a transitional zone between these southern deserts and the Great Sandy Desert to the North.

The South American deserts

The two main desert regions, including both arid and semi-arid areas, are the Atacama–Peruvian zone, and the Monte-Patagonian desert.

1 The Atacama–Peruvian deserts

The climate of this narrow but extensive zone down the western seaboard of South America combines the effects of the cold Peru (Humboldt) current moving up the coast (rather like the Benguela current off the south-west coast of Africa) with the eastern part of the sub-tropical high pressure cell. When the cold current is replaced by the warm equatorial waters flowing south from the equator (the Equatorial counter-current), humidity increases, and when the southern winds are replaced by the northern equatorial winds, unstable air conditions result and torrential rain ensues.

This desert system is the driest coastal region in the world. At Arica and Iquique in Chile rainfall averages 10 mm a year. Even at the most southerly limit of the Atacama, at Copiapo, the rainfall seldom reaches 65 mm. Coastal mists are however a common feature.

Above : **Kimberley, Western Australia**
The strong erosive effects of both wind and water have formed hill cones, whose caps are covered with rock, as yet resisting the climate. The hillsides are bare, but the valleys are vegetated, watered by run-off from the hills
PHOTO: AUSTRALIAN INFORMATION SERVICE, LONDON

Right : **San Pedro, Atacama Desert**
The demarcation between the desert and the cultivated valley is determined by the volumes of water available and the water distribution techniques used
PHOTO: ANGLO-CHILEAN SOCIETY, LONDON, EDMUNDO STOCKINS SERIES

2 The Monte-Patagonian Desert
This desert starts in Bolivia and Northern Argentina, where the Andes Mountains produce a ridge-trough pressure system. This system prevents the regeneration of cyclones once they have crossed the mountains in a westerly direction, until they have overflown the southern part of the continent.

The Monte-Patagonian Desert extends southwards from 24°35′S to 44°20′S in the centre of Patagonia, and from 64°54′W in the west to 60°50′W inland. Rainfall is less than 240 mm a year, and is not sufficient to keep the southerly rivers permanently flowing, except in northern Patagonia, where the Rios Chubut, Colorado and Negro are located.

The area between the mouth of the Rio Chubut and the Magellan Straits has a cold temperate climate, but is very dry and suffers from persistent winds. Precipitation gives between 150 mm and 300 mm rain and snow a year. The central district of the Patagonian desert is very dry, with between 100 mm and 150 mm rain a year. The mean temperatures are low, with the mean annual temperature at between 6°C and 13°C. The San Jorge Gulf area in the extreme south is the next most arid district, and vegetation covers only half the surface.

A climatic definition of desert areas
Although it seems clear that the desert areas of the world can be clearly distinguished by both appearance and vegetation, there has been considerable discussion as to how to define desert boundaries in climatic terms. From the previous discussion of the principal climatic characters, the desert boundary has been variously defined as being limited by either the 100 mm or 150 mm isohyets, or the

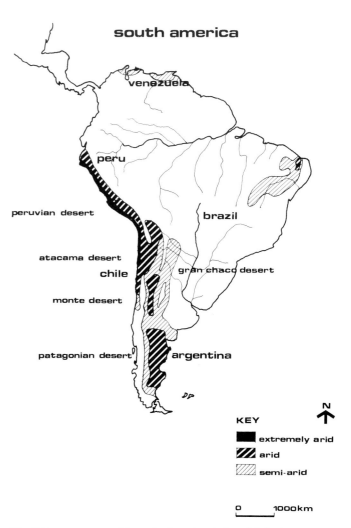

Fig 7 *Desert areas of South America (after Meigs)*

250 mm isohyets, and even the 600 mm isohyet in Australia. Although there are regional variations, it is now generally accepted that the border between arid and semi-arid lands is defined by the 250 mm rainfall isohyet, and that the boundary of the semi-arid zone is 500 mm. This has been confirmed for various regions of the world by the following authorities.[4]

Authority	Country	Arid Land Rainfall	Semi-Arid Land Rainfall
Barucha	India, Pakistan	250 mm	
Cabrera	South America		500 mm
Davies	Australia	250 mm (600 mm)	
Dyer	South Africa	250 mm	500 mm

The definitions do not include the northern Arabian and eastern Mediterranean countries, where the lower 100–150 mm limits were set. It therefore seems appropriate to suggest that rainfall records cannot be used on their own to delineate desert boundaries, but that they should be used in combination with such other factors as wind characteristics and indigenous vegetation. Since rainfall, wind and temperature together promote morphology and soils, and therefore the vegetative habitat of any area, the influence of both morphology and soils should also be considered. That being the case, there seems little point in persisting in an attempt to define a precise boundary which is dependent on so many intricately-linked elements.

DESERT MORPHOLOGY AND SOILS

The wide range of landforms in the desert is linked both to the present geological structure of the land and to the climatic patterns. The rain, sun, wind and high temperatures during the day, and the cool nights, force the Earth's surface into the variety of shapes and structures which are so typical of desert scenery. Each geological formation or parent rock-type has two effects on plant growth: the particular weathered form produces the soil type, and this in turn affects water relations and water retaining characteristics which have effect on plant growth. The rock type also influences the chemical and physical composition of the soil, and therefore its drainage characteristics. Furthermore, it can be appreciated that regional geology will often determine the pattern of surface and sub-surface drainage systems, and consequently subterranean water reservoirs (aquifers). Each rock type should therefore be analyzed to assess both how the climate has changed its form on the surface, and how its detailed characteristics will eventually affect plant colonization potential.

Although there are a number of desert zones, both of the hot sub-tropical and of the cool, or cold, temperate types, there is a wide range of landforms, structures and surface deposits that are common to most of them. Each landform develops in accordance with the predominant modelling element, be this rain, wind, sun or extremes of temperature. Each major form can modify the effects of the climate, and therefore of the ecosystem which develops within it. A desert surface which is exposed to intense heat during the day, and cold at night, gradually becomes pulverized into smaller and smaller particles. The wind, when it blows across such a surface, picks up the dust and sand grains, and having lost the cover of loose matter, the surface is open to further erosion and weathering. When the rain comes, smallish particles are either carried off by water during 'flash floods', to accumulate in lower depressions and streams, or else they are washed down through the soil profile. As the rain water drains down through the soil, it

Kalahari Desert

Kalahari sand overlying polished desert gravel. The calcrete layer is seen as a white zone below the overburden, but calcrete nodules are also found within the sand

PHOTO: DR. J. HEPWORTH

dissolves chemicals from the soil, and these chemicals are carried deeper and deeper down, to be deposited around rock fragments. As these deposits increase, a layer of chemical cement can build up, and eventually this can result in a hard layer or pan. Where the chemical involved is calcium carbonate, originating from limestone, the cement layer is known as 'calcrete', which is a common phenomenon in Middle Eastern deserts. Where the chemical is silica, this hard layer is known as 'silcrete', and is characteristic of the southern Sahara.

Conditions for establishment of vegetation

The establishment of vegetation depends on the depth of soil and its physical character, both influencing water retention, subsequent water availability, and therefore the continuity of supply. The depth of the soil will depend on its structure or its components, and the stratification pattern produced during its formation. Generally speaking, desert soils are primitive in structure, because the different layers are not well differentiated, except at the point where the surface deposits meet the bedrock. It is the nature of the superficial deposits that defines the soil's potential for plant colonization, rather than water storage; but when a clay or silt barrier develops, especially in either

alluvial or aeolian soils, drainage can become interrupted causing an increase in moisture levels, and colonization is more rapidly achieved, provided that the drainage system does not become wholly impeded.

The distribution of the various components of the soil—its texture—does however have a definite effect on water penetration patterns. Where loose-textured soils occur the fragments of rock aggregates offer little resistance to water drainage, and plants growing in such soils must have the ability of responding quickly before the water drains beyond the reach of their roots. A very fine-textured soil, with a high proportion of silt or clay, may provide such a barrier to water penetration that much of the water evaporates from the surface before it can enter the soil.

Other factors, such as the presence of chemicals like salt or other substances, can combine with the soil particles to produce micro-environments which stimulate the development of plants and their associated animals and insects. It is also obvious that under the same climatic conditions there will be a number of different growing localities, such as depressions, areas of shade created by rocks, open land exposed to the wind, or pockets of different soils: each locality may modify or be modified by the microclimate, and each will develop its own particular ecosystem.

Mount Olga, Northern Territory, Australia

Unusually rounded desert mountains showing streaks and grooves in their sides formed by water erosion
PHOTO: AUSTRALIAN INFORMATION SERVICE, LONDON

Geological features of desert areas

Desert mountains
Desert mountains are usually bare and angular, and exhibit

the primary stages in erosion and weathering. Their surfaces are washed away by rain running off the slopes in gullies or rivulets, or stripped bare by sand particles carried in the wind. The nature of the bedrock influences their ruggedness, and bare outcrops are common. Smooth, rounded surfaces, like Ayers Rock in Australia, are exceptional: here the heating–cooling process of insolation splits shallow leaves of rock away, which results in a smooth surface. Soil is rare on desert mountains, and where it exists, it is very shallow, accumulating in pockets between rocks or in fissures, and providing the only suitable medium for plant life in these mountains. Wind action is also responsible for the poor soil cover, carrying away loose particles not protected by hollows.

Desert plains

The desert mountains usually rise abruptly from the plains, of which there are three principal types:

HAMADA The hamada has an almost flat solid rock surface. Wind abrasion exceeds insolation, and soil is virtually absent, because any which does accumulate is immediately blown away. The surface is thus virtually devoid of vegetation, and when any is seen, it is usually in fissures protected from the wind. The bedrock type will influence the plant colonization potential.

REG The surface of a reg is also flat, but is covered with rock detritus or gravel. While the wind can remove the finer particles lying between rock fragments, it cannot reach the soil protected by the larger pieces, and these areas can be used by plants. The surface soils are thicker than those of the hamada plain, but unless there is adequate rainfall, plants are usually small, or only temporary inhabitants.

ERG The erg is not as flat as either the hamada or the reg, for it is the classical 'sand sea', identified by its undulating surface of crests and troughs. The sand forming the surface of an erg originates in mountains, regs or hamadas, often a considerable distance away, or from neighbouring desert zones. The undulations are wind-formed and mobile as a rule. Vegetation is sparse, especially on the more mobile surfaces, but where the surface is relatively stable, plants can be found, particularly in the troughs and hollows between the crests.

Alluvial fans

Alluvial fans are formed when the streams running off the mountains in deep gorges meet the plains below. The streams carry rock detritus and alluvium, which is quickly deposited into fan-shaped structures spreading out from the foot of the mountains. A gradation of rock particle sizes is found in the fan, with the largest boulders deposited near the mountain face, and the alluvium spread further out. The water running down the gorges flows under the boulders, so that the finer alluvium is carried along underground. Alluvial fans store large volumes of water underground, and dense vegetation can be supported. In the individual water channels, the vegetation can be even thicker. The size of the plants is regulated by the depth of the sediments and their water storage potential.

Top : **Reg Desert, Saudi Arabia**
The reg desert is composed of small rock particles on the surface, between which the soil can accummulate, but mostly it is blown away leaving an almost sterile surface
PHOTO: J. MCMAHON MOORE

Left : **Mobile Dunes, Colorado Desert, USA**
Infertile mobile dunes—the ripples on the sand surface indicate light surface winds
PHOTO: US INFORMATION SERVICE

Alluvial blanket

As the number of gorges down the mountain sides increases, the number of alluvial fans multiplies. Eventually the fans unite to form a continuous layer or blanket. Being on a larger scale than alluvial fans, the alluvial blankets, which are alternatively known as 'bajada', have a greater vegetation potential.

Pediment

The mountain faces, as they are weathered and eroded, gradually retreat and the surface left behind at their feet (the pediment) is a gently-inclined, bare rock, hamada-like surface. Pockets of soil are the only suitable spots for plant colonization. The pediment surface extends from the

Above : **Alluvial fans, Saudi Arabia**
The alluvial fans can be seen spreading out into the desert from the junction between the mountain escarpment and the plain
PHOTO: J. MCMAHON MOORE
Top right : **Inselbergs**
Inselbergs are the relics of former rocky pediments after both chemical and physical weathering under arid conditions. The face of the inselberg is very steep, forming an almost vertical surface which gradually retreats towards its crest
PHOTO: DR. J. HEPWORTH
Bottom right : **Dry Pan, Kalahari Desert**
The fringe of a dry pan
PHOTO: DR. J. HEPWORTH

mountain face until it disappears under the alluvial blanket or fan.

Inselberg

The bosses of rock rising up from a pediment, or protruding above the alluvial fan, are known as inselbergs. They are also encountered on desert plains.

Drywash

The drywash goes under various other names: in the United States it is known as 'arroyo', in Africa and Arabia as 'wadi', in Chile as 'quebrada', in China as 'chapp' and in South Africa as 'laagte'. The drywash is a water drainage channel on the surface of an alluvial fan. It can vary in width from 3 to 30 metres, and according to its age it can develop a braided or detailed branching drainage system. The soils associated with a drywash are of good quality and can support large plants. Erosion by water flow is common, and the vegetation tends to be denser on the banks than in the actual beds as a result.

Dry lake or playa

In the desert plains there are occasional depressions, where rainwater can accumulate when it runs off pediment slopes. A lake bed can form in the lowest part of a desert basin, and water can persist there for several weeks (though rarely for longer) after rain. The surface of the playa is usually flat, and can support little or no vegetation. There are two distinct types of desert dry lakes:

CLAY PAN OR CLAY FLAT This is formed in the desert valleys. When such a pan dries out, the clay surface usually cracks and eventually pulverises. The water-table tends to be well below the surface, but very deep-rooting plant species can become established, provided that they are not inhibited by poor soil or water quality.

SALT PAN, SALT FLAT OR SALT PLAYA Although the water table is usually within 3–4 metres of the surfaces in such areas, plants cannot grow because of the high salt content of the deposits. Salt crystals are found on the surface, and these are among the most hostile surfaces of the desert.

Sabkha

Sabkhas are found in desert areas which lie close to the sea, and are depressions which are not fed by either streams or run-off water. The surface of the sabkha is within 1–2 metres of a very salty water-table, and in the dry season it is covered by a salt crust which overlies a saline bog. A sabkha usually has sand dunes on its edges. It can become flooded by the sea during high tides, or flooded by rainwater after a storm. The salt crust can be broken up during periods of desiccating winds, and the crystalized salt can be blown away to contaminate the soil in neighbouring areas. While no plants can be found growing in a sabkha, a limited range of plants can grow on the periphery, if they are able to tolerate the high level of salinity.

Salina

When a dry salt lake or playa remains moist or contains water throughout the year, it is known as a 'salina'. Vegetation will grow on the perimeter, but the range of species depends on the quality of the water and the soil.

Desert flat or llano

The desert flat is found in broad valleys where the surface slopes gently between a dry lake and the alluvial deposits. The slope of a flat is 1° instead of the 7° usual for alluvial

fans. The surface deposits are finer than those of alluvial fans, and are therefore very suitable for plant establishment.

Desert pavement

A desert pavement is a type of surface which develops on desert flats, alluvial fans and alluvial blankets. It is formed when the wind blows away the sand, silt and clay deposits. The surface is almost level, and consists of rounded pebbles between 15 mm and 75 mm long. When the pebbles are rolled together by wind and rain, and become tightly interlocked, the surface is known as 'pebble armour' or 'serir'. Vegetation can become established on this surface, but is sparser than that found on alluvial fan soils. Deep-rooting species are particularly well-adapted to the desert pavement surface.

Badlands

Badland scenery is usually associated with hilly or mountainous land, which has been deeply scored by gullies created in the aftermath of the occasional heavy storms. The normal rainfall is too scant to support plants, whose roots would otherwise bind the surface and stabilize the slopes. Badlands are most common in highland areas composed of soft bedrock types. Where there are harder rocks which are better able to resist erosion, these remain as tall pillars or platforms, rising above the surrounding landscape.

Sand dunes

There are four major sand dune types:

BARCHAN The barchan dune is crescent-shaped, with the tails of the dune pointing downwind. It is constantly on the move, and progresses across the desert either on its own

Salt Pan—The Sua Pan, Botswana

The Okavango Swamp, of which the Sua Pan is part, is a unique water resource which is at present virtually untapped
PHOTO: DR. J. HEPWORTH

TRANSVERSE DUNES Whereas the longitudinal dune is formed parallel to the wind, the transverse dune develops across its path. These dunes are either an amalgamation of barchans, or they are formed when there is more sand than can be used by a swarm of barchans.

WHALEBACK DUNES Very large siefs, on which both barchans and smaller siefs can develop are called whaleback dunes. They are either an agglomeration of a number of siefs, or can be considered as erosional dunes, because of the rocky surface exposed between them. Water is stored within all the large dunes, as they tend to move quite slowly, and plants can be seen growing on them, with the roots reaching down to the sub-surface storage areas. Nevertheless, vegetation is sparse, and consists either of deep-rooting species, or those plants whose roots can survive in the moving surface, taking their moisture from dew.

Dunes can be classified according to size, environment, growth stage, origins, shape and wind direction. There are simple, compound or complex dunes, depending on the prevailing conditions. When complex or compound dunes coalesce together into larger units still, they form a 'dune field'.[1, 2]

or as part of a swarm, where numbers of dunes become linked and move together.

SIEFS OR LONGITUDINAL DUNES These dunes usually run in parallel lines, up to ten kilometres in length. They appear to have originated as barchans which have become temporarily anchored by a plant or group of plants. These hold down the tail of the dune, enabling the free end to move on its own. The dune then coalesces with other barchans, and thus forms the longitudinal dune. Another theory is that, conversely, the barchan is formed out of a sief, when the speed of the winds flowing over the sief drops, and friction on the sand causes turbulence which breaks up the continuous surface into smaller crescent dunes.

Desert soil classification

In 1962, Aubert developed a simple classification of soils,[2] relative to the aridity index of the land, and since the definitions of extreme aridity, aridity and semi-aridity were

Above left : **Badlands, Arizona Desert, USA**
PHOTO: US INFORMATION SERVICE, LONDON
Below : **Whale-back dune, Algeria**
Smaller dunes can be seen on the main dune
PHOTO: ALGERIAN INFORMATION SERVICE, LONDON

currently in use, his system corresponds to these definitions.

Extremely arid regions

The soils of these regions are severely blown, deposited and unsifted soils. They are either raw, undeveloped mineral soils, composed mostly of rock fragments, or else they have a weakly developed structure and profile, such as are found in regs, sand dunes, skeletal soils and salt pans.

The influence of rainfall is minimal, and cementation of particles occurs only rarely. The surface soil of the extremely arid regions is therefore highly susceptible to sun, wind and high temperature erosion. Plant colonization is rare, and is restricted to the ephemeral annual species which germinate rapidly after rainfall, or to deep-rooting species which can reach any available deep underlying water source. The potential for plant establishment can only be improved by increasing the volume of water available, and by providing protection to the selected zone, by erection of shelter barriers, or stabilization of any dunes likely to encroach.

Arid regions

The soils of the arid regions include the desert and steppe soils, the red and grey desert soil groups, and the sierozem soils, including the red, grey and tropical hydromorphic sierozems. Desert soils are found in areas with 200 mm rainfall, but even this volume is not sufficient to develop a well-stratified soil, because the surface layer is thin and low in organic matter. Below the surface layer, there is frequently a shallow zone of slightly weathered material, and an accumulation of calcium carbonate.

The sierozems develop in regions with between 200 mm and 300 mm of rain per annum, and are therefore found on the fringes of deserts. They have clearly differentiated soil layers: the topsoil contains organic matter, but its subsoil is weak, with calcium carbonate concretions at 300 mm to 500 mm below the surface. Gypsum deposits can frequently be found at a depth of one metre.

Higher moisture levels are absorbed by the soil to a greater extent than by the extremely arid soils, and their surfaces are less subject to wind erosion. The sierozem soils have a greater potential for vegetation establishment than the true desert soils, but both major desert soil types in the arid region can support a significant amount of vegetation cover. To improve plant cover will require less additional water than in the extremely arid regions, and the principal element for consideration should be the stabilization of the existing vegetation, either by protection, using conservation techniques, or by augmentation of the water supply, should climatic variations occur.

Semi-arid regions

The predominant colour of the soils of these regions is brown, although there are a number of sub-groups: brown steppe soils, reddish-brown tropical soils, encrusted brown, saline brown and alkali or solonetzic brown. There is a higher content of organic matter, which is to be expected with an increasing influence from rain, which ranges between 250 mm and 500 mm.[5, 2]

The semi-arid regions have richer soils and support the full range of self-sustaining plants: trees, scrub and grasses. The density of cover depends very strictly on the annual climatic patterns and variations, for in good years good growth and regeneration will occur, while in drier years, much of the vegetation will die back. Because these regions are beyond the edge of the true desert, man has been able to exploit them, and farm them, with varying degrees of success.

To improve the potential of semi-arid lands will involve the careful conservation of certain areas, while others are in active use. Their economic potential for the resident populations cannot be overstressed, but it must also be appreciated that semi-arid lands can nowhere be considered a permanent medium, capable of sustained productivity. Because these lands are so valuable, they have in the past often been exploited far beyond their potential, and it is then that they become endangered by wind and gulley erosion, which can reverse the trend from productivity to desertification with terrifying rapidity.

Soil development

TABLE 2.1 DESERT SOIL TYPES (Based on G. Aubert, 1962[2])

Aridity index	Soil types	Rainfall	Plants
Extremely arid	Skeletal soils Blown soils	less than 100 mm	Ephemerals Deep-rooted plants Very sparse plant cover
Arid	Red and grey desert soils Red and grey sierozem soils	less than 200 mm 200 mm–300 mm	Ephemerals Annual grasses Deep-rooted scrub Small deep-rooted trees Sparse plant cover with large open spaces between plants
Semi-arid	Brown soil series: Steppe soils Encrusted soils Saline soils Solonetz soils Tropical soils	250 mm–500 mm	Ephemerals Annual and perennial grasses Deep and shallow rooted scrub Large trees Good plant cover: no, or small, spaces between plants.

Soil development starts with the raw mineral soil of the hamada and reg types, proceeds through the desert steppe soils and sierozems, and terminates (for the purpose of this discussion) with the semi-arid brown soil series. It is only when the semi-arid soil stages are reached that soils with well-defined layers are found. The character of these soils is dependent on the relative dominance of physical weathering, topographical differences, scarcity of vegetation cover, the severity of wind and water erosion, the nature of the bedrock materials, the moisture patterns

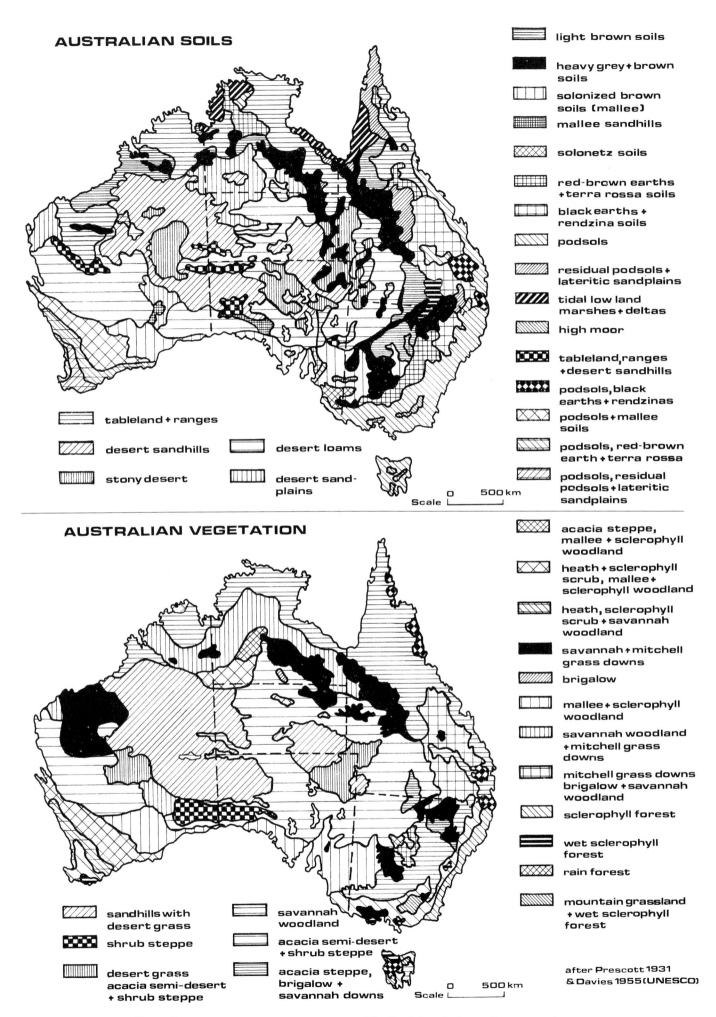

AUSTRALIAN SOILS

light brown soils

heavy grey + brown soils

solonized brown soils (mallee)

mallee sandhills

solonetz soils

red-brown earths + terra rossa soils

black earths + rendzina soils

podsols

residual podsols + lateritic sandplains

tidal low land marshes + deltas

high moor

tableland, ranges + desert sandhills

podsols, black earths + rendzinas

podsols + mallee soils

podsols, red-brown earth + terra rossa

podsols, residual podsols + lateritic sandplains

tableland + ranges

desert sandhills

desert loams

stony desert

desert sand-plains

Scale ⊢ 0 500 km

AUSTRALIAN VEGETATION

acacia steppe, mallee + sclerophyll woodland

heath + sclerophyll scrub, mallee + sclerophyll woodland

heath, sclerophyll scrub + savannah woodland

savannah + mitchell grass downs

brigalow

mallee + sclerophyll woodland

savannah woodland + mitchell grass downs

mitchell grass downs brigalow + savannah woodland

sclerophyll forest

wet sclerophyll forest

rain forest

mountain grassland + wet sclerophyll forest

sandhills with desert grass

shrub steppe

desert grass acacia semi-desert + shrub steppe

savannah woodland

acacia semi-desert + shrub steppe

acacia steppe, brigalow + savannah downs

after Prescott 1931 & Davies 1955 (UNESCO)

Scale ⊢ 0 500 km

Fig 8a *(top) Australian soils*
(after Prescott 1944 and Davies 1955, Unesco)

Fig 8b *(above) Australian vegetation*
(after Prescott 1931 and Davies 1955, Unesco)

particularly in local depressions, or the retention of wind-blown salt.

In regions where the climate is known[2] to have changed from wetter to drier conditions, such as the western Sahara, Mauritania, North Africa and the Arabian Peninsula the soils and the environment can be seen to have degraded. The skeletal soils, with sparse vegetation, on the mountains have disappeared. However the alluvial soils on the upper slopes, although coarse, will have had a gradation of soil particle sizes, from boulders to sand, and will have formerly supported deep-rooting species and ephemeral plants. Organic matter will have been low, but would have been sufficient to encourage the perpetuation of vegetation. The onset of drier conditions, causing the death of plants, loosens the soil, and the smaller soil particles and organic matter are blown away. Similarly, the alluvial deposits on the footslopes degrade, and lose their valuable soil components to the winds which drive them into the lower valleys to form sand dunes. Vegetation cover, binding the former soils into a stable habitat, disappears and its return can only be accomplished by climatic improvement.

Plant life on desert soils is dependent on the depth of the soil, the structure and components of that soil, and its ability to allow water to drain down through it and to store it at levels which can be reached by the plant roots. Accordingly the soil type controls the range of plants able to establish in it.

DESERT VEGETATION TYPES

The gradual building-up of desert soils, either by accumulation of blown soil (which increases water-storage potential) or by increased weathering (which decreases it) defines the structure of the plants associated with them. The removal of soil layers by wind, man or other agencies changes the direction of the plant development process. A typical sequence following increasing soil depths starts with the plants whose roots actively dissolve rocks by acid secretion. These plants are known as *rhizophagolitho-phytes*, and they are followed by the *chasmophytes*, plants whose roots penetrate the fissures in the rock, then by ephemerals growing on the thinnest soils, succulent plants on less shallow soils, then desert grassland species, and finally the development of scrub and open woodland. Should the surface soil be displaced, the sequence can be reversed through successive stages, a process which can be triggered by a worsening of the climate, or by the removal of the plant cover by animals or man. The contributing element is the extent of soil character change that occurs when such a disturbance takes place.

Arid land plants

In simple terms, which will be discussed later in more detail, there are three basic categories of arid land plants: ephemerals, succulent perennials and woody perennials.[6]

Ephemeral plants

50–60% of all desert plants are ephemerals. They have extremely short life-cycles and are herbaceous, i.e. non-woody, in character. Their growth is rapid: the time from germination to death is telescoped into 6–8 weeks. Their

activity has to coincide with the moist season: they deal with the dry season and drought quite simply by by-passing them altogether. Therefore they have no need to develop xerophytic or drought-resistance properties. Their roots are shallow, they are small plants, they grow very fast and flower quickly. The seeds can remain dormant in the soil until the next important rains, and even if there is no rain for several successive years, the seeds are not damaged. Went established in 1953[6] that 10 mm of rain was not sufficient to promote germination, but that some seedlings would appear after 15 mm of rain had fallen; germination is only complete after 25 mm of rain has fallen. He also observed that a cloud-burst producing 75 mm of rain did not automatically ensure germination, and from this evidence he concluded that the seed contained some agent which inhibited germination unless the circumstances were all favourable. Shreve discovered[2] in 1957 that germination was also related to the number of sunny days following rainfall, and also realized that the two classes of ephemerals—winter and summer ephemerals—had different temperature requirements and optimums. For winter ephemerals, the optimum was between 15·5°C and 18°C, while the optimum for summer ephemerals was 26°C to 32°C.[6]

Ephemerals are the first colonizers of most kinds of desert terrain (but see the note in the first section of this desert vegetation discussion about rhizophagolithophytes and chasmophytes) as their seeds may be spread by animals, insects and the wind. When the plants die and decay, they are attacked by soil organisms, and soil fertility is thereby gradually improved, enabling the establishment of other plant types, should other conditions allow this to happen. In good years, the plants produce a larger number of seeds than are produced in poorer, drier years, and in this way, the species ensure their survival.

Succulent perennial plants

The phenomenon of succulence occurs when the parenchyma or outer cells of the plant stem or leaf enlarge or proliferate. The evolution of this characteristic means that the volume of the plant's stem or leaves is increased, which enables the plant to store an increased volume of water within its structure. The deposition of a water-proofing layer of wax or similar substance on the external surface of the plant reduces the risk of loss of water from leaves or stem, and this, in combination with the cell proliferation, enables the plant to reduce its overall water requirement.

Succulent perennials are either spiny, like the cacti, or non-spiny but physiologically swollen plants. The cacti of the American continent, the succulent euphorbias of the African dry zones, and certain other succulents have a further quality which fits them to life in their dry environments: they are able to close their stomata during the heat of the day, to avoid excessive loss of water through transpiration, and open them during the coolness of the night instead. This phenomenon is being intensively researched, especially in the U.S.A.

It has now been established that there are three distinct aspects of desert plant physiology, and these will be discussed later in this chapter, when the specific adaptations of desert plants to their environment are examined.

Succulent perennial plant, Yemen Arab Republic
PHOTO: DR. J. HEPWORTH

Woody perennial plant, Kalahari Desert
PHOTO: A. SOBOTT

Woody perennial plants

Although the ephemeral plants make up 50–60% of the total number of plants in the desert, the woody perennial is the dominant plant type. Woody perennials are composed of a number of morphologically different forms of plant, ranging from grasses and woody herbs, through shrubs to trees. They are all very hardy, for they have to cope with the major characteristics of the desert environment: drought, heat and wind. They can be evergreen or deciduous—drought-deciduous in the hot deserts and cold-deciduous in the case of the cooler deserts. They grow most actively after rain, and become dormant either during periods of drought, or during the cold season. Many of the woody perennials are spiny or harsh-textured.[6]

The seeds of woody desert perennials have a particular germination characteristic in many cases, and Went researched into this, when he was working on the germination patterns of desert ephemerals.[6] He found that many perennials produce seed which will only germinate if the seed coat is damaged in some way. This damage can occur in a number of natural ways, for instance by the action of stones and boulders pushed along wadi beds after sufficiently large volumes of water have accumulated, these stones having a grinding effect on the coats of such seeds as may be amongst them, and cracking the coats open. Other seeds rely on the effects of the digestive juices in animal intestines to soften their coats, prior to germination. Once the seeds of woody perennials in the desert have germinated, they produce only a few leaves before they appear to stop growing. This is because activity shifts to the root structure, which grows deeper and deeper down into the soil, to penetrate the moister layers below. Once the roots are well-established, the plant starts to produce more leaves and expand above its surface growth.

THE MECHANISMS OF PLANT ADAPTATION TO ARID CONDITIONS

Xerophytic plants have the ability to resist or evade drought in some manner. One factor, or a combination of several factors, can provide the plant with its defence mechanism. As mentioned earlier, there are three distinct xerophytic systems: morphological systems, anatomical characteristics, and physiological adaptations. The morphological characters are, however, the external expressions of the internal physiological processes and the anatomical structure.

Morphological processes

All plants have two morphological zones: the root and the shoot.

Root growth

The spread of the root, in desert and arid land plants, is generally larger than the spread of the shoots. The plant can thus preserve its water balance. The roots grow in a vertical or a horizontal direction or both, and their network is usually influenced by the soil type or its depth.

The deepest roots are found on the deeper alluvial soils, like alluvial fans and the banks of ephemeral streams, where they grow down to reach the underground water-table. Some plant roots can reach to a remarkable depth: mesquite roots up to 20 metres long have been found; lucerne (alfalfa) roots can reach 35 metres in length and tamarisk roots up to 50 metres. It is not uncommon to find plants with roots of between 10 and 15 metres in length.

Horizontal roots are usually found in the shallow, sandy desert soil types, or in shallow soils overlying rock. They are usually spongy and tough, radiating outwards from the stem for up to 15–20 metres, and lying just below the surface. The creosote bush (*Larrea divaricata*) in the Argentine has roots 6 metres long, lying only 300–500 mm below the surface, and the desert scrub plant *Retama raetam* can develop roots over a surface area of 40 square metres.

After rain, some plants put out 'rain roots', which grow from their main root systems. Their function is obvious, but the speed with which they appear demonstrates the ability of these plants to react very fast to changes in soil moisture levels. Such roots can even be found after an exceptionally heavy dew. Once these 'rain roots' have exhausted all the extra available moisture, they die back, and only reappear when there is another shower or dew.

Rocks, such as limestone, that are natural storers of water, attract the rhizophagolithophytes and chasmophytes mentioned earlier on.

Shoot growth
The large root–small shoot ratio is prevalent throughout the desert flora. The Russian botanists, Sveshnikova and Zalensky,[6] studying plants in the Pamir mountains west of the Takla-makan desert, found that certain root systems exceed the shoot systems in the ratio of 1:30 and occasionally even 1:50, although the commonest ratio is 1:6.

Some plants found in the Israeli desert are considered seasonally dimorphic, having both long and short shoots. As they grow, they are able to shed different types of leaves and branches, according to seasonal variations. The shedding of leaves is a typical method by which a plant can reduce its transpiring surface area. Other plants are able to produce smaller leaves when it seems necessary, or have evolved to a point where they have no leaves at all ('aphylly').

The reduction of leaf surface area lessens the pressure on the limited water supply available, and this helps the plant's survival chances. Noteworthy are *Zygophyllum dumosum, Artemisia monosperma,* and *Helianthemum ellipticum,* which can reduce their leaf surface area by 87%, 76% and 62% respectively (Orshansky, 1954).[6] Other leaf-shedding plants are the ocatillo (*Fouquieria splendens*) of the U.S.A., and *Encelia, Artemisia, Noaea, Haloxylon* and *Anabasis* in Israel. Mediterranean species, like the ones found in Syria, are *Poterium spinosum, Cistus salviaefolius,* and *Thymus capitatus* (all chasmophytes). Some plants like *Ephedra trifurca* in New Mexico survive as leafless green twigs. Some grasses, on the other hand, roll their leaves into tubes, to protect the stomata.

Several plant species with relatively long leaves and small spines can change with increasing aridity to producing smaller leaves and more prominent spines: *Alhagi maurorum, Nitraria retusa, Lycium arabicum, Zilla spinosa* and *Euphorbia cuneata* are examples of plants with this ability.

Adventitious buds can form on some roots when wind erosion of the soil exposes the roots, and these buds can develop into new shoots, for instance *Lycium arabicum, Zilla spinosa, Echinops spinosissima, Pityranthus tortuosus, Iphiona mucronata* and *Heliotropium luteum* are examples here.

Adaptation to dry conditions
The Baobab Tree (Adansonia digitata) *adapts to the dry season by dropping its leaves, and by storing water in its trunk*
PHOTO: SATOUR, LONDON

In the Sonora Desert of Mexico, several of the plants found have rigid thorny branches, and no leaves at all. The necessary photosynthetic processes take place in specially-adapted stems and branches, for example *Canotia holocantha, Holocantha emoryi, Koeterlinia spinosa* and *Dalea spinosa*.

Cercidium floridum carries out photosynthesis in its bark, and it can improve its photosynthetic performance by producing many chlorophyllous branches of small diameter.

An interxylary sleeve of cork can be developed over the previous year's growth of xylem by *Artemisia incana*. This layer retards the process of desiccation, especially near wounds, and slows the upward movement of water, by restricting it to a narrow channel.

Anatomical characteristics which aid survival
There are six main anatomical adaptation systems:[7, 8]

1 Resins and varnish-like coverings of stems and leaves: these exudations from the plant's surface cells help to isolate them from the surrounding atmosphere and reduce the danger of excessive dehydration of the surface cells

2 Lignification of the inner cells: this is due to the deposition in the cell wall of lignin, which becomes mixed into the middle lamella between the cells and into the cellulose layers of the cell wall. Lignified cell walls are generally dead, but have increased rigidity and strength

3 A high ratio of volume to surface area: the proliferation of internal cells ensures that the highest possible volume of water is preserved within the plant, and desiccation pressure on the plant surface is reduced by the smaller surface area

4 Hairs on the leaf or stem surfaces: the air that is trapped between the hairs creates an insulating layer which keeps

C₃ plant, Kalahari Desert

Capparis spinosa: *being a C₃ plant it can only survive if there is adequate moisture for the plant to fulfil its normal functions*

PHOTO: A. SOBOTT

the dry atmosphere separated from the plant surface. This trapped air layer is saturated with moisture and thus prevents further evaporation losses from the stomata in the plant leaf or stem

5 Stomata in deep grooves: the moisture and gaseous exchange relationships of the plant are controlled through the stomata. By being set in deep recesses protected by large guard cells, the stomata are prevented from opening excessively wide, which would allow the loss of moisture

6 Cutinization of the epidermal and hypodermal cells: cutin is a waxy substance which is secreted through the cell walls and deposited on the external surface of the cell walls. It is almost impenetrable to water, and therefore protects the cells below it from excessive water loss. By the extension of cutinization (or cuticularization) to the hypodermal cells under the epidermal cells, further reductions in water loss are achieved.

Physiological processes

Although both the morphological and the anatomical adaptive mechanisms affect the internal processes of the plant, they deal mainly with its water relations, as controlled by its structure. It has, however, recently been realized that because a number of plants are able to withstand desic-

cation for several consecutive years, there must be other processes within the plant which support the morphological and anatomical mechanisms, and so improve its xerophytic potential further.

Research into these physiological characteristics has been carried out principally in the U.S.A.:[8] at the University of California at Riverside, the Philip L. Boyd Deep Canyon Research Center and the Carnegie Institute. Between them, they have studied the phenomenon of plant survival in a wide range of arid and semi-arid land plants.

By tracing the Carbon 13 radioactive isotope, it has been proved that the photosynthetic pathway can follow two separate routes in desert plants. When the carbon dioxide pathway within the plant was measured, different processes which resulted directly from certain physiological and anatomical activities were discovered. Normal plants, those living in a balanced environment with no exceptional stresses on them, take in carbon dioxide during the day through the stomata in their leaves. From there it is quickly transferred to the chloroplasts in the cells, where it is immediately used in photosynthesis. This pathway uses the standard 'Calvin Cycle' and has become known as the 'C₃ pathway', and the plants exhibiting this characteristic are accordingly known as 'C₃ plants'.

The plants with a particularly strong resistance to arid conditions were found not to conform with this normal C₃ pattern. In these plants there is a delay in the transfer of carbon dioxide because it is stored instead in organic acids present in the plant, malic acid being the most important. Furthermore, it was found that the stomata acted in reverse of the normal pattern, and in this way the plants were able to avoid heavy transpiration losses during the day, and absorbed carbon dioxide through their open stomata at night. These plants were designated 'C₄' plants.

C₄ plant

Spinifex Grass (Zygochloa hirsutus): *although rainfall is adequate for the large trees, the open soil surface does not retain moisture and plants with C₄ characteristics will survive under these conditions*

PHOTO: AUSTRALIAN INFORMATION SERVICE, LONDON

Above: **C₄ plant**
The saltbush (Atriplex nummularia) *has evolved to produce hairy leaves which reduce transpiration and therefore water need*
PHOTO: AUSTRALIAN INFORMATION SERVICE, LONDON
Right: **CAM plant**
Saguaro Cactus: Carnegea gigantea
PHOTO: US INFORMATION SERVICE, LONDON
Below: **CAM plant**
Welwitschia mirabilis (bainesii): *the unique plant of the Namib Desert. The plant develops in virtual isolation. It depends on dew supplementing the very scarce rainfall*
PHOTO: SATOUR, LONDON

Subsequently, it was found that some plants could select either the C_3 or the C_4 pathway, according to prevailing conditions. The option chosen was found to be closely related to water shortage, high temperatures or high salinity. Since water shortage is generally the major factor in the survival of desert plants, most attention has been given to mechanisms by which the plants resist drought, and to those plants which are able to make the most efficient use of the available moisture. The greater efficiency of the C_4 plants in using water is related strictly to the physiological and chemical functions of the plant. The carbon dioxide, taken up at night, enters a carboxylase reaction,in the plant and is converted into organic acids. The following day, while the stomata are closed, the carbon dioxide is transferred to the normal C_3 pathway for use elsewhere in the plant. This ability to function in direct response to the environment and so select the most appropriate way to avoid harm from the hostile environment has been given the name 'Crassulacean Acid Metabolism' (CAM), from its initial discovery in the *Crassulaceae* family.

Since this initial work, Szarek and Ting have published a report (1977)[9] reviewing the occurrence of CAM in plants. So far, CAM has been found in one gymnosperm (*Welwitschia mirabilis* of the Namib Desert), two ferns and a number of families of flowering plants: *Agavaceae, Aizoaceae, Asclepiadaceae, Asteraceae, Bromeliaceae, Cactaceae, Crassulaceae, Cucurbitaceae, Labiatae, Liliaceae, Orchidaceae, Piperaceae, Portulacaceae*, and *Vitaceae*.

The evolution of the C_4 and CAM plants is now receiving more attention, as it indicates the hierarchy of plants in the arid environment. The species *Atriplex* and *Euphorbia* are receiving the most attention. From various studies it appears that the C_3 plants are the most primitive, for they have no special drought-resisting qualities. The development of the C_4 pathway is the first step in the isolation of the chemical functions of a plant from its habitat. However, once a plant has evolved with a C_4 pathway, it becomes restricted to the particular arid environment. The evolution of the CAM process, giving the plant two environmental choices, is therefore the most recent and most sophisticated in evolutionary terms.

A simple method for identifying C_4 plants is examination of the leaf cell structure. To reduce transpiration and to improve the isolation of the moist inner cells from the parched atmosphere, C_4 plants have developed the 'Krantz anatomy' of chlorochymatous bundle sheath cells, instead of the normal palisade layering. (Philpott and Troughton, working on *Atriplex* in 1974.)[8]

All this has relevance in terms of plant competition. Where conditions are normal, and in particular where there is a regular pattern of rainfall supporting a perennial plant population, C_3 plants are commonest. With an increasingly irregular rainfall pattern, the C_3 plants gradually thin out, losing their potential of forming a continuous canopy or cover of either roots or branches, and C_4 plants take over the open spaces. CAM plants follow when increasing aridity occurs and water starts to be at a premium. Therefore the sequence is: C_3 plants dying out with increasing aridity and being replaced first by the C_4 plants and subsequently by the CAM plants. Even though the mechanisms of the C_4 and CAM plants are more highly

sophisticated, they are only of a special and restricted value to arid lands: when moisture increases, the C_3 plants will gradually return.

In practical terms, any activity, such as over-cropping or over-grazing, which precipitates the elimination of C_3 plants from arid areas, will in due course promote the establishment of C_4 and eventually CAM plants. Generally speaking (and excluding the few edible succulents and cacti) such plants are of no value in fodder terms. However they are significant in that, once established, they can improve the soil's structure and stability by the binding action of their roots, and add to the soil's organic content, so assisting the return of the C_4 and C_3 plants. This should make it easier to select plants for land restoration works in arid lands, once reasonably fertile conditions are provided. The use of the CAM–C_4–C_3 sequence would make most efficient use of resources, and would eventually lead to the re-establishment of the indigenous flora of a territory, without the expensive techniques involved in the usual land restoration procedures. (See Appendix 3.)

NOTES

1 Fairbridge, R. W. *Encyclopedia of Geomorphology*. Reinhold Book Corporation: New York 1968

2 McGinnies, W. G., Goldman, B. J., Paylore, P. *Deserts of the World*. University of Arizona Press: 1968 (information reproduced by kind permission of the publishers and editors)

3 Le Houerou, H. 'The Nature and Causes of Desertification', *Arid Lands Newsletter No. 3*. University of Arizona, USA: 1976

4 Unesco. *Plant Ecology, Vol 6, Arid Zone Research* © Unesco: Paris 1955 (information reproduced by kind permission of the publishers)

5 Russell, E. W. *Soil Conditions and Plant Growth* (9th edition). Longmans, Green and Co: London 1961

6 Hills, E. S. *Arid Lands: A Geographical Appraisal*. Unesco/Methuen: London 1966 (information reproduced by kind permission of Unesco)

7 Lowson, J. M. *Text Book of Botany*. Howarth and Warne, University Tutorial Press: London 1953

8 Briggs, W. R. *Annual Reports of the Director of the Department of Plant Biology*. Carnegie Institute, Stanford, California, USA: 1973–4, 1974–5

9 Szarek, S. R. and Ting, I. P. *Review: The Occurrence of Crassulacean Acid Metabolism among Plants*. Department of Botany and Microbiology, Arizona State University, USA; Department of Botany, University of California Riverside, USA: 1977

3 Desert vegetation

It has been seen that each of the three basic categories of plants found in desert habitats shows its own particular methods of adapting to the dry conditions. Each plant's physical characteristics are therefore a good indication of the degree of intensity the plant can withstand. All of them demonstrate different means of avoiding, resisting or withstanding drought: the ephemerals germinate and grow only after rain, thus 'avoiding' the drought; the succulent perennials, by storing water in their leaves, 'resist' it, and the woody perennials, shedding their leaves or branches, 'escape' from it.

The distribution, and the survival, of these plants is not only a question of their morphological, anatomical or physiological aptitudes—it is also related to the locality where the plant is growing. As has already been described, this is influenced in turn by the morphology of the land and the way the climate moulds it. Therefore the plants that appear, establish and survive, mirror these interactions.

To understand this, a detailed examination of each of the elements that combine to produce the individual plants and their associates is required, but it should be realized that no one element within the ecosystem works on its own: each is linked to all the other factors, and each influences the others, so that the plant lives with, and affects the whole environment. In order to start the process of analysis, it is necessary to return to the habitat, and look at the way it influences plant establishment, then to examine the way the plant communities develop, before the individual plants are looked at in detail. It is further necessary to study the way the history of plants has influenced their present-day distribution, and finally to examine the implications this has for the way we use, or should use, plants within our environment.

DESERT HABITATS AND ASSOCIATED PLANTS

Each desert habitat has a distinct type of plant community associated with it. The nature of the habitat determines the precise manner in which plants are able to exploit its potential. There are differences of opinion about whether the flora of the desert should be studied from the point of view of the botanist or the ecologist, as will be seen later, but nonetheless, if the potential of the desert environment is to be achieved, the basic medium—the soil—should be explored first, to establish the potential for food production programmes, animal pastures or simple conservation.

Types of desert ecosystem
In 1955, M. Kassas, working for the Arid Zone Research Programme of Unesco, distinguished nine different desert ecosystems:
1 Desert plateaux
2 Desert wadis
3 Desert mountains
4 Erosion surfaces
5 Erosion pavements
6 Gravel deserts
7 Desert plains and playas (lakes)
8 Desert sand drifts
9 Dunes.

Not all of these ecosystems can be found in every desert. Dunes for example, need not necessarily exist, nor need the dry lakes or playas, but these nine are the basic types to be found in most deserts.

Ozenda,[1] working in the Sahara in 1958, managed to distinguish only seven biological habitats there:
1 Ergs, and other sandy soils
2 Regs with clay or rocky soils
3 Hamadas and rocky soils
4 Non-saline depressions (not inundated)
5 Saline soils
6 Aquatic habitats
7 Oasis habitats.

Emberger,[1] who was also working in the Sahara, found eight habitats:
1 Hamadas—denuded plateaux with depressions
2 Mountains and hills, e.g. Tibesti Mountains
3 Regs—bare, except in depressions
4 Gypseous and clay regs with depressions
5 Gravelly regs and ergs (absolute desert) in the southern Sahara
6 Gypseous deserts interspersed with ergs and sabkhas
7 Ergs and dunes with valleys, drier than (1) above
8 Dunes—bare except in depressions.

Emberger's classification took Ozenda's basic order and expanded it slightly, to include, wherever possible, further details of the structure of the desert surface and sub-surface.

Types of desert soil
M. Petrov,[1] studying the Central Asian Deserts in 1966 and 1967, distinguished nine different edaphic (soil) communities, and he assigned to each the climatic type of desert its edaphic type, and its vegetation. The climatic types he

identified were the Dzungaro-Kazakhstan, the Irano-Turan, and the Mongolian. The edaphic types are:

1 Typical sandy deserts on the desert-sandy sierozem and grey-brown soils of the palaeoalluvial and coastal plains
2 Sandy-pebbly deserts ('gobis') on gypsumed grey-brown soils of the Tertiary and Cretaceous plateaux
3 Gravelly gypsumed deserts on grey-brown soils of Tertiary plateaux
4 Stony and gravelly deserts on hillocky and low-mountain areas
5 Loamy desert on slightly carbonate grey-brown soils of stratified plains and plateaux of northern deserts
6 Clay-loess desert on sierozems of piedmont plains
7 Takyr deserts on piedmont plains and in ancient river deltas
8 Badlands
9 Solonchak deserts of saline depressions of lake and sea coasts.

M. Kassas and El-Abyad working in the Sahara in 1962 and 1963[1] broke the edaphic communities down to an even smaller scale:

1 The lower courses of the main channels of drainage systems
2 The channels of drainage systems where the ground surface is covered with coarse materials
3 Communities occurring within the drainage channels
4 The main channels of drainage systems, in particular on limestone areas, where the stream (wadi) beds are covered with mixed rock detritus
5 The wadis of limestone areas on the eastern edges of the Cairo–Suez Desert
6 The downstream parts of main wadis where the soil is mixed sand and silt, which is mostly water-borne
7 The channels of the upstream part of the wadis
8 The major drainage channels of the main drainage systems
9 The distantly-isolated drainage systems
10 The smaller tributaries of the drainage systems
11 The small upper runnels where the surface veneer of sand is thin and discontinuous.

This remarkable analysis indicates the detailed survey required to relate plants to their micro-habitats, and therefore to the micro-climates. Of greater importance, this classification demonstrates how closely water distribution patterns have to be examined to find how the volume of water available to plants varies, in terms of both surface distribution and sub-surface storage.

Hassib in 1951[1] approached the Saharan vegetation from the point of view of plant associations, though he assigned to each an edaphic habitat:

1 Sandy plains and broad valleys
2 Deep sandy soil
3 Sandy desert
4 Rocky desert plateaux and shallow depressions on the margins of deep valleys
5 The sandy floors of shallow wadis and on small dunes
6 The rocks and high cliffs of deep wadis
7 Loose stony areas, or banks of wadis
8 Sandy soils with drifting sand collecting around plants
9 Depressions or exposed plateaux
10 Sandy ground of broad shallow wadis

11 Within broad shallow wadis.

Again, this researcher understands that the relationship of the micro-habitat is a vital part of the explanation of why plants become established in certain locations.

Factors influencing plant distribution

It is not always possible to identify either the plant habitat or the form the plant community takes, even with careful study, and so to establish how both or either developed. This was the sort of dilemma faced by Dr John Smith in the Sudan in 1949,[2] and his surveys show his brilliant analytical methods.

He found in his initial research that, except in certain cases where plant distribution was related clearly to climate and altitude, most plants were found in widely differing rainfall zones, and it was difficult to establish what factors limited or promoted the distribution of plants. His idea was to examine this problem by using four transects: contour, rainfall, site and belt.

The contour transect

Records field ecology in an area of one rainfall regime, and it shows how species vary with contours and with the character of the soil surface, and how each species is limited to a certain site type.

The rainfall transect

Was developed for a single species, and indicates the different types of site on which a particular species occurs at different parts of its rainfall span. It is a contour section across the rainfall levels and demonstrates how the type of site occupied by a single species varies with changes in volume of rainfall, and what site type is required in each rainfall level by each species.

The site transect

Records sites which are equi-conditional in available moisture, and shows the values in terms of the available water of the various soil types in whatever one rainfall level they occur. It extracts the various types of site found in the rainfall transect and places them in order of water availability.

The belt transect

Describes the sequence whereby one plant succeeds another on any one type of site in gradually changing rainfalls. It establishes a list of type species in order of their moisture demand derived from the resources in several site series, crossing the isohyet (equal rainfall).

After analyzing the transects, Dr Smith found that:

1 Species occur in a definite succession on the same type of site, from the wet end of the country to the dry end
2 The species preserve this order of occurrence if examined on one type of site across several rainfalls
3 The types of site can be arranged for any rainfall in order of water value. This order is the same as that on which the sites carrying a given species occur in the rainfall transect for that species
4 A species is no indicator of soil or rainfall until its transect is known. Then, the use of its occurrence site type makes the plant a reasonable indicator of rainfall.

Furthermore, on datum soils, the volume of rainfall is a precise indicator of the expected clay content of the soil

5 For any given water condition, there is a very limited range of textures on which a given tree species will survive

6 For a given soil texture, there is a very limited water range, which is, for the texture of the soil, the necessary water demand for that species.

In other words, provided the various transect surveys have been carried out, the soil texture directly influences the range of species that will establish, and Dr Smith concludes that '. . . these principal ecological sub-divisions are more constant than their species composition . . .', further emphasizing that the habitat controls the form of the plant ecosystem. His subdivisions are shown in table 3.1.

TABLE 3.1 PLANT COMMUNITIES IN THE SUDAN
(Based on study of Dr John Smith 1949)

Type	Rainfall	Species	Soil
Desert	25–50 mm	*Acacia flava*	Coarse sand
	25–50 mm	*Capparis decidua* *Maerua crassifolia* *Leptadenia spartium*	Favoured locations
Acacia desert scrub	50–250 mm	*Acacia tortilis*	Sand
	50–400 mm	*Acacia raddiana* *Maerua crassifolia* *Capparis decidua* *Acacia flava* *Boscia senegalensis*	Clay
	50–400 mm	*Salvadora persica* *Leptadenia spartium*	Sand dunes
Acacia short grass country	300–400 mm	*Acacia mellifera*	Clay soils
	300–400 mm	*Acacia senegal* *Albizzia aylmeri* *Albizzia sericocephala*	Sand
Acacia tall grass country	400–800 mm	*Acacia mellifera* *Acacia fistula* *Acacia senegal* *Acacia seyal* *Balanites aegyptiaca*	Clays
Mixed deciduous fire-swept forest	800–1200 mm	*Acacia hebecladoides* *Tamarindus indica* *Albizzia zygia* *Albizzia anthelmintica* *Albizzia sericocephala* *Dalbergia melanoxylon*	Sand

From these analyses, it is evident that there are differences in approach to establish the character of the habitat, and research therefore is defined by the state of knowledge obtaining and by the purpose behind the research. If information is available, such as the analyses of Kassas, Ozenda and Emberger, only micro-habitat studies will be required, but if there is no data forthcoming, and visual analysis does not help, research will have to be modelled on the intensity shown in Smith's work. Moreover, unless research is carried out to the required extent, serious errors in decisions could be made.

THE CLASSIFICATION OF PLANT COMMUNITIES

Desert plant communities have a number of common features of which the main ones are:

1 Each community is generally dominated by one species, which gives it its visual uniformity

2 Each community has a number of species associated with it which may or may not be linked to any particular community type

3 Each community is characterized by the frequency or density of the species rather than by the presence or absence of any particular species

4 Each habitat has a distinct community associated with it.
   Küchler, in 1949,[1] established that vegetation cover varies in accordance with the depth and stability of the surface soils, and described the principal forms of desert vegetation as:

• Barren
  Sparse shrubs and grass
• Scattered shrubs and grass
• Scattered shrubs and/or scrubby trees with or without scattered third storey of trees
• Dense shrub and/or scrubby trees
    with scattered third storey of trees
    with grain-herb cultivation
• Palms, with or without grain-herb cultivation
• Steppe
• Steppe savannah
• Grain-herb cultivation
• Marsh.

Increasing soil depth is indicated by the first six forms.

Conditions for the occurrence of various plant communities

F. Shreve,[1] working in the Sonora Desert in Mexico, found that the frequency of large desert communities is affected by the severity of the habitat conditions, and because the same few species occur over and over again, the repetition of a particular environment encourages a repetition of its characteristic associations. He also realized that the term

Top right: **Desert Plant Community dominated by one species**
A desert plant community of deep-rooting trees in Piura, Peru. The surface soil is stabilised by uniform plant coverage. The sub-shrub layer is inhibited by competition and shading
PHOTO: J. LEON OLAVARRIA

Middle right: **Plant community characterised by the frequency or density of species**
This community is colonizing a reg-like desert floor in the Northern Frontier Province of Pakistan. The plants can only use pockets of soil and their roots spread out horizontally to tap moisture in other pockets, or under nearby stones. Here the plants are fighting a losing battle for they are not vigorous enough to prevent soil loss
PHOTO: PAKISTAN INFORMATION OFFICE, LONDON

Bottom right: **Each habitat has a distinct community associated with it**
Kokerboom trees (Aloe dichotoma), *sometimes known as quiver-trees, in the Karroo exploiting deep water reserves*
PHOTO: SATOUR, LONDON

'climax' cannot correctly be used for desert vegetation, because each habitat in each sub-division of the landscape has its own climax, and is merely the particular group of species which is able to occupy a particular habitat under its present environmental conditions. Therefore, he recognized that the desert habitat, including climate, is prone to fluctuations which influence the structure and relationship of the plant associations, so that even if there is an adequate rainfall, unless there is a soil which can take advantage of it and store it, the plant communities are severely limited in their scope and range.

The pattern of root penetration into the surface and sub-surface layers of the soil is also vital. Just as the shading effect of vegetation precludes or encourages plant elimination or survival, so the differences between plant root patterns encourage or prevent the inclusion of species into a plant community. The different species within a desert plant community survive by exploiting the different sub-surface layers, according to their water demand.

In the extreme desert, vegetation is only expected after rain, and because rainfall is low and its frequency very unpredictable, and the evaporation rates are high, which reduces water availability still further, the only plants that are capable of germinating are the ephemerals. Their shallow roots can take immediate advantage of any rain that falls, and, extending down to only 100 mm, these roots are perfectly adapted to exploit the limited water supply.

In the less extreme deserts, the succulent perennials, because of their special moisture-storing ability, can develop deeper roots, which tap the moister layers. Often these deeper roots develop horizontal side-roots, which run along just under the surface. Once established, they are therefore more efficient than the ephemeral species, for they can make use of very low rainfall volumes and dew, which are inadequate for the germination of ephemeral plant seeds, as well as the deeper moisture sources the ephemerals cannot reach.

The woody perennials have a higher water demand, and are found in different and generally less arid conditions.

The sequence of root penetration will follow this order:
1 Ephemeral plants: shallow surface roots, no deep penetration
2 Succulent perennials: both deep and shallow roots
3 Woody perennials: predominantly deep roots, with some shallow roots.

Consequently, the community is built up according to the water supply and root penetration patterns. As aridity increases, the plants, while they generally dispense with their aerial (above ground) shoots, expand their root systems. The community stabilizes where the optimum density of plants can be supported by the rainfall/soil conditions. This often results in open spaces between plants, but these are not as barren and unexploited as they appear: the soil below them is colonized by the roots of the plants around the space. Provided the network of roots is not disturbed, nor the plants killed, the surface will not erode as might be expected.

Returning to the Kassas and El-Abyad[1] classification of the dry stream habitats in the Sahara, this layering of vegetation can be appreciated:
1 In the lower courses of main channels of drainage

DESERT VEGETATION
Natural spacing and rooting patterns

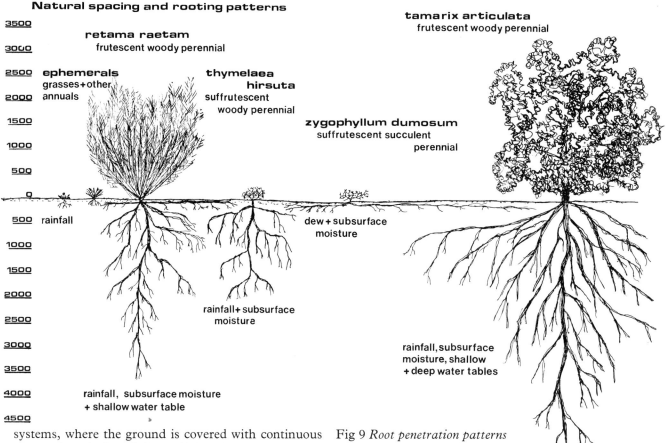

Fig 9 *Root penetration patterns*

systems, where the ground is covered with continuous sheets of sand of negligible salinity, the land is covered with the grass *Panicum turgidum* in a pure stand, giving the ecotype 'desert grass-land'. The land surface character is uniform, the rainfall likewise, and a community of *Panicum* establishes throughout.

2 The channels of drainage systems where the surface is covered with coarse materials promotes a scrub layer, dominated by the deep-rooting *Haloxylon salicornicum* and the shallower-rooting grass, *Panicum turgidum*. The grass establishes on the soil held below the coarse rock litter, while the shrub penetrates deeply below.

The communities occurring within the drainage channels have co-dominants of *Haloxylon* and *Panicum*, and in this instance, it can be deduced that the channels are composed or rock detritus, boulders and sand. In the rain channels of the drainage system, in particular in limestone areas where the streams are covered with mixed rock debris and sand, the species mentioned above are joined by *Zygophyllum dumosum*, particularly suited to a rocky limestone surface.

Thus, with a knowledge of the way in which species are associated with the habitat, it is possible to deduce from the dominant plant within the community the basic characteristics of the habitat.

Hassib (1955)[1] noted the following distribution in the Sahara:

Panicum turgidum association: widely distributed in sandy plains

Zilla spinosa association: widely distributed in deep sandy soils

Pithuranthus tortuosus association: (often with *Zilla spinosa*) covers large areas of the Libyan desert, indicating both rocky and deep sandy soils.

Zygophyllum coccineum association: found on rocky desert plateaux and in shallow depressions on the margins of deep valleys. In the pockets of soil, and in the deeper soil in the depressions, the deeper-rooting shrub *Reaumuria hirtilla* is found

Haloxylon salicornicum association: widely distributed on the shallow floors of wadis, and on small sand dunes, demonstrating deep-rooting under rough surfaces and showing that moisture reserves are available in the dunes

Capparis spinosa association: found on rocks and high cliffs of deep wadis

Odontosperma pygmaea association: loose stony areas and banks of wadis

Cornulaca monacantha–Convolvulus lanatus association: sandy soils, where drifting sand collects around the plants

Reaumuria hirtilla association: in depressions and exposed plateaux with little soil on the surface; on very rocky ground, in deep wadis, *Zygophyllum coccineum* (see above) becomes associated with it

Salsola foetida association: on sandy ground in broad shallow wadis

Cleome droserifolia association: in broad shallow wadis

Aristida coerulescens—Danthonia forskalii association: these grasses accumulate sand and form small dunes in drifting sand areas.

This type of classification can be widened, as shown by Dr Smith's work cited earlier, and by J. G. Davies in Australia[3] (see table 3.2), and writing in 'Soils and Men', *U.S. Department of Agriculture Yearbook, 1938,*[3] Baldwin, Kellogg and Thorpe produced a similar categorization for arid and semi-arid lands in North America, summarised in table 3.3.

M. Petrov (1966 and 1967),[4] having established nine different edaphic communities for the central Asian deserts, broke the plant community down into different

TABLE 3.2 PLANT COMMUNITIES IN AUSTRALIA *(Based on study of J. G. Davies, © Unesco, 1955)*

Communities	Rainfall	Soils	Temperature
Desert communities			
Sclerophyllous grassland	200 mm or less	Desert sandhills and stony desert	not recorded
Desert steppe	200 mm or less	Desert sandhills and stony desert	
Arid communities			
Sclerophyllous grass steppe	not recorded	Desert sand plains, stony hill and brown soils	21°–27°C
Mulga scrub	125–200 mm	Desert loams	10°–21°C
Scrub steppe	125–200 mm	Desert loams	
Grass scrub	250–400 mm	Brown soils of light texture	21°–30°C
Arid scrub	200–250 mm	Desert loams	10°–21°C
Semi-arid communities			
Savannah	400–750 mm	Grey-brown soils	21°–30°C
Mallee scrub	250–375 mm	Solarized brown soils	10°–21°C
Savannah woodland	400–750 mm	Rendzinas, black earths, podsols, red-brown earths, and terra-rossa	10°–21°C
Mallee heath	400–750 mm	Sandsheets with solarized subsoil	10°–21°C
Sub-humid community			
Dry sclerophyll forest	750–1000 mm	Podsols	10°–21°C

TABLE 3.3 PLANT COMMUNITIES OF NORTH AMERICA
(After Baldwin, Kellogg and Thorpe, and W. G. McGinnies, Unesco, 1955)

Zonal soils	Vegetation	Climate
Desert	Scattered shrubby desert plants	Temperate to cool
Red desert	Desert plants, mostly shrubs	Warm-temperate to hot; arid
Sierozem	Desert plants, scattered short grass and scattered brush	Temperate to cool; arid
Brown Chernozem	Short grass and bunch grass prairie	Temperate to cool; arid to semi-arid
Reddish brown	Tall bunch grass and shrub growth	Temperate to hot; arid to semi-arid
Chestnut	Mixed grasses and short grass prairie	Temperate to cool; semi-arid
Reddish Chestnut	Mixed grasses and shrubs	Warm-temperate to hot; semi-arid
Chernozem	Tall and mixed grass prairie	Temperate to cool; sub-humid

Sandy desert vegetation, Northern Territory, Australia

Red spinifex grass predominates in the valleys between the rough, rocky and harsh ridges in the Simpson Desert. Trees can be seen fringing the water courses

PHOTO: AUSTRALIAN INFORMATION SERVICE, LONDON

classes. In his analysis of the vegetation found on the 'typical sandy deserts on the desert-sandy sierozem and grey-brown soils of the palaeoalluvial and coastal plains', for example, he distinguishes:

1 Brush psychroxerophyte psammophytes
    Calligonum species, *Pterococcus* species, *Ammodendron karelinii, Ephedra lomatolepis, Salix caspica, Salix rubra, Eleagnus angustifolia, Haloxylon persicum, Haloxylon aphyllum*

2 Psammophyte grasses and sub-shrubs
    Elymus giganteus, Aristida pennata, Agropyron sibiricum, Artemisia santolina, Artemisia arenaria, Agriophyllum arenarium, Horaninovia ulicina.

This incidentally shows the split between deep-rooting brush psychroxerophytes and the shallow-rooting psammophytic grasses and sub-shrubs. Later, in 1971, Petrov sub-divided these plants further, giving the plant type, its edaphic habitat and the species associated with them (see table 3.4).

Although a community in the desert is characterized by the frequency or density of the species rather than by the presence or absence of any particular species, the communities in the semi-arid areas are more clearly defined by the predominant plant species. M. Zohary[5] split the vegetation of Palestine into thirteen different communities (see table 3.5).

TABLE 3.4 SHRUBS OF CENTRAL ASIAN DESERTS *(Adapted from M. Petrov,* Wildland Shrubs: Their Biology and Utilization, USDA, *1971)*

Aridity	Plant type	Soil formation	Soil type	Plant species
Extremely arid	Psammophytic shrubs	Desert sands	Moving and overgrown sands and barchans	*Ammodendron* *Aristida* *Calligonum* *Caragana* *Eremosparton* *Hedysarum*
Arid	Halophytic shrubs	Solonchak depressions and coastal solonchaks	Sulphate-chloride saline soils and close-lying saline groundwaters	*Halocnemon* *Halostachys* *Kalidium* *Siedlitzia*
Arid	Petrophytic shrubs	Arid mountains	Rocky and stony locations	*Ammopiptanthus* *Rhamnus* *Tetraena* *Zygophyllum*
Arid	Gypsophytic shrubs	Sheet plains and plateaux	Rocky and sandy calcareous soils	*Anabasis* *Hammada* *Salsola* *Sympegma*
Semi-arid	Mesophytic shrubs	Steppe	Deep steppe soils	*Amygdalus* *Caragana* *Cerasus* *Spirea*

Left : **Scrub steppe, Northern Territory, Australia**
This dry, arid land surrounding Ayers Rock borders the extremely arid desert. No large trees can grow, but a uniform stable scrub community has developed geared to the available water and the character of the surface soil
PHOTO: AUSTRALIAN INFORMATION SERVICE, LONDON

Below : **Cold desert vegetation**
Saxaul Woods (Haloxylon persicum) *in Turkmen, USSR. Sand blow is reduced by the deep-rooting saxaul. Little suffrutescent (sub-shrub) vegetation can compete with the wide-ranging roots of the saxaul*
PHOTO: NOVOSTI PRESS AGENCY, LONDON

TABLE 3.5 PLANT COMMUNITIES IN PALESTINE *(After M. Zohary, Ronald Press, 1962)*

Climate	Community	Species
Semi-arid	Coniferous forest belt	*Pinus* spp.
Semi-arid	Sclerophyllous oak and maquis	*Quercus calliprinos*
Semi-arid	Deciduous broad-leaved oak forest	*Quercus macrolepis*
Semi-arid	Evergreen maquis	*Ceratonia siliqua* & shrubs
Semi-arid	Deciduous steppe maquis and steppe forest	*Pistacia atlantica* *Crataegus azorollus* *Amygdalus communis* *Rhamnus alaternus* Shrubs and dwarf shrubs
Semi-arid	Mediterranean batha and garigue	*Cistus* spp. *Phlomis* spp. *Salvia* spp. *Satureia* spp. *Poterium* spp.
Arid	Deciduous thermophilous scrub	*Zizyphus lotus*
Arid	Halophytic forest	*Tamarix* spp. *Suaeda* spp.
Arid	Saxaul woods	*Haloxylon persicum*
Arid	Savannah forest	*Acacia* spp. *Zizyphus spina-christi* *Moringa aptera* *Salvadora persica* *Thymus* spp.
Arid	Dwarf shrub steppe	*Artemisia herba-alba* *Noaea mucronata* *Helianthemum* spp.
Arid	Steppes of aphyllous broom-like shrubs	*Retama raetam* *Periploca aphylla*
Arid	Leaf and stem succulent, dwarf shrub formations	*Suaeda* spp. *Salsola* spp. *Atriplex* spp.

In the United States of America, Weaver and Clements[3] divided the semi-arid grassland into six associations (with two sub-associations):

TABLE 3.6 COMMUNITIES IN NORTH AMERICAN GRASSLANDS (After W. G. McGinnies, Unesco, 1955)

Formation	Association
True prairie	*Stipa—Sporobolus*
Sub-climax prairie associes	*Andropogon*
Coastal prairie	*Stipa—Andropogon*
Mixed prairie	*Stipa—Bouteloua*
Short-grass associes	*Bulbilis—Bouteloua*
Desert plains	*Aristida—Bouteloua*
Pacific prairie	*Stipa—Poa*
Palouse prairie	*Agropyron—Festuca*

Of these, the last two formations, including the short-grass plain associes, are considered truly semi-arid, while the others from higher or lower topographical levels dovetail into the other formations, and therefore influence them to a certain extent.

It is also worth noting that the climate and the influence it has on the soil affect root patterns and plant establishment, even in regions where regular rainfall patterns can be expected. Mesa grassland soils, for instance, occur where the climate is too dry to support forests. They are characteristic of regions subject to summer droughts sufficiently severe to deplete the available moisture in the root zone before the droughts cease. They can be roughly divided into three types:

1 Prairie soils
   The summer rain is too low for deciduous forest, but is sufficient over the rest of the year for adequate leaching throughout the soil profile to occur
2 Chernozem soils
   Formed under more arid conditions so that there is little leaching out of the root zone
3 Chestnut soils
   Typical of greater aridity, and rainwater only rarely leaches through the profile.

The moister, deeper prairie soils therefore support the deeper-rooting tall grasses, i.e., *Stipa*, *Sporobolus* and *Andropogon* species, while the drier, shallower chernozem soil supports the short grasses—*Bulbilis* and *Bouteloua* species. It is also possible to say that the strongest evidence for the antiquity of a grassland formation is to be seen in the soil. For instance, it would have been virtually impossible for the shallow carbonate layer found in chernozems to develop under middle or tall grasses, because these penetrate more deeply and require higher moisture levels, and the calcium carbonate layer would not have formed (see table 3.7).

So, in such a manner the history of plant colonization and the stability of the plant community reflects, and is reflected by, the structure and composition of the soil. If there are adequate indicators in both soils and plants, a further concept can be added to the analytical methods— any change imposed on a soil which changes its form will, under the existing climatic regime, automatically change the nature of the plant community associated with that soil.

NATURE OF DESERT PLANTS

It is possible, as exemplified by M. Kassas,[6] to separate the vegetation of dry lands into four major orders: accidental form, ephemeral form, suffrutescent (sub-shrub) perennial form and frutescent (shrub) perennial form. Each of these orders has a number of classes, and the predominant orders are the ephemeral form and the suffrutescent perennial form. Each contains a sequence of classes, developing from the more primitive to the more sophisticated, dependent as they must be on soil quality.

Accidental form

Only ephemeral plants are included in this order (though not all ephemerals are of the accidental type). Growing only when rain occurs, the formation cannot be considered

TABLE 3.7 RAINFALL AND GRASS GROWTH *(After W. G. McGuinnies, Unesco, 1955)*

Formation	Soil group	Water Penetration	Plant root penetration	Period of sustained growth
Tall grass	Prairie	600–900 mm	600 mm	2½ months
Short grass	Chernozem	200–400 mm	250 mm	Few weeks

permanent in any way. It is determined by extremely erratic rainfall, as is found for example in the Libyan Desert, where, in the Dakla region, only 10 mm of rain can be expected every ten years.

Ephemeral form

There are three categories in this group: succulent-ephemeral, ephemeral grassland, and herbaceous ephemerals. When any of these are found, rainfall is known to occur annually. The plants are ephemeral in the main, but perennials can be found occasionally. There is therefore some moisture, but, because the soils are not water-retentive, it does not last throughout the year. As aridity decreases and rainfall regularity improves, the ephemerals become displaced by the perennials.

Succulent-ephemeral form

The growing season for succulent ephemerals is longer than the 6–8 weeks typical of the non-succulent ephemerals, for they have the ability to store some moisture in their tissues. They can tolerate the severe conditions prevalent in soils that develop on erosion pavements, such as pediments, regs and hamadas.

The typical plants can be further sub-divided into three types: the winter ephemerals and the summer ephemerals, and salt-marsh ephemerals.

• *Winter ephemerals*
Growing after winter rains such as in those deserts influenced by the Mediterranean climatic types.

The SPECIES are *Aizoon canariensis, Aizoon hispanicum, Mesembryanthemum crystallinum, M. forskali, M. nodiflorum, Trianthema crystallina,* and *Zygophyllum simplex.*

• *Summer ephemerals*
Growing after summer rains such as in those areas influenced by the Indian Monsoon, or tropical climate systems.

The SPECIES are *Salsola inermis, S. kali* and *S. volkensii.*

• *Salt-marsh ephemerals*
The SPECIES are *Halopeplis amplexicaulis, Salicornia herbacea.*

Ephemeral grassland form

This form can develop into grassland over large stretches of ground, and in particular on shallow sand drifts. The predominant species are: *Aristida, Bromus, Cenchrus, Eragrostis, Poa, Schismus, Schoenfeldia, Stipa* and *Tragus.*

Herbaceous ephemeral form

These herbaceous ephemeral plants are only found on soft deposits in good locations, where a water supply is preserved even if for only a short while.

Suffrutescent perennial (sub-shrub) form

This is the most widely-spread order. There is a permanent flora of perennial species, and it includes a perennial grassland form. There are three layers: a suffrutescent layer 300–1200 mm high, a grassland layer of the same height and a ground layer. The suffrutescent flora usually predominates, and the ground layer of dwarf and prostrate perennials is sometimes augmented by some ephemerals.

Succulent sub-shrub form

These plants have evolved sufficiently to have an internal moisture reserve system. Where salt-marsh communities are found, the dominant species are *Arthrocnemum, Salicornia* and *Suaeda;* otherwise they are *Anabasis, Haloxylon* and *Zygophyllum.*

Perennial grassland form

Soils which are capable of storing some water are the habitats of these plants. They are particularly valuable for sand-sheet and sand-dune stabilization, and the different soil types encourage different plant associations. This type is dominated by *Hypparhenia hirta, Lasiurus hirsutus, Panicum turgidum, Pennisetum dichotomum* and *Poa sinaica.*

Woody Perennial form

This order is a transitional order falling between the succulent and the grassland forms. Plant cover is always thin, in particular in the more arid locations, and many of the species which grow on rocks—the chasmophytes and rhizophagolithophytes—are included here.

Frutescent perennial (shrub) form

This form is typical of all the vast desert scrublands. There are three layers: frutescent (1200 mm–3000 mm), suffrutescent (below 1200 mm) and ground.

Succulent perennial form

The cacti of the American deserts, and the succulent Euphorbias of tropical Africa and Arabia are part of this category. The saxaul, *Haloxylon persicum,* is also included.

Scrubland form

Scrubland can only be found in good locations where there is adequate soil and rainfall, and where there are mountains around to supply run-off water. Scrubland indicates the highest level of water reserves available in the desert, and is particularly relevant to semi-arid areas. The dominant plants are *Acacia, Larrea, Pistacia, Prosopis, Retama, Tamarix* and *Zizyphus.*

Classification of plants by morphology

While Kassas's system identifies the basic groups or orders of plants within the arid environment, it is possible to break them down to identify the particular characteristics of each plant form. Plants can be classified according to

TABLE 3.8 THE CLASSIFICATION OF DESERT PLANTS BY THEIR MORPHOLOGY *(After Cabrera, Unesco 1955)*

Order	Sub-order	Morphological characteristics
Holoxiles		Woody plants with persistent stems and boughs
Arboriform		Plants with a main trunk, or plants with branches some distance above ground
	Trees	Microphanerophytes 1–8 m high, evergreen and deciduous species
	Resulates	Stems with few or no branches, or divided, as in palms
	Cereiform	Tall plants with thick leafless trunks or branches; very spiny
Arbustiform		Small woody plants which branch at ground level (nanophanerophytes)
	Upright shrubs	Arrow or spiniform leaves
	Creeping shrubs	Stems and branches hug the soil
	Cushion shrubs	Adapted to windy conditions
		(i) Convex cushions—rosettes
		(ii) Convex cushions—highly ramified
		(iii) Subterranean shrubs—twigs form a compact mat on the surface
	Thick-stemmed shrubs	Branches are thick and practically leafless
Hemixiles		Lower part of the stem is woody and the upper part is herbaceous
Herbs		Plants with woody stem above the ground
	Hemicryptophytes	Annual resting buds at soil level
		(i) Graminiform: resting buds at soil level
		(ii) Rosular: rosette of leaves at surface
		(iii) Caulifoliates: without rosettes but with leaves growing directly from stems
		(iv) Creepers: creeping stems
	Geophytes (cryptophytes)	Herbs with subterranean resting buds
		(i) Rhizomata: resting buds on rhizome
		(ii) Tubers: buds on underground tubers
		(iii) Bulb geophytes: resting buds protected by thick bud sheaths, forming bulbs
		(iv) Radicemagas: resting buds formed on the roots
	Therophytes	Annuals without resting buds

TABLE 3.9 THE CLASSIFICATION OF DESERT FLORA BY THEIR MORPHOLOGY *(After Shreve, 1942)*

Longevity type	Morphological character	Species
Ephemerals		
Strictly seasonal	Winter ephemerals	*Daucus, Plantago*
	Summer ephemerals	*Pectis, Tridestromia*
Facultative perennials		*Verbesina, Baileya*
Perennials		
Underground parts perennial	Perennial roots	*Penstemmon, Anemone*
	Perennial bulbs	*Allium, Hesperocallis*
Shoot base and crown perennial		*Hilaria, Aristida*
	Shoot reduced, a caudex:	
	(i) Caudex short, all or mainly leafy	*Agave, Hechtia, Nolina, Dasylirion*
	(ii) Caudex long, leafy at top	*Yucca, Inodes, Washingtonia*
	Shoot elongated:	
	(i) Plant succulent and soft	Leafless stem succulents:
		Ferocactus, Thelocactus, Pachycereus, Carnegia, Pedilanthus, Mammilaria, Cylindropuntia, Platyopuntia
		Leafy, stem not succulent:
		Sedum, Talinum
	(ii) Plant woody and not succulent	Low bushes, shoots with leaves, wood soft:
		Encelia, Franseria
		Shrubs and Trees, leaves perennial, wood hard:
		Larrea, Mortonia
		Leaves deciduous:
		(a) Drought deciduous:
		Fouquieria, Bursera, Idria, Jatropha, Plumeria, Cercidium, Euphorbia
		(b) Winter deciduous:
		Populus, Ipomea, Olneya, Prosopis

Shreve's classification includes 25 sub-divisions, rather than the 14 shown in this table, but the flora included above covers the important categories.

their morphology, in other words. A. L. Cabrera, working in South America in 1955,[3] and basing his study on Du Rietz (1931), produced the classification system shown in table 3.8. Forrest Shreve,[3] working in the North American desert in 1942, took this one stage further, and established a key for desert flora based on the form of the plants. In brief, his key is as shown in table 3.9.

M. Zohary,[7] working in the Arabian Desert in 1952, realized the importance of the xerophytic adaptations of desert plants, and although Shreve obviously appreciated these valuable attributes, it was Zohary who managed to separate the characters.

TABLE 3.10 XEROPHYTIC ADAPTATIONS OF DESERT PLANTS (After Zohary, 1962)

Adaptation types	Species
Herbaceous whole shoot shedders	*Acacia raddiana*
	A. spirocarpa
	Tamarix spp.
Phanerophytic summer leaf shedders	*Lycium arabicum*
Petiolate leaflet shedders	*Zygophyllum dumosum*
Aphyllous leaf and branch shedders	*Retama raetam*
	Calligonum comosum
Aphyllous branch shedders	*Ephedra* spp.
Basiphyllous branch shedders	*Artemisia* spp.
Brachyblastic leaf shedders	*Reaumuria* spp.
Aesticladous leaf shedders	*Noaea mucronata*
Articulate shoot splitters	*Anabasis articulata*
	Haloxylon articulatum
Articulate branch splitters and shedders	*Haloxylon persicum*

From the preceding table, it is evident that a close knowledge of the overall basic orders of plants and their detailed morphological, anatomical and physiological adaptive mechanisms gives a clear indication of the type and range of plants which will survive in a given environment, and it will help in recognition of what types of plants can be successfully introduced. It further emphasizes the close correlation between climate, soils and plant form.

PHYTOGEOGRAPHY (Plant Geography)

From the plant names so far mentioned, it will be apparent that certain plants have repeatedly appeared, i.e. *Acacia, Anabasis, Artemisia, Calligonum, Haloxylon, Salvadora, Zygophyllum,* etc. A closer look will show that they belong to one major desert zone, and are dominant within it, and also that they have spilled over into other desert regions. However a plant dominating one habitat or region may not necessarily be the chief species in another.

A number of authorities, including Petrov, Zohary, Boyko and Ozenda, by carefully plotting the distribution of a certain plant and measuring the climatic influences on it, defining the soils in which it grows and examining its basic morphological structure (whether it is dwarf, stunted or full-grown), have been able to establish the extent of the distribution of that plant. By surveying an increasing number of plants, it became possible to define vegetation regions from where the plants originated, the dominance of certain plants, their associates, and more important, the

TABLE 3.11 PHYTOGEOGRAPHY OF IRAN, ISRAEL AND TURKEY (After Boyko, Unesco, 1955)

Formation	Phytogeographic region	Plant species
Humid forest belt		*Fagus orientalis*
		Gleditschia caspica
Sub-humid Mediterranean forest belt		*Quercus ilex*
		Q. calliprinos
		Q. coccifera
Arid border forest belt	Mauretano–Iranian Anatolic–Iranian	*Pistacia mutica*
		Amygdalus spp.
		Juniperus macropoda
		Quercus macrolepis
Mountain steppes	Kurdic–Iranian	*Acantholimon*
		Astragalus
		Tragacantha
	Afghano–Iranian	As above, but with additional Afghanic elements
Steppe regions	Anatolian	Vegetation transitional between Pontic–Pannonic & Irano–Turanian
	Mauretano-Iranian	*Artemisia herba-alba*
		Stipa tortilis
		Zizyphus lotus
	Central Asiatic and Turanian	Turanian species predominate
Deserts and semi-deserts	Central Asiatic	*Haloxylon aphyllum*
		H. persicum
		Tamarix spp.
	Saharo–Sindian	*Anabasis articulata*
		Phoenix dactylifera (in oases)
	Sudano–Deccanian	Sudano–Deccanian influences

extent they have spread away from their origins.

Although their research obviously started with the individual plant species, it is simpler to understand their work, if not appreciate it, by accepting that these phyto-geographical regions exist and are confirmed, rather than taking a close look at the plants and developing the regions from them.

Ozenda, in 1958,[1] described the phytogeography of Africa and Asia by defining six floristic regions:
1 The Eurosiberian region
2 The Mediterranean region
3 The Sudano–Deccanian region
4 The Irano–Turanian region
5 The Saharo–Sindian region
6 The Humid Tropical region.

Petrov,[4] referring to previous work by Lavrenko, in 1971 defined the regions more clearly, although he concentrated on Asia and the Mediterranean:
1 The Eurasiatic Steppe region
2 The Sahara-Gobi Desert region
  • Central Asiatic sub-region
  • Irano–Turanian sub-region
  • Saharo–Sindian sub-region
3 The Mediterranean Evergreen region.

TABLE 3.12 PHYTOGEOGRAPHY OF PALESTINE
(After Zohary, 1962)

Phytogeographical region	Distribution and derivation	Plant species
Eurosiberio-Boreoamerican region		
Boreoamerican		North American species have only a marginal influence on the separate Eurosiberian region
Eurosiberian		15 species: hydrophytes of little value
Mediterranean region		Climax communities: Evergreen sclerophylous forest Maquis
Sub-Mediterranean	Littoral species	*Cakile flavum* *Euphorbia paralias* *Eryngium maritimum* *Statice limonium*
	Enclaves in the Irano–Turanian region	*Juncus subulatus* *Pinus brutia* *Juniperus oxycedrus* *Psoralea bituminosa* *Stipa aristella* *Oryzopsis coerulescens*
Omni-Mediterranean	Widespread over the Mediterranean region	*Pinus halepensis* *Juniperus phoenicea* *Ceratonia siliqua* *Pistacia lentiscus* *Lavandula stoechas* *Thymus capitatus*
	Coastal plains	*Matthiola tricuspidata* *Statice sinuata* *Ajuga iva* *Sporobolus arenarius* *Cyperus mucronatus* *Narcissus serotinus*
East Mediterranean		Leading tree species: *Quercus calliprinos* *Q. boisseri* *Q. ithaburensis* *Platanus orientalis* *Acer syriacum* *Arbutus andrachne*
	Garigue and batha formations	*Poterium spinosum* *Euphorbia thamnoides* *Phlomis viscosa* *Thymbra spicata* *Teucrium creticum*
West Mediterranean	Relics of a more humid period	14 species: play little part in Palestine flora
North Mediterranean		30 species: unimportant
South Mediterranean		14 species: unimportant
Saharo-Sindian	Mediterranean derivatives	*Matthiola* *Medicago* *Erodium* *Thymus*
	Sudano or Tropical derivatives	*Capparis* *Cleome* *Caralluma* *Iphiona* *Varthemia*
	Irano-Turanian derivatives	*Calligonum* *Suaeda* *Salsola*

Phytogeographical region	Distribution and derivation	Plant species
Saharo–Sindian *(cont'd)*		*Haloxylon* *Tamarix* *Aizoon*
	South African derivatives	*Mesembryanthemum* *Notoceras* *Citrullus* *Aristida*
	Saharo-Sindian endemics	*Gymnarrhena* *Pteranthus* *Anastatica* *Zilla*
Irano-Turanian	Restricted distribution. Centre of origin of a number of endemic species	309 species: Irano-Turanian derivatives
Mauritanian steppe sub-region	Belt in west of North Africa	*Ephedra alte* *Haloxylon articulatum* *Pistacia atlantica* *Zizyphus lotus* *Artemisia herba-alba* *Achillea santolina*
Mesopotamian sub-region	Region includes the Syrian desert, Upper Mesopotamia and plains of southern Anatolia and south-western Iran	100 species: Irano-Turanian derivatives
Irano-Anatolian sub-region	Mountainous areas of inner Anatolia, Armenia, and the Iranian plateau. It is one of the largest centres of speciation	Endemic species: *Astragalus*—1000 species *Acanthophyllum* *Acantholimon* *Cousinia*: 160–180 spp. *Centaurea*: 200 species *Helichrysum* *Onobrychis* *Hedysarum* Other species: *Euphorbia macroclada* *Daphne linearifolia* *Thymus syriacus* *Phlomis orientalis*
Turanian (Aralo-Caspian)	Halophytic and Psammophytic habitats	*Calligonum* *Haloxylon* *Suaeda* *Anabasis* *Nitraria* *Zygophyllum* *Tamarix*
Sudano-Deccanian variable classification		Northerly limit of species in Palestine: *Zizyphus spina-christi* 38°20′
Western Sudanian		*Acacia albida* 32°30′ *A. tortilis* 31°51′
Eritreo-Arabian	Tropical Africa, Yemen, Southern Iran, Baluchistan to Deccan Plateau	*Moringa aptera* 31°50′ *Maerua crassifolia* 31°28′ *Acacia lacta* 31°3′ *Capparis cartilaginea* 30°40′

N.B. The plant lists included in the above table are only an indication of the range of relevant species

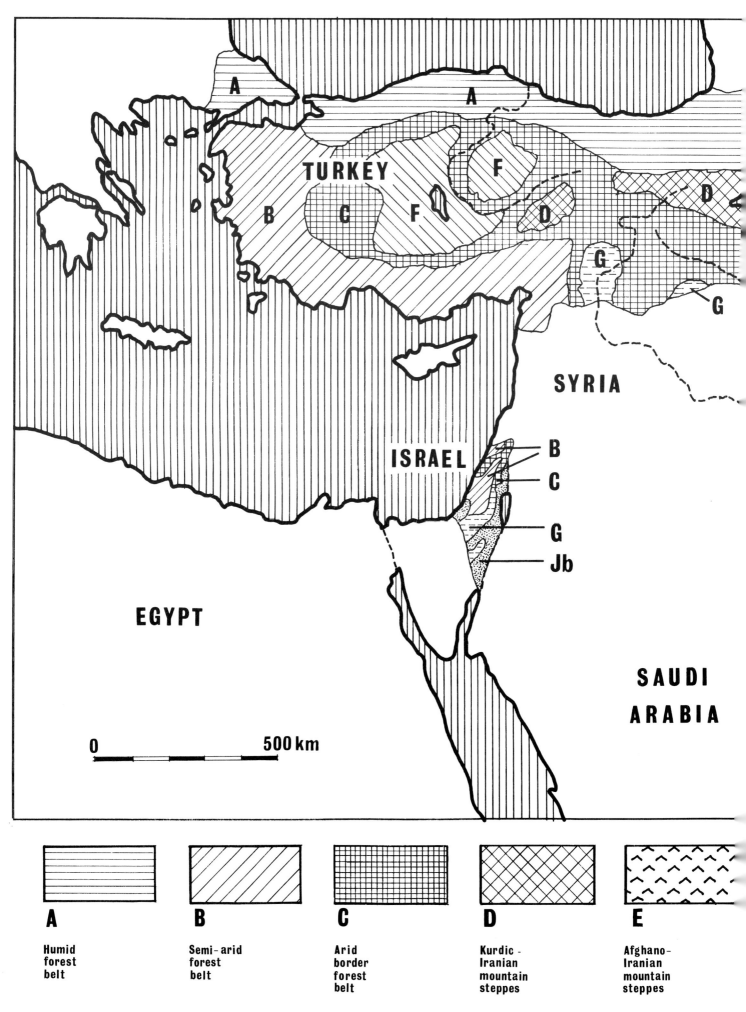

Fig 10 *Phytogeographical regions (after H. Boyko 1955—Unesco)*

Legend:

A — Humid forest belt

B — Semi-arid forest belt

C — Arid border forest belt

D — Kurdic-Iranian mountain steppes

E — Afghano-Iranian mountain steppes

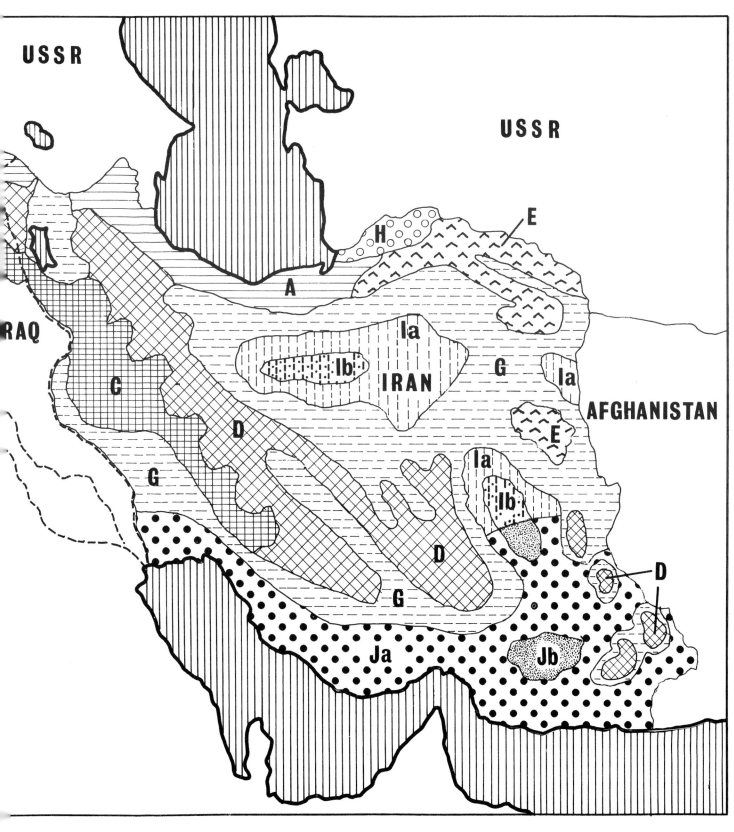

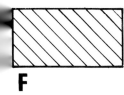

F

Anatolian
steppe
region

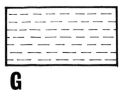

G

Mauretano-
Iranian &
Irano-Tura-
nian steppe

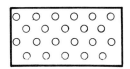

H

Central
Asiatic or
Turanian
steppe

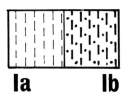

Ia   **Ib**

Central
Asiatic
Ia) semi-
    desert
Ib) desert

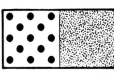

Ja   **Jb**

Saharo-
Sindian
Ja) semi-
    desert
Jb) desert

The fact that Petrov considered that the Sahara–Gobi was a major region means that the Saharo–Sindian region is relegated to the status of a sub-region, while full recognition can be given to the Sudano-Deccanian region. This division makes sense, as the climatic patterns of the Sudano–Deccanian region are tropical, and are separated from the Mediterranean climate by the great expanse of the Sahara Desert. Also, the subdivision of the Sahara–Gobi into three sub-regions is logical because one climate is replaced gradually by another, rather than being forced apart by a major topographical feature.

Hugo Boyko[3] specialising in the Middle East, has produced an extensive analysis of the region covered by Iran, Israel and Turkey (table 3.11).

Boyko's system describes both the species of plants which predominate in each region, and the regional floristic influences. The vegetation indicated also describes changes in the climatic patterns, for instance, the sub-humid forest belt, with its regular Mediterranean rainfall patterns, hugs the coastline of Turkey and Israel, and is indicative of semi-arid conditions, but even so, the rainfall is sufficient to support oak trees (*Quercus ilex* and *Q. calliprinos*) as well as oak scrub (*Quercus coccifera*). The zone of the central Asiatic deserts and semi-deserts found to the south and east of Tehran supports the saxauls (*Haloxylon persicum* and *H. aphyllum*) and tamarisk, which because of their drought adaptation mechanisms and their ability to produce long roots which can reach the sub-surface moisture reservoirs, indicate that the regular Mediterranean climatic influences are receding and that the vegetation is typical of a more continental type of climate with severer winters and hotter drier summers.

M. Zohary,[5] in his researches, refers to a number of authorities, including Alechin, Eig, Engler and Diels, Boissier, Braun-Blanquet, Markgraf, Grisebach, Grossheim, Popov, Gajewsky, Maire, Hayek and Meusel, when discussing the phytogeographical influences on the Palestinian flora, and distinguishes the following regions:
1 Eurosiberio–Boreoamerican region
2 The Mediterranean region
3 The Saharo–Sindian
4 The Irano–Turanian
5 The Sudano–Deccanian or Sudanian Region.

The consequence of Zohary's work is that, as far as the Palestinian flora is concerned, detailed information about plant communities and their historical development is now available, giving a very clear picture of how the present-day flora evolved. Furthermore, it holds the key to the secrets of the flora of the whole Saharo–Gobi desert region, because the wide range of influences from the central Asian Irano–Turanian region to those of the Saharo–Sindian have finally been identified in botanical terms.

Phytogeography is the ultimate weapon in the hands of those selecting plants suitable for environmental programmes in the dry lands. Until it is accepted that these lands have a great potential, and are capable of sustained productivity, greater emphasis will always be placed on the exploitation of the desert fringes. Unless detailed phytogeographical assessments, like those of Zohary, are made on the desert floras, and attempts made to appreciate their history and environmental requirements, any solutions proposed for the fringe lands will inevitably be prone to risk of failure.

NOTES

1 McGinnies, W. G., Goldman, B. J., Paylore, P. *Deserts of the World.* University of Arizona Press: 1968 (information reproduced by kind permission of the publishers and editors)

2 Smith, J. *Distribution of Tree Species in the Sudan.* Ministry of Agriculture, Khartoum: 1949 (source: Meteorological Office, London, No 59047)

3 Unesco. *Plant Ecology, Vol 6, Arid Zone Research* © Unesco: Paris 1955 (information reproduced by kind permission of the publishers)

4 *Wildland Shrubs—Their Biology and Utilisation.* US Department of Agriculture, Ogden, Utah: 1971

5 Zohary, M. *Plant Life of Palestine.* Ronald Press: New York 1962

6 Hills, E. S. *Arid Lands: A Geographical Appraisal.* Unesco/Methuen: London 1966 (information reproduced by kind permission of Unesco)

7 Cloudsley-Thompson, J. L. *Biology of Deserts.* Institute of Biology, London: 1954

4 Plant selection

The selection of indigenous plants, rather than introduced species, is of great importance in the fragile arid lands, where the preservation of the ecological balance is a prime necessity. Their use is essential to ensure that the disastrous effects of desertification are reduced to a minimum wherever possible: the aim should be to preserve soil stability and fertility. Using the criteria outlined in chapter 3, it is possible to select plants which will encourage appropriate land uses, that will least disturb the natural resources.

The function of research

The ultimate purpose of all research into arid land vegetation must be to provide guidelines:

1 To improve land use potential
2 To select plant species which will contribute to, not destroy or impoverish, the habitat
3 To ensure that plant ecological principles are understood.

The potential of all land use can be maximized by identifying its resources, and selecting a use which fits both the resources and the function that is required from the land.

The selection of plant species so that they do not harm the habitat will depend on detailed knowledge of their history, evolution and potential, before a function or target can be achieved.

The identification of plant ecological principles will pinpoint any interactions that are likely to occur when new plants, new water regimes, or new soil structure manipulations are introduced into the habitat.

At present, man is deeply involved in the problems of desertification, and in improving the productivity of the semi-arid lands to ensure the survival of people in these hostile habitats, to the extent that 'survival at (almost) any cost' is becoming the by-word. Great advances have been made, particularly in Russia and America, but the suspicions of environmental disturbance remain. We simply do not know what will happen when large rivers are diverted from one region to another to provide irrigation waters for vast, formerly virtually empty lands. What will happen to the areas through which these rivers originally flowed? We know too little about the effects on the land surface of extremely heavy cropping systems, except through the example of the dust bowls of the American mid-west, and the struggle to right these. However, we do know that alien plant introductions, inaccurate water use and lack of control of land exploitation do alter the land's surface and have put large populations at risk, as for example in Australia, Mesopotamia and the Sahel.

The processes required to solve the multitude of environmental problems man is facing are complicated and require many interactions between numerous disciplines. Hence it is more important than ever, in order to find the answers, to return to first principles.

Principles of plant selection

As has already been said, the plants which are selected must contribute to the environment, and once included in the ecosystem must not endanger the indigenous floras.

Ledyard Stebbins produced a logical thesis in 1971[1] concerning this point, which strikes at the root of both

Amu Darya River diversion, Karshin Steppe
This very large water conservation and diversion programme is for the reclamation of millions of hectares in the Kara-Kum Desert for food production
PHOTO: NOVOSTI PRESS AGENCY, N. KLYOCHNEV

commercial land productivity systems and the relationship of wild plants to such systems. He discusses the evolution and diversity of arid land shrubs from the basis of the theory that there are special evolutionary trends on islands, in particular the development from herbs to shrubs. From the consideration of this characteristic type of isolation, he developed the hypothesis that there can be ecological islands, surrounded by natural, even vegetative barriers. He explored the possibility that these ecological islands developed during the Tertiary Era, with its more arid climate, and he called them 'xeric (dry) islands': the competitive ability of the vegetation of the more humid surrounds restricted the natural progression of vegetation from one area to another following normal evolutionary trends. The vegetative boundaries became impenetrable, and the enclaves became firmly enclosed. The vegetation within xeric islands therefore came under a natural but aggressive pressure from the surrounding vegetation, while if the boundaries had been open, and normal evolution were able to occur, the full range of species would remain unaltered. But even though evolutionary changes take many hundreds or thousands of years to become fixed, there is no knowledge of precisely when the first genetic mutation occurs. To this extent, artificially increasing pressure on these natural enclaves could force the indigenous species contained within them to mutate. Changes could occur there at a faster rate than under normal conditions, so that the plant is able to survive. Instead of alien plants spreading into the enclave, which is normally the case, they would be prevented by the wild mutants so that there is a danger of the original plants changing their nature in perpetuity, and so of being lost.

Therefore, quite apart from identifying the possibly useful plants in the wild, there is a serious need to explore the area needed by particular species to fulfil their normal evolutionary requirements, and so remain in the natural, normal state. It should also be remembered that it is not only the leaf canopy that should be considered, for in the arid environment, the roots play a highly significant role: 'canopies' operate both below and above ground level.

The mixture of species in arid plant associations clearly demonstrates this root 'canopy' or layering effect. It has already been shown that certain plant species have root systems that are wide-spreading and/or deep, e.g. the broom-like *Retama raetam*, whose roots cover up to 40 square metres. The roots of other plants associated with it must develop and spread either above the roots of the *Retama*, or below them. In nature, such a balance does develop, but the artificial inclusion of more efficient species, with wider-spreading roots, can eliminate the indigenous plants, so opening the land to the risk of erosion, and also reversing a process which may have taken hundreds of years to stabilize. It is therefore not enough to assess the characteristics of the plant to be introduced: it is also essential to assess the effects such an introduction is likely to have on the dominant species and their associates within the existing plant communities.

The introduction of deeper-rooting plants amongst shallower rooted species poses two problems: either they will grow at the expense of the other species, or if the latter are able to survive as well, they must be given additional

water to enable them to thrive. When deeper-rooted plants are introduced into an existing natural environment, the water regime in the soil, and possibly the area, can be expected to change, and the other plants, being unable to compete by penetrating so deeply or expanding their roots so far, will be destroyed, or will have to undergo extraordinarily rapid mutation to survive. As the deeper-rooting plants flourish and the others change or die out, the plant community will change. The species formerly associated will likewise be affected, and instead of a wide range of species occurring, it may gradually become one which is restricted to the deeper-rooting plants, leaving only ephemeral species capable of colonizing the open spaces.

Deep-rooting plants
A mono-species community of Retama raetam *in Jordan. The spaces left between the dominant species can be colonised by plants which can compete with* Retama, *or, like ephemerals, can establish before the* Retama *has used all the water*
PHOTO: DIRECTORATE OF FORESTRY AND RANGE, JORDAN, MAHMOUD JUNEIDI

Should the introduction of deeper-rooting plants be the requirement, and should the addition of water be the only way of ensuring their survival, profound and marked changes will occur: the soil structure and its chemical composition will alter, and the greater the watering requirement, the greater will be the change to the soil, its composition and its potential ecology. The use of plants from parallel phytogeographical zones, whose characteristics within a known environment are understood, will necessarily involve less environmental manipulation and less water use. Maintenance and after-care will be reduced, and the chance of survival consequently increased, especially since they would be more resistant to any major interruption in water supply which might occur, or should the water-supply suffer a quality change. The likelihood of such occurrences must be assessed before such planting is carried out.

There are cases where plants have been transferred from one zone to another by enthusiastic plant collectors, for their intrinsic, aesthetic or practical qualities, but the introduction of such alien plants as the *Agave americana*, *Carpobrotus edulis* and *Opuntia ficus-indica* has put the landscape, and therefore the ecosystem, at risk, and it has been necessary to institute eradication procedures to enable the indigenous species to return. It is no longer acceptable to translate any plant exhibiting suitable requirements from one region to another for any particular purpose, except under the most strictly monitored conditions, because unless they come from a parallel phytogeographical zone they will generally require land modifications which can be costly in terms of both initial outlay and maintenance, or they will impose unacceptable modifications on the land. It would be better instead to encourage the expansion of species within a phytogeographical zone; such species would in any case adapt to the habitat more quickly and efficiently. Even so, before such introductions are made, there should at least be surveys into the indigenous flora, to identify those plants which may form the basis for new environmentally-adapted species, and at the same time select the areas where valuable wild plants should be protected, not only for the reasons already given, but to eliminate the possible dangers arising from random cross-pollination and hybridisation.

Hybridisation

Hybridisation holds the key to the production of food and animal fodder crops, and, so that the introduction of new plants will not disturb ecological balances, it is essential that the artificial enclaves mentioned earlier on are so located that random hybridisation, both within and without the enclave, is avoided. The main danger is that random hybridisation could produce new species that will eliminate the local species, or will multiply to such an extent that they will isolate the individual plants so that they can no longer hybridise with each other, and be eliminated in this way as well.

However, the value of hybridisation cannot be overlooked in human survival terms, provided certain conditions are imposed, for, using the preserved 'gene banks', new, fully-adapted species can be created; these species could make more satisfactory use of particular locations. Although the enormous potential value of wild 'gene banks', composed of wild plants fully adapted physiologically to their environment, holding within their hereditary potential all the adaptive genetic characteristics, has been appreciated, few people have established them or are currently using them. It is worth honouring the work of C. V. Malcolm, in Australia, at this point, though his emphasis is on translocating special fodder species. Research at the Carnegie Institute in America has recently been looking at the possibilities of hybridising C_3 and C_4 plants of the *Atriplex* (salt bush) family.

Methods of assessing plant use potential

An alternative to the costly research of hybridisation to select new plants for arid environments has been developed by both Boyko and Emberger. Emberger, working in north west Africa,[2] and using data by G. Long, established the relationship between indigenous vegetation and the cropping potential which could be associated with them as shown in table 4.1. V. J. Chapman extended this research, and his findings, which are published in *Salt Marshes and Salt Deserts of the World* (1960)[3] are shown in table 4.2.

TABLE 4.1 CROPPING POTENTIAL INDICATED BY INDIGENOUS VEGETATION (After Emberger, Unesco, 1955)

Ecological association	Cropping potential
Eragrostis papposa *Zizyphus lotus* *Artemisia campestris*	Almond, olives and apricots
Stipa retorta *Erica sativa* *Plantago ovata* *Eryngium illicifolium*	Olives (*Olea europea*)
Retama raetam	Almonds (*Amygdalus communis*)
Plantago lagopus *Silybum burneum*	Irrigated cultivation
Aristida pungens *Rumex tingitanus* var. *lacerus*	Prickly pear (*Opuntia ficus-indica*) plantations
Salsola vermiculata var. *villosa*	Pasturage crops, possibly figs (*Ficus carica*) and almond
Limoniastrum guyonianum *Suaeda vermiculata* *Salsola cruciata*	Cereals (saline ground conditions)
Suaeda fruticosa and *Salsola tetrandra* or *Limoniastrum guyonianum* and *Halocnemon strobilaceum*, or *Arthrocnemum* spp.	Date palm (*Phoenix dactylifera*)

TABLE 4.2 CROPPING POTENTIALS IN SALTY CONDITIONS (After Chapman, 1960)

Ecological association	*ppm NaCl	Cropping potential
Salicornia fruticosa	7,000	Limit for *Cynodon dactylon* and *Polypogon monspeliensis*
Suaeda fruticosa and *Sphenopus divaricatus*	4–8,000	Can be cultivated, if leached
Suaeda fruticosa and *Salicornia fruticosa*	4–8,000	Limit for cotton, wheat barley and oats. Good for cabbage, beet, and sweet clover. Maize sterile
Suaeda fruticosa	3–5,000	Good for cotton, beet, artichoke, pomegranite, oats, lucerne. Olives sterile
Suaeda fruticosa and *Calendula algeriensis* and *Ormensis praecox*	2–3,000	Maize fairly satisfactory
Suaeda fruticosa and *Atriplex halimus*	2–3,000	Tomatoes, melons, marrows, and olives
Atriplex halimus and *Suaeda fruticosa*	2–3,000	Flax difficult, but olives satisfactory
Atriplex halimus	1–2,000	Upper limit for potato, carrot, onions, pimento, and peppers. Citrus difficult

*ppm = parts per million

Potential of ornamental plants

Emphasis so far has been on the conservation and use of plants in the wild, but another aspect—the introduction of plants for their ornamental, rather than functional value—deserves consideration. Because the desert environment can be combated, albeit at some cost, urban settlements in arid areas are now rapidly expanding. Although the Middle East is the prime example of this, other countries (e.g. Russia, Australia, Sudan) are building and planning urban developments in arid regions, whether they are needed for new residential, commercial or industrial growth, or simply to provide 'second homes'. These developments have stimulated the desire for vegetation, especially ornamental trees and shrubs, to soften the built image. New design criteria, whether for flowers, leaf shape or colour, or plant form, are selected, and because indigenous plant species are seldom available locally, and moreover often lack these aesthetic qualities, they tend to be overlooked, especially as publicity tends to be more forthcoming for the particularly spectacular introductions. With reference to the Middle East and the Arabian states in particular, because of the lack of knowledge about indigenous plants greater encouragement is given to the importation of the more dramatic plants, and little is given to the production of indigenous plants. The introduced plants necessarily come from different environments, and so require land modification and specialist treatment, involving the physical changing of the character of the land to suit the plants, modifying soil structure and texture, and requiring additional water to help them adapt to their new habitats.

That being the case, greater attention is needed to ensure that the species used will eventually satisfy an alternative function, like provision of timber, when they have reached their maturity, so that they repay their initial cost of establishment and maintenance. Trees and shrubs likewise should also contribute to preserving or improving the quality of the soil. They should not use resources for which man could find alternative more valuable uses. The concept of using vegetation in urban settlements for 'beautification' should be widened so that the plants can be 'farmed', in order to promote benefits to the economy, as well as to the psychological requirements of the residents.

As populations expand, towns and cities use more and more land which may have a productive alternative; but it is man who must eventually be able to survive in these conditions, and as water is his prime requirement, he should ensure that wherever water is used for crops, shelter belts or ornamental parks, each in their own way significant to man, additional functions must be satisfied wherever and whenever possible.

Plants for arid climates then must serve a number of purposes, and their selection should satisfy a number of conditions:

1 They should be heat, drought and wind resistant
2 They must, in many cases, be resistant to salinity
3 Plants chosen for urban use should serve an economic, as well as an ornamental, function wherever possible
4 They should, when introduced, come from the same phytogeographical zone, unless they are required for particular functions which cannot be satisfied by the regional flora.

The most important criterion, then, is not 'Will the plant grow?', but 'Will it use the resources efficiently in the long term, without forcing modifications to the habitat?' While plant stocks are in short supply, or even non-existent, expedient choices will have to be made, but if continuous publicity is given to rational selection, to encourage research and development, the propagation of indigenous species will eventually be brought about. The new landscapes can then serve new social and economic functions, as well as suiting their new environments. Landscapes with national, regional, and local identities will then be created, providing people with environments geared to their own particular needs, and which they can recognize as their own.

New Regional Landscape
This kibbutz in the northern Negev, Israel is totally dependent on its water supply. All land which can be cultivated is served with water by the National Water Carrier, and now, after a number of years, a new functional landscape is stabilising
PHOTO: ISRAEL EMBASSY INFORMATION DEPARTMENT, LONDON

NOTES

1 *Wildland Shrubs—Their Biology and Utilization.* US Department of Agriculture, Ogden, Utah: 1972
2 Unesco. *Plant Ecology, Vol 6, Arid Zone Research* © Unesco: Paris 1955 (information reproduced by kind permission of the publishers)
3 Chapman, V. J. *Salt Marshes and Salt Deserts of the World.* Leonard Hill (Books) Limited: London 1960

5 Man and dry-land ecosystems

Man's greatest enemy in the arid lands is himself. The ecological balance in the dry lands is continually responding to, and evolving with, changes in climate, soil and water, and plant and animal populations. But above all, man is rapidly changing the land for his own ends.

Man has always been the exploiter. When the nomad or the shifting cultivator had exhausted his immediate environment he moved on, leaving nature to rebuild the ecosystem. Man has always needed shelter, food, and comfort from cold and all types of adversities and natural enemies. As a passive food gatherer, and later a hunter, he took food from the land and used trees and caves as shelter, but caused very little change to the ecosystem he inhabited. Nature was still in control.

However, as we shall see, as populations grew larger and colonized lands less conducive to survival and a passive existence, man's inventiveness began to change the land to suit human requirements and eventually created the quest for improved 'standards of living'. Human motivation now had a greater impact upon the land. But this vital fact was forgotten: man is no outside species acting independently upon the land—his every-day actions are inextricably linked with all the components of the ecosystems he inhabits; the food he eats, the clothes he wears, his shelter and tools, all originate in the environment around him. Whether as a passive food gatherer half a million years ago or a present day nomadic pastoralist, man is an integral part of the ecosystem, as affected by changes in the ecological balance as any other organism. For example, if he takes too many trees for fuel, his sources of food and fodder are affected, and there is less shelter and recycling of nutrients to encourage the growth of food species beneath the trees. The resultant bare soils encourage soil erosion, sand blow and almost irreversible loss of fertility and vegetation, especially in very arid areas.

It was therefore necessary in areas of extremes and sparse resources such as dry lands, for man, like other organisms, to adapt his way of life in order to survive different degrees of aridity and availability of food and water. His nomadic lifestyle, his clothing and style of housing, designed to reduce heat and humidity and increase cool air circulation, can be compared to adaptions made by other animals in similar environments; but in one important respect man began significantly to differ from the other organisms. His powers of memory, enquiry and comparison, together with his dextrous skills, experimentation and co-ordination, enabled him *actively to change his environment* to a much greater degree than any other organism. Innovations such as the use of tools, the construction of irrigation systems, reservoirs, canals, catchment areas, the digging of wells, the prediction of seasonal weather changes using astronomy, and the capacity to record these events and calculate for new situations all equipped man to modify his environment to his own benefit. However, many of these operations set up an unforeseen series of chain reactions within the ecosystem, reactions which are not always beneficial to the ecosystem and man himself.

Human populations in the past were regulated by three major mechanisms—death from tribal warfare, death from disease and death due to starvation in a time when the population exceeded the food supply, notably in drought periods. In recent years these regulating mechanisms have been largely removed. Modern medicine has reduced deaths from disease, and national and international aid programmes have considerably reduced deaths from starvation. The effects of the resultant population increases on the dry-land ecosystems have been enormous, and soils have been denuded of their topsoil rendering the land even less able to support larger populations.

As long as man allowed nature sufficient time to restore the land, the whole system was in a form of balance. But now, as the length of crop rotations decreases, fallows shorten, and grazing and cropping intensities increase, the land is forced to support larger populations than ever, and man is giving nature less and less time to recharge the resources he needs. A new balance results, which is often deleterious to man, and he is faced with two alternatives—to leave the degraded site, which may never return to its former status, and develop another area, or to maintain the site artificially, so that it is ecologically out of balance but in a productive state for himself. To achieve this he must supply large inputs from outside the ecosystem, such as water, minerals, fertiliser, power and labour, and the massive extraction of these inputs can endanger the ecological balance of other areas.

Desertification has been described in the introductory chapter. Its causes are attributable to man and climate. Climatic theory and future predictions are still being investigated, but more is already known about man. The conclusions which are drawn from our existing state of knowledge show that we must develop more positive solutions to man's problems—ones which protect the land as well as man's immediate interests. We are progressively developing the ability to identify the land's natural capabilities, the populations it can support, and the interdependences within the ecosystems. Could we not use such tools as these to work with nature rather than against it? In this spirit we could assess the site prior to development and regulate the direction of future developments from an ecological basis, so that man can remain in harmony with the land and the resources he needs.

This suggests that modifications to land use development, new settlement patterns and new techniques of implementation will be required, incorporating appropriate traditional and modern ideas and translating them into practical, useful and flexible solutions on the ground. This can only be achieved by understanding

MAN—his drives, comforts, needs: and these are different for different communities and regions

LAND—its carrying capacity, fertility and resources, especially of water

MAN/LAND INTERACTIONS—for example to give sustained productivity or desertification, regeneration or denudation of vegetation

MAN/LAND RESPONSES TO CHANGES IN ENVIRONMENT—decreased rainfall causing man to increase irrigation and possibly exhaust underground water supplies; advances in medication increasing settlement size and over-grazing on the settlement periphery and many other examples.

We must therefore turn inwards and critically examine our motives and our place within the ecosystem. In this way we may begin to understand how we can retain the balance of the forces of nature within the system and simultaneously realise our aims.

The last century's increase in industrial urbanisation with separation of towns from the countryside has been accompanied by an erosion of man's natural instincts. He has developed the ability to step outside the self-generating mechanisms of nature and artificially hold and apparently

sustain his own environments, even when these are out of balance with their surroundings. Recent catastrophes, like the silting-up of dams or the gradual declines in productivity, as with salinised soils in Egypt, have shown that man is merely holding back time until a massive regulation of nature takes place. Witness the gradual exhaustion of water supplies until the aquifer dries up and whole oases are no longer productive.

Man can also 'accelerate' time by evolving established plant communities and vegetation and soil types within the space of a few decades, a process which normally would have taken centuries. When this evolution has taken an opposite direction to the natural one determined by site conditions, and if it is out of phase with other components of the ecosystem, it may eventually fail or degenerate from the man-made and regenerate to the natural. It is only with a high degree of maintenance and cost to man that such systems can be sustained.

It is therefore of vital importance for modern man to be able to interpret his effect on arid environments and to develop the skills of forecasting the outcome of new technologies. Changes in the ecosystem can be interpreted only with an understanding of man's aims and how he uses the ecosystems.

MAN'S DEPENDENCE ON PLANTS

Man has always depended upon plants for food and shelter, and later for fuel, extraction of medicines, chemicals and fibres and many other purposes: the main uses we make of plants are summarized in the list below. Certain plants even became sacred if they had special properties or religious connections—e.g. *Ficus religiosa* and *Prosopis spicigera*. If the climate was so arid that trees were very scarce, these

Trees creating shade around the tomb of Hafiez, Shiraz, Iran

were often individually named and highly revered. The shade and cool cast by a tree in the heat of the day has always been hallowed with a reverence which is retained in special gardens in modern cities.

Plant use: Some of the ways in which man has used plants and plant products to his benefit

FIRE	charcoal, wood, tinder, for warmth and energy
FOOD AND FODDER	roots, stems, leaves, fruits, pods, flowers, seeds, salts, oils, fats, gums, bark, roughage
MEDICINE	beneficial drugs for man and animals and now also natural insecticides and fungicides for other plants
SHELTER	timber for construction and providing shade, shelter belts, fencing
STABILISATION	of sandy, rocky, water eroded soils, regulating catchment areas for water
INDICATORS	of soil and water conditions, presence of minerals e.g. gold, oil
POISONS AND ANTIDOTES	for man, animals, fish, e.g. insecticides, vermicides, antihelminths
WATER	for man and animals, e.g. in cacti and succulents
BEVERAGES	water substitutes, water purifiers, sweet drinks, alcohol, milk substitute, tea, coffee, cola, cocoa, *etc.*, bitters, stimulants
MANURE	rotted organic matter or green manures, particularly legumes which fix nitrogen in the soil
RELIGION	specimen trees
AESTHETICS	ornamental species for gardens, landscape architecture, country parks and recreations, social benefit; grass or ground cover areas, also cosmetics, paints, perfumes
FURNITURE	wood, raffia, coconut matting, basketing, brushes, stuffing
FABRICS	linen, paper, silk, floss, fibre, thread
INDUSTRY	fats, oils, fibre, gums, alkaloids, resins, waxes, tannins
CHEMICALS	creosote, turpentine, latex, rubber, dyes, stains, inks, resins
ENERGY	protein from sunlight, heat, chemicals, drugs, electro-potential

Food gathering

Man's earliest relationship with plants was naturally as a food gatherer. In the dry lands where the available vegetation is minimal compared with that in wetter lands, it is necessary to range over large areas of land in order to find sufficient food. It is therefore unlikely that the dry lands were used to any great extent by food gathering peoples in search of edible grains, fruits, leaves, nuts and roots and hunting animals, birds and fish. Indeed it is generally accepted that such peoples as the bushmen of the Kalahari and Namib, and the Bandibu of central Australia have been forced to inhabit the arid areas as a result of invasion of their traditional, more fertile homelands by tribes stronger than themselves.

In the very arid areas such food gatherers had very little overall impact on the environment, although they most certainly have affected individual plant species which were useful to them. In the semi-arid areas, however, they did have significant effects. The principal of these was the use of fire to burn off grassland, either to stimulate new flushes of the grass itself and improve the grazing for the animals they hunted or to encourage the growth of food plants, particularly those with tuberous roots. Natural succession to savannah scrubland in these areas was prevented by burning, and regeneration of scrub growth was slow

compared with those seeds which were stimulated into germination by fire, e.g. some Australian eucalypts. The harvesting of wild plants is still an important activity in many areas. Not only do such plants provide food in times of crop failure, they are often the primary source of medical compounds as well as providing fibres and building materials.

Farming and pastoralism

The history of man's development of more organised forms of land use is still not fully worked out. Some authorities have proposed that the herding of domestic animals was intermediate between hunting and settled farming. Others postulate the reverse—that pastoralism resulted when farmland could no longer support the local populations as a result of climatic change, of population growth or of man's over-exploitation of land.

It seems probable that both routes of development were followed according to the environment in which man found himself. Thus land use evolved as a response to the productivity of the land, itself determined primarily by climate and population density. The historical development of land use therefore parallels the land use we see today. Simplifying this to its basic essentials we can say that farming is carried out wherever the moisture supply is adequate, whereas in the more arid areas pastoralism, generally synonymous with some form of nomadism, predominates.

Each land use until the extremely urbanised and industrialised modern ages, depended upon man's relationship with plants. Initially, only the easiest lands, where water and vegetation were more plentiful, were used as settlement areas for food gathering and the later cultivation of crops. Very arid lands were inhabited only if advantages such as trade outweighed the difficulties of poor climate and low soil fertility, or peoples were forced into the area after warfare or due to their criminal attributes. Populations grew and spread, more arid areas became inhabited, and each different degree of aridity supported different lifestyles.

Table 5.1 illustrates how ecological zones, climate and natural vegetation affect the types of land use that can be carried out in West Africa.

In the subsequent pages we consider land use in semi-arid areas (Sudanian/Sahelin type), arid areas (sub-Saharan type) and the arid interior areas (Sahara type).

FARMING IN SEMI-ARID LANDS AND DESERT FRINGES

In these areas (e.g. the Sudanian and Sahelian Deserts) rainfall is more predictable than in the truly arid areas and natural vegetation is more abundant in the savannah areas. The greater the rainfall, the more densely the trees and shrubs grow, the more leaf litter decomposes to plant nutrients and the deeper they are recycled—all resulting in a greater build-up of soil fertility than in the drier regions.

These factors encouraged the raising of crops in many areas; the savannah woodland was cleared and crops grown on the residual fertility until it was exhausted. The settlement then moved on and allowed nature to restore the

TABLE 5.1 TRADITIONAL LAND USE PATTERNS FROM THE SAHARA TO THE EQUATOR ASSOCIATED WITH CHANGES IN CLIMATE AND VEGETATION (*After E. S. Hills,* Arid Lands: A Geographical Appraisal, *Unesco, 1966*)

Zones	Countries	Approx. rainfall (mm)	Vegetation	Chief tree spp.	Major land uses	Main crops	Livestock
Saharan arid	Mauritania, Mali, Niger, Chad, Sudan	less than 100 dry all the year round	Desert		Nomadic grazing		some camels
Sub Saharan arid	Mauritania, Mali, Niger, Chad, Sudan	100–250 dry 11–12 months	Sub-desert steppe with *Aristida* grass community		Nomadic grazing		camels, sheep, some cattle
Sahelian semi-arid	Senegal, Mauritania, Mali, Upper Volta, Niger, Chad, Sudan	250–600 9 months dry season	Wooded steppe thorny savannah with *Cenchrus* grass community	*Acacia* *Commiphora*	Semi-nomadic grazing. Some semi arid cultivation and tree cropping for fodder, fuel, shelter	sorghum millet irrigated rice	goats, cattle, sheep
Sudanian	Senegal, Mali, Upper Volta, Niger, Northern Nigeria, Chad, Sudan	600–1250 6–8 months dry season	Open woodland, savannah with *Andropogon* grass community and relatively drought tolerant undifferentiated tree and shrub communities	*Anogeissus* *Sclerocarya* *Balanites* *Prosopis* *Butyrospermum* *Adansonia* *Bombax*	Semi-nomadic grazing and arable cultivation with fallows often of medium to long duration. Tree cropping for fuel, fodder, minor products	sorghum millet groundnuts yams maize irrigated rice	cattle with some sheep and goats
Guinean	Senegal, Gambia, Portuguese Guinea Guinea, Mali, Ivory Coast, Upper Volta, Ghana, Togo, Dahomey, Nigeria, Cameroon, Chad, Central African Republic, Sudan, Congo	above 1250 3–6 months dry season	Seasonal (deciduous) forest spp. abundant *Isoberlinia* in north, undifferentiated moist spp. in south; also savannah with *Hyparrhenia* grass community	*Isoberlinia* *Berlinia* *Uapaca* *Lophira* *Brachystegia*	Arable cultivation with fallows often of medium to long duration. Forest utilization for local consumption, some planted forests	sorghum millet groundnuts cassava yams maize irrigated rice	cattle depending on absence of tsetsefly; goats and some sheep
Guinea equatorial	Sierra Leone, Liberia, Ivory Coast, Ghana, Nigeria, Cameroon, Rio Muni, Gabon, Congo, Cabinda	above 1800 with very short dry season	Closed rain forest with woodland and associated *Pennisetum* grass	*Khaya* *Entandrophragma* *Lovoa* *Piptadenia* *Lophira* *Mytragina* *Sacrocephalus* *Aucoumea* *Triplochiton* *Tarretia* *Chlorophora* *Terminalia*	Arable cultivation with fallows often of a long duration. Permanent tree crops for export; forest utilization for export and local consumption (natural stands and plantations)	upland rice plantains bananas yams taro maize oil palm cocoa rubber robusta coffee	goats, with cattle in forest-savannah, mosaic on coast

The association between climate, natural vegetation and land use can easily be seen—increasing rainfall supporting greater numbers of forest trees which increase soil fertility and the possibility of arable cultivation.

Shifting cultivation in the Sudanian zone of Northern Nigeria

The land immediately behind the cultivated area was previously cropped and has been allowed to return to bush fallow

Jojoba—a promising new crop for arid lands

Top : Harvesting a wild stand of Jojoba on the San Carlos Apache Indian Reservation, Arizona

Bottom: Jojoba development trials at the University of California, Riverside

PHOTOS: OFFICE OF ARID LAND STUDIES, UNIVERSITY OF ARIZONA

woodland and hence the soil fertility. This could take 15 years or longer depending on the dryness of the seasons. Where rainfall was sufficient for a number of crops to be grown, farm animals were grazed on crop residues, on natural pasture and near the farmsteads. As the dry season progressed the animals were herded over large areas of the surrounding savannah. In dry years, or nearer the desert fringes, fallows of 1–2 years were used, not to restore soil fertility so much as to retain soil moisture. Where fallows were omitted both soil moisture and fertility decreased until the land could hardly support even the less demanding indigenous vegetation. In these areas the exposed soil surface became dry and this, together with the lack of stabilising vegetation and organic matter, allowed the topsoil to erode and be blown to adjacent areas, and the process of desertification began.

Soil stability and fertility can be monitored and maintained by only partially clearing the woodland, by crop rotation and ploughing in crop residues and green manure crops and addition of plant and animal compost. Soil and leaf analyses will determine if more manuring is needed. In this manner, the need for a fallow period can be decreased. Soil moisture can also be monitored and moisture levels conserved if seen to be decreasing below a critical level. This can be achieved by minimising soil disturbance and mulching the soil surface to prevent moisture evaporating; improved farming techniques such as minimum tillage and direct drilling are being developed for such areas to achieve this. Crops can be matched to moisture conditions, e.g. barley will grow on drier soils than wheat, millet and sorghum will give good yields on even drier soils, but cash crops such as cotton or tobacco will need irrigation in the dry season. Plant breeding methods are adapting more and more crops to the growing season and, particularly, soil moisture status. The use of indigenous plants such as the buffalo gourd and jojoba bean in North America is being further investigated.

The types of land use chiefly seen in these areas are dry farming (i.e. using the wet season and residual soil moisture for cropping without irrigation), irrigated farming (irrigating only in the dry season), and pastoral nomadism and ranching in the drier parts.

Dry farming

Dry farming is an economic proposition in areas where the seasonal rainfall exceeds 300 mm. Thus the origins of dry farming are in the forest and savannah zones rather than the arid areas. Cropping depends on the amount and distribution of rainfall, the season in which it falls and the potential of harvesting large rainwater run-off areas and spreading the rainfall over the more fertile soils. The sowing period depends on the correlation of rainfall and potential evaporation. Aridity occurs even in areas with significant rainfall if evaporation losses exceed rainfall gains. Where cropping is co-ordinated with climatic and soil conditions and natural recycling processes are encouraged, a dry farming land use is productive but does not exhaust natural resources.

Indigenous plant and animal communities thrive alongside dry farming but care must be taken by terracing, contour ploughing and mulching to prevent soil erosion in the dry and fallow seasons.

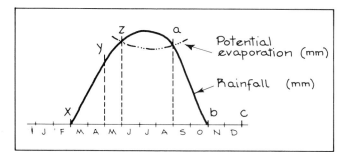

Fig 11 *Cropping seasons for dry farming*

Figure 11 shows a typical rainfall pattern for the areas under discussion. Selected crops such as wheat and barley can be sown at the end of the dry period (x). Where the risk of crop failure due to uncertain rainfall is too great, this period is used for preparing the soil. At (y), germination should have taken place, and sowing can continue until (z) when it often becomes too wet to cultivate and the incidence of disease increases.

Other crops can be sown at (a) and (b) if the land has remained fallow during the wet season and the soil moisture reservoir is replete. These crops will survive until the remaining soil moisture is exhausted after (c).

Permanent tree and shrub crops grown for fruit, berries, pods, *etc.* are listed in the tables of plant uses (Appendix 4.1, 4.2). Others which have been bred for greater productivity and which will require some irrigation include mulberry, paw paw, guava, mango, citrus, pistachio, cashew nuts and olives.

Irrigation of crops increases yields and numbers of harvests, e.g. alfalfa can be cropped 10–12 times per annum. The longer the rainy season, the more intensive the cropping and the less the movement of livestock away from the crop residues and farmsteads. The increased rainfall does however bring increased pest and disease incidence for plants and animals alike.

Irrigation agriculture

In the semi-arid areas irrigation is not generally essential to support life since dry-land farming produces sufficient food. Historically, therefore, irrigation has not been afforded high priority since it generally requires a higher labour input than dry farming. One reason for this is that irrigation is generally practised in river valleys on heavy alluvial soils which hold moisture well. Cultivation of such soils is tedious and difficult compared to that of lighter upland soils. Two types of irrigation are commonly practiced:

1 Drawdown agriculture, where crops are planted following uncontrolled recession of seasonal floods

2 Irrigation proper, where river water is diverted or controlled for at least part of the crop year.

The crops grown are often cash crops, commonly vegetables, and rice in sub-tropical areas. Food crops—grains and roots—are grown on upland areas under dry farming, although in more advanced communities grain and fodder crops may also be irrigated. This traditional pattern of cropping frequently presents problems where attempts are made to modernise agriculture in such areas. Subsistence farmers naturally give priority to food crops—cash crops are planted and tended only when the food crops have received sufficient attention. In a subsistence economy with low investment in irrigation facilities this is not important. If crops are planted late or neglected then cash income is lower. However where investment is made in irrigation facilities such as dams, canals and pumps, a reasonable return on capital has to be earned. Farmers can then no longer neglect irrigated crops and generally have to intensify irrigated cropping to generate sufficient revenue to show a profit. Unless their food supply is underwritten, subsistence farmers are often unwilling, and indeed unable, to make the necessary changes in their patterns of farming.

A large proportion of irrigation projects in semi-arid areas have failed to achieve economic viability. A commonly stated reason is that they failed to realise the

TABLE 5.2 CROPS WHICH CAN BE GROWN IN WET SEASON, DRY SEASON, AND DRY SEASON WITH IRRIGATION

Climate type	Wet season	Dry season
Mediterranean type: e.g. Jordan and Algeria	(Winter) Wheat Barley Chick peas Lentils Vetch Vegetables (cool climate types)	(Summer) Vegetables (warm climate types) Tobacco Sunflower Safflower
Subtropical type: e.g. northern Nigeria	(Summer) Sorghum Millet (Maize) Cowpeas Groundnuts Cassava Vegetables + Supplementary irrigation: Cotton Tobacco	(Winter) Crops grow only in isolated cases without irrigation as soils too hard to cultivate when dry + Irrigation: Rice Wheat Vegetables

predicted crop yields or cropping intensities. Incomplete understanding of farmers' needs is certainly a major contributing factor.

Pastoralism

In the semi-arid areas rainfall is insufficient to support domestic animals in one place without irrigated fodder production. Few areas have suitable water supplies together with the facilities and organisation required to make this economically viable. Livestock, in the dry season, are therefore ranged over large areas of land to find fodder. Many intermediate stages between, and combinations of true pastoral nomadism and farming have developed in response to climate and the extra income which can be obtained through trading meat, milk and hides.

The majority of nomads follow relatively fixed patterns of seasonal movement, determined by rainfall patterns. In the Sahel zone, for example, the herds are at their furthest south during the dry season. At the start of the rainy season, they follow the onset of the rains northwards, grazing the flush of new grass. During the main wet season they graze on the pasture lands in the northern areas, returning southwards at the end of the rains and grazing the vegetation which has grown during that season, as well as stubble and residues from arable cropping. This type of seasonal movement brings nomads into contact with farmers during their periods in the wetter savannah areas.

Some nomads plant crops in wadis or other areas where moisture supplies are adequate, and cereals such as barley and millet may be grown. The true nomad does not however husband these crops but merely sows them in one visit to the area, returning later in the season to reap any harvest.

In areas where rainfall or moisture supply are higher, a permanent residence may be maintained at least for a few years and a variety of crops grown around the residence. Where pastoralism forms the main source of revenue with arable cropping being only supplementary, this is termed semi-nomadism. Where cropping predominates, it is identical to that of a settled farmer who also has livestock

Cattle collecting area outside Khartoum Sudan
Stock are assembled here for final fattening prior to being sold in Omdurman Market. Although adjacent to the Nile, all ground cover vegetation has long since gone, and feed has to be brought in from irrigated farms

and is termed partial nomadism. Transhumance (the seasonal moving of livestock) involves two separate seasonal residences—one occupied during the dry season and located in a dry season grazing area, the other occupied during the wet season. Whole villages may practice transhumance, and supplementary cropping during the wet season is common.

In all these forms of nomadism the pastoral element is essentially the same, the only differences being the extent to which crop residues are used to supplement grazing.

Present developments with livestock

Ranching is a relatively recent development in pastoralism. It treats pastoralism as an 'agribusiness' rather than as a way of life and is characterised by large numbers of animals looked after by a small number of people. The system is essentially the same so far as the plant ecosystem is concerned, the fundamental difference being that stock movement is largely controlled by fences rather than people.

Concentration of single species of livestock in this manner carries potential dangers of overgrazing and particularly of disease. FAO/Unesco in 1963 therefore suggested that game farming is preferable to ranching. A number of different species cohabit and feed on different plants, maintaining the diversity and vigour of a natural system and conserving over-exploited species. This enables the land to support a higher liveweight of animals per hectare than ranching since wild ungulates are more efficient feeders than domestic stock, and less likely to overgraze areas due to the way they 'nibble' foliage rather than eating it nearly to soil level as goats do. The replacement of the wild gazelle with the goat is a sad loss to the ecosystem in many arid areas.

Nomadic pastoralists such as those of the Sahel have substantially increased their herd sizes during climatically favourable years. This has occurred in response both to increased population size and to increased revenue from the large numbers of the tribes who have obtained work outside the community. However, when the drought years came the ecosystem could no longer support the animal population. The death of large numbers of their livestock put the human population at risk. This prompted aid programmes in the form of food distribution centres and the drilling of new wells to provide vitally needed water for the herds. The result however was the concentration of the pastoralists around these fixed points. Within a very short time the vegetation in the surrounding area, up to distances of hundreds of kilometres, was totally denuded. Soil became directly exposed to the desiccation effect of the sun and wind, and the pounding of the livestocks' hooves created a fine surface dust which easily blew away. Soil degradation and further decreases in vegetation followed. The herds, as in Botswana, eventually died, and continue to die, of starvation rather than thirst.

Dry farming is pushing further and further into areas of marginal rainfall as a result of pressures of land availability. Crop production is rarely successful in such areas but this is usually not discovered until the original pasture vegetation has been destroyed. This puts further pressure on the nomadic pastoralists. They are often attracted to marginal areas along the routes and roads developed by the existing farming community and by the aid organisations for their food distribution operations. Government policies attract pastoralists to such areas since the infrastructure also serves to dispense benefits such as medical services and to administer political and financial control.

Around Niamey, in Niger, for example, there are now no trees for a radius of 200 km. The demands of the population for wood as fuel have completely stripped the area in the absence of any development of fuel plantations. As a result it now costs as much to purchase fuel to heat the cooking pot as it does to buy the food to go into it.

It is on these areas on the fringes of the true arid areas that attention is particularly focusing at present, as their ecosystems progressively deteriorate and desert-like conditions take over. The necessity for planning land use and population sizes to match the land's capabilities is vital, and surveys are being carried out to establish land carrying capacity of the existing ecosystems and tailor uses to them.

FARMING IN ARID AREAS

Historically, the predominant form of farming in arid areas (for example, the sub-Saharan type) has been nomadic pastoralism, but present-day needs for more food have placed greater emphasis on the use of irrigation farming. The two forms of farming are discussed separately below.

Nomadic pastoralism
The predominant form of land use in arid areas is nomadic pastoralism. This form of land use can be considered as a refinement of food gathering. Since man is unable to obtain sufficient food from plants himself, he employs animals which can utilise plant species which he himself is unable to digest. Forms of total nomadism vary considerably. They include peoples such as the Tibus of the Libyan desert who live in small groups with only a few sheep and goats ranging over hundreds of square kilometres, and tribes such as the Tuareg who roam from Libya to Timbuktu and cover much larger areas with huge herds of goats and camels.

In the cold pastureland of west Eurasia and central Asia, perennial grazing can be carried out on xerophytic and halophytic vegetation such as *Artemisia* species and *Salsola* species. Sheep and goats migrate to various altitudes to find temporary fodder. In the hotter dry lands, perennial and ephemeral vegetation provides food and fodder. In Arabia and the Sahara the nomads travel to areas of successive rainfall and increased fodder. This successful subsistence adaptation to aridity is seen in the severe climatic deserts such as the Atacama, Arabian, Eurasian and central Asian and the Iraq Deserts, as well as in the man-assisted dry lands such as North Africa and the Near East.

Where the human and animal populations are appropriate to the carrying capacity of the land, the nomadic system is claimed to be one of the best adaptations to harsh arid conditions. A Unesco study concludes that '. . . Nomadism as a careful pastoral continuum is the least traumatic of human influences and as a form of husbandry utilised areas which could not be utilised by man in any other way'.[1] However this statement ignores the fact that nomadism is capable of supporting only a relatively low standard of living by modern standards, unwelcomely low for those who have come into contact with the consumer society.

Alternatively, should all the nomads be settled in order to take advantage of these facilities, a large area of land would be left completely unproductive and the skills of living in arid conditions would be lost. It would therefore seem practical to encourage those with a strongly developed nomadic instinct to remain nomads whilst also having the opportunity to enjoy some of the comforts of settled existence. This could be achieved by setting up education services, information programmes on radio and portable television, weather and grazing forecasts and possibly mobile markets and clinics to service nomads en route.

Even the total nomad is not, however, entirely free simply to follow the available grazing. Both he and his herds must have water. Camels, for instance, require water every 2–3 days in hot weather although only at 2–3 week intervals during cooler periods. For the total nomad this means that rather than roam in direct response to the availability of vegetation he has to move from one water source to another.

Only in extremely arid areas where rainfall is particularly unpredictable are nomadic movements completely dictated by the availability of pasture. Even here nomads come into contact with oasis dwellers and exchange meat, milk and hides for dates and crops.

Irrigation agriculture
Crop production without irrigation is possible only in very limited circumstances in the truly arid areas. Occasional catch crops of barley can be grown in wadi beds or depressions in very wet years. Using stored soil moisture in this manner is similar to the drawdown agriculture of the semi-arid areas. Consistent and reliable crop production normally requires irrigation for the complete crop season.

As a result considerable expertise in irrigation has been developed historically by various peoples as discussed in the examples below.

Mesopotamia

8000 years ago, the centre of crop domestication moved from the mountains of Iraq, Iran, Turkey and Galilee to the drier alluvial plains of the Tigris and Euphrates rivers. This move from semi-arid to arid areas stimulated the development and building of dams and canals for storing and distributing flood water originating from the melting of mountain snows in April and June.

Irrigation innovations evolved as the Tigris river cut down into the bedrock, and the water for irrigating adjacent fields had to be lifted. The flooding Euphrates deposited a fertile layer of silt on fields adjacent to its course, but, as the new silt raised the level of the surrounding fields, water still needed to be lifted and the canals continually kept free of silt. Salinisation and waterlogging occurred in many soils with time, and wheat was replaced by salt-tolerant barley, with the result that when the network was neglected in the Mogol period the system collapsed. In the twentieth century the Turks constructed a barrage on the Euphrates, and, together with the Greater Zab Dam, there is now reputed to be a reservoir of water sufficient to irrigate 3 million hectares.

Egypt

In Egypt, the basin system of irrigation was introduced in 3000 BC in order to store and regulate the supply of water from the erratic flooding of the Nile following the summer monsoons. Dams and reservoirs were constructed to regulate the flow of the river, and drainage into a series of basins was facilitated by the use of carefully placed levées and dykes. Today the basin system is used for wet rice, and water stands in the basin for most of the crop's life cycle. The floods deposited fertile silt in the basins, and a single winter crop was sown. With time, silting up of the Nile gradually increased until there was a danger of inundation from the sea. Barrages were built unsuccessfully in the nineteenth century. As technology progressed the Aswan Dam and new barrages, together with drainage installation, regulated flooding, salinisation and waterlogging and produced hydro-electric power. Lake Victoria became a storage reservoir to obviate flood catastrophes. However, as sedimentation has now ceased, salt water is penetrating the Nile delta margin, cultivatable land is being lost, and the fishing industry is in decline due to the decrease in nutrients from the Nile. Fertilisers now less efficiently replace the rich silt and schistosomiasis (bilharzia) has increased.

The original primitive basin system had several factors to its advantage: regular silting maintained fertility, and good drainage initially prevented salinisation. The land dried out in the hot, fallow period, killing weeds and disease pathogens and aerating the soil. Disadvantages included the unpredictable size and duration of the flood and the diseases it spread.

There were also problems with perennial irrigation, and here the raised water-table caused much waterlogging and salinisation. Dams, barrages and drainage provided an answer to these problems but only at the expense of high maintenance and massive disturbance to the natural ecosystems of the site and its surroundings.

Jordan

One of the most interesting historical examples of great irrigation systems is the ingenious run-off and rain-water harvesting of the Nabateans who cultivated areas of the Negev desert in Israel and Jordan using only 100 mm of rainfall per year. The principles of their efficiency of water-use serve as an example for our present situation.

The Nabateans were Arabian nomadic pastoralists who in 2 BC–AD 2 settled on the trading routes between Syria and Arabia. They founded the great city of Petra where goods were marketed for reshipping to Africa, India and China. Their settlement in the desert was fraught with problems—amongst them the lack of water for producing food for their expanding populations. This was overcome by the development of huge water catchment areas and underground water cisterns carved into the barren rock of the hills and mountain slopes. Aerial photographs today show the massive extent of stone mounds and gravel strips, water traps and dams, run-off terraces and collection conduits connecting them. Levées trapped silt to form fertile terraces for cereal production, and crosswalls diverted water from the main wadi to flat terraced strips on either side. Other walls were built to prevent crop and silt erosion—the whole a regulated maze of channels and terraces, all superbly co-ordinated with the run-off from the mountains.

Avdat Farm, Negev Desert

Reconstruction of this ancient farm has yielded much practical data on how run-off systems functioned. Unreconstructed areas are on the right while the blocks in the centre of the photo are terraced fields being rebuilt. Run-off channels can be seen on the hills to either side of the farm

PHOTO: ISRAEL EMBASSY INFORMATION DEPT

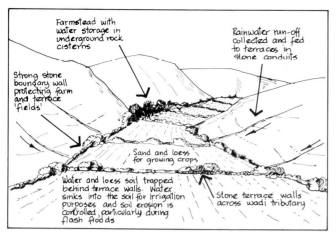

Fig 12 *Schematic view of Nabatean terracing system on a wadi tributary*

In this manner, wheat, barley, grapes, dates, figs and vegetables were grown on less than 100 mm annual rainfall. Agriculture developed as the skills of engineering, architecture and marketing progressed, until Petra was captured by the Romans in AD 106. Lack of motivation as trading routes changed and neglect of the irrigation systems caused agriculture to decline and the desert to regain its stronghold.

Prosperity then passed for a short time to Palmyra, an oasis in the central Syrian desert, where the 'qanat' or 'Kaviz' method of water supply was used. This had been developed in Iran nearly 1000 years before and consists of a chain of wells trapping the water-table in the sand and gravel of the mountain foothills and linked to an underground horizontal tunnel sloping to the surface on the plains beneath. Any mountain run-off or water-table recharge was channelled underground into these qanats which lead to irrigation channels or drinking water cisterns. Their routes can be seen today by the molehill-like mounds of stones placed at regular intervals along their length. These are the rubble from construction of the qanat itself, and the vertical shafts which ventilated and allowed access to the qanats for maintenance and for tapping-off water.

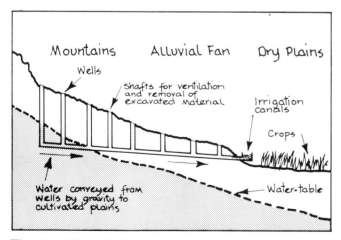

Fig 13 *Schematic longitudinal section through a qanat system showing how the chain of wells taps the water-table*

As with the Petra irrigation systems, the qanats became neglected under Roman and also Christian and Moslem rule. The vertical shafts collapsed and the qanats became blocked.

The Americas

Flood water farming was also carried out by American Indians. Water was trapped behind the silted mouths of rivers such as the Gilat and Colorado, and maize and squash were grown in the silt. The unpredictable flooding made cropping erratic but yields of fodder for livestock were always greatly improved.

In Peru and Mexico the great Toltec and Aztec Empires fed their peoples using irrigated agriculture. The complex social and agricultural organisation and technological powers parallel the great Sumerian, Egyptian and Chinese civilisations of the Old World. There have been many hypotheses citing the causes of the decline of these great civilizations. It can be demonstrated that the declines were not only due to a loss of central authority and conquest by stronger nations, but also to the deterioration of soils and crops under waterlogged and salinized conditions. Each successive dynasty required more inputs of drainage, maintenance and crop management to maintain productivity—improvements lasting for a short time only.

Present-day irrigation agriculture

The continuing development and expansion of irrigation schemes is putting greater and greater strain on water resources. In many areas, of which Saudi Arabia, the United Arab Emirates, Texas and Libya are but a few examples, water-tables are falling at rates as high as 1 metre per year. The rate of extraction of water from the aquifers is exceeding the rate of recharge, and in many cases the quality of the water is deteriorating.

Modern irrigation systems in areas where labour is scarce or too expensive have become more automated and cover as large areas as possible, sometimes at the flick of a switch. There is always, however, a high maintenance input and a necessity for monitoring the water quality and quantity. Any problems that arise can result in the loss of huge areas of crops, diminishing of soil fertility or spread of disease. Shortages of water have more recently encouraged systems which have a higher water use efficiency than flood irrigation, e.g. sprinkler and trickle systems (see chapter 8). Mass production of these systems has reduced their capital costs, and the production of various types of plastic pipe has greatly increased ease of installation. As with traditional irrigation techniques, the water source, soil moisture, texture and fertility, and the movements of salts within the soil are all affected by permanent water application and each must be monitored to avoid degradation. The time interval between water applications is also significant.

Plant survival can be directly or indirectly affected by permanent irrigation. The water used for crop production increases and changes mixtures of plant species on the surrounding land and permits exotic species to be introduced. This in turn affects other organisms and the build-up of pests and diseases. Some of the new species may be more vigorous and displace many of the valuable indigenous species. Plant diversity and its varied interactions with the soil to maintain soil fertility may also decline as

nutrient cycles change. It is therefore essential that long-term effects of irrigation techniques on surrounding land uses, as well as the irrigated area itself, be understood and monitored for adverse long-term change.

The effects of irrigation on the complete hydrological cycle must also be considered, and, in particular, the links between drainage, run-off and ground water supplies should not be broken or polluted. Extraction of water from one area can cause a depletion and loss of vegetation in another.

FARMING IN THE ARID INTERIOR

The numbers of people inhabiting the deep desert interiors (for example the Saharan type) were and still are very low. The sparseness of vegetation means that even nomadic pastoralism is too precarious an existence. Farming is only feasible where crops can obtain moisture from sources other than rainfall.

Oasis agriculture

Traditionally these sources were the desert oases where springs or high water-tables were found, or the banks of rivers from which water could be easily extracted. Natural vegetation was more abundant, for a limited amount of grazing and methods of trapping and regulating the flow of water to crops increased the efficiency of water use. Indigenous vegetation is rarely found in these oases today as native tamarisk, oleander and sometimes olives have long been replaced by date palms, fruit trees, vegetables and fodder crops.

Above : **Raingun irrigating alfalfa at Karaj, Iran**
PHOTO: BRUCE MACNALLY
Below : **The modern oasis**
Irrigated fodder for dairy cows growing under date palms in Saudi Arabia

Palm culture probably originates from before Roman times and is a skilled job requiring artificial fertilisation and the roguing of male plants. Young plants are selected as 2-year offshoots from the base of the parent tree (sexing can be determined at this stage). These offshoots are severed from the parent at a specific time of year, wrapped in hessian and planted in well prepared tree pits. They need

careful nurturing for several years including defoliation by removing the old fronds. These fronds have a variety of uses for fencing (e.g. 'barusti'), making houses, shelter for young plants, and fibre ropes. The live palm tap root will quickly penetrate to the water table and will survive on very saline water although fruit production will decrease.

Underneath, in the shade and humidity created by the palms, fodder, citrus, guava, mangoes, figs and even bananas are grown in the Middle East, often together with apricots, pomegranates and vines in North Africa. The number of trees in the oasis is directly related to the yield of the water-table and little over-extraction occurs.

Modern irrigation and controlled environment houses

The latest techniques of irrigation in the desert interior include the use of controlled environment polythene houses, hydroponic plant culture and the massive irrigation of fodder for sheep raising in Libya.

Large polythene complexes in Arizona, Mexico and Abu Dhabi are producing tonnes of fruit and vegetables under controlled conditions of temperature, humidity and soil moisture, isolating the crops from the adverse arid land conditions and creating optimum conditions within a polythene structure. These houses are cooled by air fanned through a wall of wet straw and chippings, the evaporation of the water cooling the air which is blown from one end of the house to the next. Any moisture condensing on the polythene walls can be recycled. Water is often obtained from an adjacent desalination plant and a minimum amount of water is used for irrigation purposes by selecting trickle or hydroponic irrigation systems. Hydroponic culture recycles a nutrient solution over plant roots which

Top: Aerial view of desalination plant and controlled environment greenhouses at Puerto Penasco, Mexico
PHOTO: ENVIRONMENTAL RESEARCH LAB, UNIVERSITY OF ARIZONA
Above: Aubergines growing in a controlled environment house on Sadiyat Island, off Abu Dhabi in the Arabian Gulf. The outside environment is barren sand
PHOTO: ENVIRONMENTAL RESEARCH LAB, UNIVERSITY OF ARIZONA

are growing in a mat at the bottom of plastic troughs. Research is investigating the optimum nutrient requirements for different crops and the risk of disease spreading through the whole crop from the recycled solution. Although the cost of the polythene structure is relatively low, the equipment and controls that are needed for good crop yields not only greatly increase the cost of the crop but are also reliant upon oil-based products.

Hydroponics can also be carried out without the polythene houses, using coarse dune sand and underground trickle irrigation to reduce the evaporation of water; only $\frac{1}{2}-\frac{1}{3}$ of the water used in flood irrigation is required.

Asphalt barriers can also be placed underground about 0·5 metre below the soil surface in order to isolate vegetables from saline water-tables and to decrease losses through drainage and percolation.

The Kufra scheme in Libya uses huge centre-pivot irrigation sprinklers which water great circles of alfalfa for sheep raising in the depths of the desert. Costs of production are high and the water used is 'fossil' water laid down in the rainy part of the Quarternary period of geological history. It is unlikely that this water is being recharged as the water-table has been thought to sink at an average rate of about 0·9 metre/year. The huge lake underlying the central Sahara may well be recharged by rainfall on the Atlas Mountains, but the aquifers supplying Kufra appear to have little or no recharge. Once this fossil water is used, it may be lost for ever. This indicates that developments such as these should be related to the rate of recharge of ground water sources in order to maintain the long term feasibility of the project and also to maintain the surrounding ecosystems in a viable state.

In attempts to keep down the ever increasing costs of irrigation, other projects are being developed without adequate consideration of the consequences of irrigation and installation of appropriate facilities such as drainage systems. Fertile soils are becoming waterlogged and eventually saline. This is the same problem which contributed to the downfall of the great civilisations in the Tigris and Euphrates valleys, yet modern man appears to believe that by ignoring the problem it will somehow not affect him.

Solar and wind energy

Considerable attention is now being directed towards solar and wind energy, which are particularly appropriate to desert areas. While at present 1 KW to 25 KW solar pumps have been constructed, particularly in Africa, 100 KW pumps are being planned. Solar and wind pumps are used for extracting water from aquifers and for distributing it for whatever purpose, but until the energy produced can be realistically and economically stored, they will be limited to this type of application. However, there is evidence in Australia of improved power storage methods, and this could prove to be of immense value to the rising populations of Africa and the urban centres of the Middle East. If the harnessing of solar energy on a scale to support desalination plants proves feasible, water shortages for coastal communities will become a thing of the past. Until then, however, the traditional methods will continue to be used.

Ingenious new methods of solar stills, condensing water on the inside of ground or flying polythene structures, are also proving feasible. Solar energy can be used to power, cool, recycle and pressurize its own systems, and com-

Top : Centre pivot irrigation units create 'green circles' in the Libyan Desert at Kufra. Each circle represents 100ha. of crops
PHOTO: SPP SYSTEMS LTD
Above : Traditional values combined with modern technology. Due to shortage of water, drip irrigation has replaced traditional open channels in this small, recently planted courtyard garden in Al Ain, UAE

pletely automatic sun powered machines are being produced for the irrigation of remote areas. Hydrological and meteorological recording stations may also be automated for the desert interiors.

FORESTRY, GARDENS AND URBAN LANDSCAPING

When wealth from trading encouraged the expansion of populations and the building of cities in civilizations such as the Sumerian, Egyptian, Chinese, and South American, the degree of organization required to run the city infrastructure and maintain the irrigation and water supply systems which became necessary, also stimulated the innovations of writing and reading, the wheel, architecture, engineering, astronomy and many other technologies. As the cities grew in size their agriculture similarly expanded, or intensified if land was inadequate, and the lifestyle in cities gradually became separated from living on the land in direct contact with soil and climate. The various rural and urban land uses became more distinct from each other until they were connected merely by lines of communication and transport. As a result, different communities evolved, each having distinct needs, drives and qualities. Even then, the power of water (the life giver) and trees (the shade and fruit producers) was never forgotten, and these life forces were epitomised in the city gardens. There are still many fine examples in the Near and Middle East and Mediterranean areas.

Forestry

The natural woodlands surrounding cities were used initially for hunting and 'country parks', but the requirements of wood for fuel and construction, tree crops for food and paper for writing eventually exhausted many of the natural woodland reserves, sometimes causing soil erosion and decreases in efficiency of water catchment areas in the process.

Reafforestation in dry lands chiefly began as a means of stabilizing soil, improving water catchment and providing shelter for agriculture and fodder for livestock, timber being imported for the driest areas. Productive timber still cannot be grown in the very arid areas due to the lack of water and the low financial returns where irrigation is required. However, current development work on the Mondell Pine, which has considerably lower rainfall requirements than comparable species, may extend the penetration of industrial forestry further into dry areas.

In the savannahs, reafforestation is being carried out to provide supplies of firewood and to decrease the effects of denudation of the natural woodland on soil stability and fertility, and colonisation of less desirable vegetation. Species producing the best timber or pulp for paper in the shortest length of time have been later introductions, as techniques of forestry production have been able to overcome the shortages of water. Ecologically, the beneficial effects of trees on soil fertility and stability, water catchment and microclimate cannot be overstated. However, mass planting of single species as has been carried out in the past does little to maintain a balanced wildlife and soil fertility.

Ideas are therefore changing towards mixed planting to maintain the diversity of indigenous forests, together with their use for amenity purposes. Sholto Douglas[2] has recently proposed, for ecologically suitable areas, the production of food by '3-D agriculture', where tree and field crops are grown together, exploiting different soil depths and moisture reserves and different intensities of light and solar radiation (i.e. using different heights above soil level in the same way as different areas of land). Where these crops are compatible, and may even have a synergistic effect upon each other, the system is successful. For example, trees—rather than shrubs or grass—are able to mobilise and recycle plant nutrients to much greater volumes of both soil and air; they are also capable of beneficially improving microclimate for wildlife and man.

Douglas states that a natural ecological climax forest is a *mixed* forest—one with different species contributing in different ways to the ecosystem. Soil nutrients, for example, increase in calcium where oak, buckwheat and nettles grow; increases in nitrogen occur with legumes such as acacias and beans and in saponin with spinach beet, potatoes, tomatoes and runner beans. Mixtures of certain species can have a beneficial effect on each other regarding soil nutrient and moisture status, decreasing pests and diseases and increasing wildlife—which may usefully feed on harmful pests. He advocates that any amenity tree planting should also include useful tree crops for man and wildlife, such as *Prosopis* species whose pods make excellent fodder, *Ceratonia siliqua*, the carob, which occurs in the Near East and N. Africa, whose fruit makes excellent food and fodder in rocky areas where citrus cannot be grown, and persimmons in China for man and animals; pine and hazel nuts and acorns can also be usefully grown. Walnuts have deep roots and a thin canopy and in semi-arid areas of the Mediterranean and Iran have allowed crops or grass pasture to be grown in the shade beneath them.

Douglas' examples are chiefly confined to temperate and semi-arid areas. However, where re-afforestation or shelter planting has been carried out successfully in arid areas it has included species which provide shelter, shade, soil stabilisation, fodder and nurse trees and shrubs for the timber species in the most protected part of the belt. Trees and shrubs include species of *Acacia, Tamarix, Casuarina, Eucalyptus, Calligonum, Prosopis, Populus, Nitraria* and *Salsola* which are renowned for their soil binding abilities and many of which provide fodder from leaves or pods.

When close to cities, as has recently been recognized, woodlands can also structure surrounding green belt areas and link one part of the city to another, providing cool and shady walkways for pedestrians, reducing reflection and, to some extent, modifying pollution if tolerant species are planted. The species used for replanting city woodland and green belt areas therefore differ from those selected for economic purposes. Urban species are required not for their food productivity but for their appearance and ability to cast shade and give shelter from sun, wind, noise and pollution. Root growth is often restricted, and species with fast growing tap roots (as many of the desert species living on low water-tables possess) should be avoided. In intensively used pedestrian areas near to traffic, plants with fleshy fruits and heavy leaf fall, e.g. *Terminalia catappa*,

Street trees creating shade for parked cars and separating pedestrians from traffic (Tehran, Iran)
PHOTO: RICHARD HARRISON

should be avoided so that accidents are prevented. Suckering trees can also be a nuisance, e.g. *Schinus molle*. New ideas for urban design are continually being developed, although most are based on traditions relating to garden design throughout the centuries.

Gardens

The earliest stimulus to create gardens is thought to be religious, each different religion having its own mythical garden. The garden evolved as an extension of the productive enclosure for growing food, but feeding man's spiritual rather than physical appetite. Its conception was to create a garden of paradise for spiritual rest and contemplation, often protected by wild or functional woodland or hunting forests.

The earliest recorded gardens are Egyptian, where the idea of paradise centred on the oasis garden. As water was the precious giver of life to man and the plants and animals he fed upon, it also became the centrepiece for his gardens. The irrigation patterned gardens of Asia, Arabia, Persia and India originated from Egyptian models and spread west through Greek and Roman invasions and finally to Spain with the Moorish conquest, as is exemplified by the stunningly beautiful garden of the Alhambra in southern Spain.

The basic structure of this type of garden is an enclosed courtyard protected from excessive sun and sand, with a central irrigation canal or rectangular pool, planted on each side with trees and flowering plants. Many intricate patterns of water canals, planting and hard-surfacing originated from this simple form, and in India for example symbolised the four rivers of life. In Persia water flowed over blue or mirror tiles and was surrounded by fruit trees, cypresses and almond flowers—each plant symbolic in some way. Many such gardens are recorded on the beautiful Persian carpets seen today, and others remain

Above : Traditional Persian garden at the palace of a former mayor (Shiraz, Iran)
Below : Small public garden in Abu Dhabi, UAE
PHOTO: JOHN TOWNEND, MINISTER AGRICULTURE

Fountains used as a major feature in a modern urban landscape in Mexico City

commemorating special poets and prophets. In the early sixteenth century, the idea of the Persian garden was developed by the Moghul conquerors in India, and the small channels of the Persians became large expanses of tranquil water, as seen in the Taj Mahal.

Where gardens were divided into eight *parterres*, this often represents the eight divisions of the Koran. The love of shade and colour originated in response to the arid, glaring and monotonous buffs and beiges of the open desert and is perpetuated in all modern gardens today, together with the overwhelming appreciation of scent and tranquility.

In the Hispano-Arabic gardens in Spain, mixtures of eastern and western traditions took place, and the enclosed courtyard opened to reveal beautiful views of mountains and seas, a different paradise from the harsh desert surroundings usually encompassing the eastern garden. One courtyard or patio leads to another through proportioned arcades lined with plants growing in pots and tubs, and fountains playing cooling water over stone and marble. Some of the large expanses of water were used as still ponds, to reflect the strong and simple lines of the architecture. Each garden 'room' gives a sense of solitude and calm contemplation with its simplicity and restraint, the water and plants symbolic of the wonders of life and guiding the eye to glimpses of the huge paradise outside. As darkness descends in early evening in many of the Arabian deserts, the focus of interest is for colour and scent so that the cool of the evening is also emphasised.

All of these interests are retained today, although the hustle and bustle of traffic in busy town and city centres has caused the emphasis to move to shelter, shade and colour in public gardens, rather than quiet solitude. Scarcity of water restricts the use of water features, although fountains are still seen in many gardens and urban open spaces. Plants are also used to provide shaded walkways from one shopping area to another or to residential areas as well as play spaces. They play a role in reducing noise, pollution, visual artifacts, discomfort due to humidity, dust, lack of air movement and reflection from hard surfaces. The reverence for water and plants is still incorporated into the design of all public and private gardens, and in this way can educate man towards an understanding of his spiritual and physical dependence upon the world around him.

Urban landscaping

The use of exotic planting and high-technology methods of irrigation in city gardens does not usually contribute to the maintenance of natural ecosystems. This is better achieved by the development and protection of existing large scale green belt systems of indigenous species, established on natural water supplies. These green areas can greatly assist in maintaining and propagating natural systems close to cities that help to purify the air and give peace and freedom for man to appreciate his relationships with nature.

Planting in cities and industrial areas to develop both urban landscape and city ecosystems is relatively new. Gardens in cities have always existed where people could afford the space to develop them. However, the use of masterplans to co-ordinate all landscape activities and provide a basic framework and guidelines for development and planting is less than half a century old. Strategies for

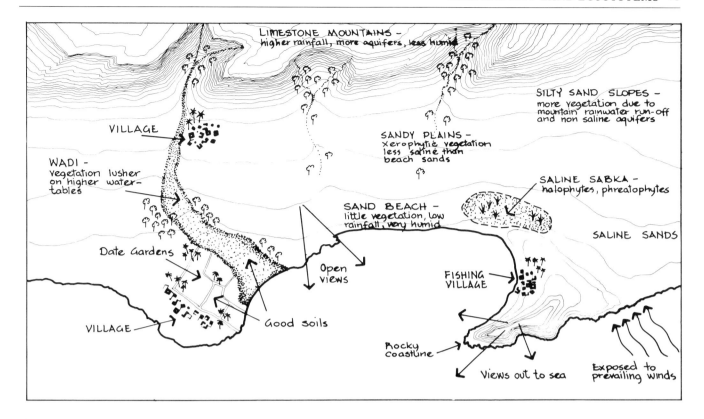

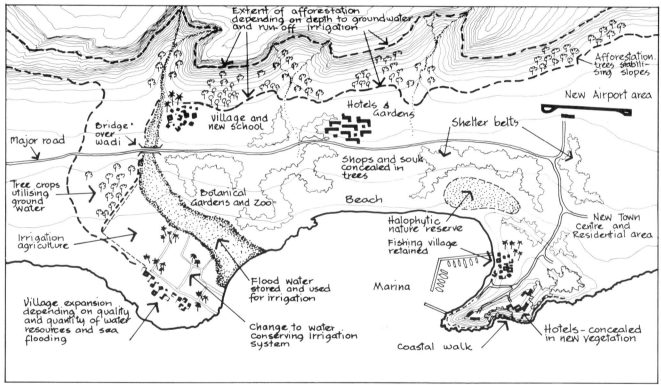

Fig 14 *Landscape masterplan for a coastal development site*

urban landscape planting are only recently being considered in arid areas. This is often due to the lack of water resources and the speed of construction and industrial development overshadowing other aspects of city life. The aim of developing an urban landscape is to provide an attractive foil of foliage against built form, to link one area with another, creating vistas to stimulate pedestrian movement and defining and protecting, if necessary, one land use from another. Screening and vistas encourage people to go from residential areas to recreation, shopping centres, offices or ceremonial areas but to avoid industrial

and dangerous regions. A distinctive character is created for each space and land use, and its atmosphere and appearance will establish its importance within the city. For example, very formal, distinctive planting defines ceremonial and civic regions, whereas more intimate, lush planting creates privacy and variety amongst houses. The choice of hard-surfacings and street furniture should also be in keeping.

Above: The selection of plants suited to site conditions can curtail the need for irrigation or expensive site amelioration
PHOTO: MINSTER AGRICULTURE
Facing page: Designs for urban open spaces
BY COURTESY OF ORLANDO JONES, DEREK LOVEJOY AND PARTNERS

Fig 15 *Landscape design for an urban area incorporating hardy structure planting to protect more sensitive ornamental plants*

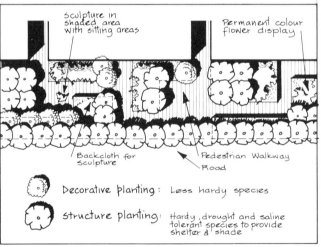

Since a cohesive relationship must be established between natural resources, plants, people and architecture, landscape potential must be assessed from a survey of the different site conditions occurring in the city and the size, character, history and use of the existing open spaces. From this information, policies can be formulated to guide the development of an ordered, unified landscape, suited to site conditions and also providing imaginative environments for people at work, home and play.

The harsher environment of most dry-land cities requires special attention to site conditions. Shelter belts will be required to deflect the hot, desiccating winds and provide cool shelter, as well as for their noise, pollution and screening capabilities. Soils polluted by saline water-tables or seepage from septic tanks must be leached, good backfill added and salt tolerant plants used if salts cannot be completely eradicated.

It is often useful to devise a backbone of very hardy 'structure planting' which can survive extremes of temperature, wind, drought and salts. These plants will survive in the most adverse conditions. In time the improved microclimate offered by these hardy plants will allow less tolerant and more decorative plants to be introduced.

Due to the restricted area between buildings, and hard-surfacings within cities, most plants need irrigation, especially if the water-table is at great depth. Where salt tolerant and drought resistant species are used water conservation and use of brackish water can be employed. Non-tolerant plants would increase the labour required to give extra water and cope with leaching of salts and tending after salt damage had occurred. Sprinkler and trickle irrigation systems require less labour and water application than flood systems. The continuous leaching effect of trickle irrigation applying small, frequent applications and maintaining a low soil-water tension in the root zone, enables more saline water to be used than for flood and sprinkler systems.

Desalinated water is used for urban water supplies in many cities in arid areas, but this water is usually too expensive for use on street planting. Most schemes are now using treated sewage effluent or brackish groundwater and encouraging water conservation and recycling of storm water drainage and sewage. The health hazards and salinity of these waters must be continually monitored, as process breakdowns can rapidly result in the death of plants and the spreading of disease or illness for city inhabitants. A co-ordinated landscape strategy will therefore permit the creation of a more pleasant life style within the city whilst tailoring plant requirements to the city's natural resources and the projected use of the open space. The development of ugly, sterile surroundings can be avoided and the discomfort of being in the hot, humid, dusty outdoors alleviated.

NOTES

1 Unesco. *Use and Conservation of the Biosphere*. Unesco: Paris 1970
2 Douglas, Sholto. *Forest Farming*. Robert A de Hart: 1976

6 Interpreting and forecasting man's effect on dry-land ecosystems in rural and urban areas

In many cases planning and forethought have been able to alleviate some of the problems facing dry lands today. However, some plans have gone badly astray, creating more havoc than originally existed. These plans were only tackling part of the problem, rather than relating it to the complete situation with all its complexities and interactions.

In summary, it can be seen that man can have the following adverse effects in rural and urban areas:

Water
Water-table depletion—extraction exceeding recharge
Salinisation/contamination by overcropping or using 'greedy' exotic species
Waste of water through inefficient cultural practices
Pollution—from septic tanks, industry, waste tipping, quarrying
Hydrological changes—due to excavation, damming, re-routing water

Soil and topography
Erosion, sand blow—from grading (earth moving), bare fallows and over-use
Salinisation/waterlogging—poor irrigation practices
Loss of fertility—poor crop husbandry
Spreading disease/pollution—from salts, industry, wastes, septic tanks, extraction

Plant and animal communities
Overgrazing and overcropping
Introduction of competitive species
Denudation and consequent soil erosion from over-use
Monoculture and increases in pests and disease
Introduction of exotics that change the organisms feeding on the original community, pollution

Microclimate
Exposure—clearance of woodland shelter
Too wet or too dry—changes in moisture status, humidities
Air pollution—industry, domestic fires, cars

Geology
Erosion from quarrying, mining
Changes in moisture status due to cities, structures, bridges, dams, underground works

It is therefore essential to interpret man's effect on natural ecosystems as he pursues his many land uses. It is necessary to know the current situation and how it may alter in the future. A forecast of the possible effects on the ecosystem before implementation of future strategies and projects begin, would alleviate the occurrence of overgrazing, salinisation of soils *etc.*, and continuous monitoring of site changes could prevent their occurrence in the future.

How can this be achieved? Man must know his ecosystems in relation to land and climate.

SURVEY—LAND AND CLIMATE

Unfortunately, many of the deserts and their semi-arid fringes are virtually unmapped, and where maps do exist, they are generally on too small a scale to be relevant to detailed studies. Unesco and the 1977 UN Plan of Action to combat desertification is beginning to correct this omission. While such surveys may not be important in the heart of the deserts, where very few people live, they are critical for the desert fringes where nomadic people are being pressurized to increase food production. Continuous surveys, especially by aerial photography, are needed to recognize increasing desertification.

Surveys into the hydrological resources have been carried out in a number of countries. Hydrogeological surveys are still needed to locate underground water resources which depend on the hydrological cycle. As knowledge of the hydrological cycles is increasing, it is becoming apparent that the water resources of one country often depend on catchment areas in another. For instance, the Hajar Mountains in the State of Oman are known to be the source of the water which feeds the aquifers in many of the United Arab Emirate States. It is also suspected that parts of the Empty Quarter in Saudi Arabia are catchment zones for the Abu Dhabi aquifers. The Nile, of course, is the prime example of an international water resource.

International control
It is becoming increasingly urgent to establish international agreements to ensure that catchment areas are protected. Further aquifer exploitation similarly must be controlled. While numerous shallow wells are difficult to monitor, the catchment areas are larger land forms, like mountains, and are more easily identified and monitored. The anger generated between India and Bangladesh over the rights to use the water from the Ganges, and the clashes

between Egypt and Libya over oasis rights are clear evidence in favour of such international agreements. With proper controls and accurate meteorological data, volumes available for aquifer penetration can be calculated, and will establish the volumes which can be sensibly extracted. Discussions on international water policy (as in the UN Water Conference) are being initiated to cover aquifer management, international and inter-state agreements on water use and conservation, control and monitoring of extraction of resources, improvement of catchment areas and the development of alternative sources and their relationship to the maintenance of soil fertility and its capacity to hold moisture.

Interpretation of surveys

Much information is now available on deserts and their semi-arid fringes. The Arid Zone Research Unit of the United Nations, under the auspices of Unesco, the University of Arizona, the University of California at Riverside, the University of North Wales at Bangor, and the Governments of Iran, Israel and Australia (not by any means an exhaustive list) have undertaken extensive research. The problem is collating and re-assessing the information and making it available in a usable form; this aspect of arid lands research is now being dealt with by the Office of Arid Lands Studies (OALS) at the University of Arizona, and is the most promising development in the appreciation of the problems of these lands. OALS has available a computer-based retrieval system for research information covering a broad spectrum of disciplines, at both national and international levels. It issues regularly *Abstracts of Arid Lands Studies and Research* plus newsletters on matters of arid lands interest and is experimenting with the use of satellite transmissions of its arid lands information resources through remote terminals. The complex interactions of ecological systems and the problems of subjectivity have encouraged the use of computer techniques to analyse much of the data to make future predictions.

More interpretation techniques and implementation of ideas are needed in order to put the assessment of survey data into practice. A pragmatic approach is essential.

Implications of new technologies

Technology is continually evolving new ideas with considerable potential for the development of dry lands. However, the environmental implications are often relatively unknown. Cloud seeding is one of the most publicised methods of harnessing climate. This has proved reasonably successful in North America where there is adequate moisture in the air but topographical reasons prevent its falling on the lands most needing it. Where there are no clouds or air moisture is very low, as in many of the arid areas, cloud seeding is not successful. Repercussions could occur should one country take another's rainfall.

There have also been suggestions for much larger schemes, such as diverting the rivers from the Himalayas to the Russian steppes. This could, however, produce drought in south Asia. Pumping water over a dammed Bering Strait would melt some of the Arctic ice, but also affect climatic change and cause increases in sea level that might flood many of the important regions of the world. It has also been proposed to divert the Zambesi to recreate the lakes that existed in the Pleistocene period. This would also flood a large area of fertile land, and the ecological implications, as with all of these schemes, would be greater than we could ever anticipate at our current stage of understanding. Most recent ideas have included using nuclear explosions to blast a canal from the Mediterranean to the Qattara depression in the western Sahara, and the towing of icebergs to the Middle East for drinking water. The economics of the latter suggestion appear to be more viable than one would expect.

The latter types of technique would certainly bring more dry lands into productive use, but mostly at the expense of flooding existing fertile areas. None of them is based on sound ecological principles, although ecological strategies for their implementation could be worked out if future knowledge and methods of interpretation, with the aid of a computer, progress sufficiently. The ecological chaos that might result from implementing any of the schemes on a large scale with our present degree of knowledge would be too high a risk to take. Strategies are therefore needed, and some are already being compiled on an international and community basis, to regulate water use, mineral extraction and pollution, record meterological and hydrological data, improve land management and planting techniques and base land use upon land capability. These must all be correlated with long-term socio-economic plans.

Reserves for use in times of drought, and disaster-relief operations must be planned in advance. It is essential that the communities themselves, as well as the national bodies, should be involved in the planning and implementation of these strategies, as idealistic plans which do not have the support of the people involved have not succeeded to date. Institutional and financial support must be thoroughly organised before implementation.

Whilst shortages of resources have promoted research into alternative energy sources, new settlement patterns and cropping systems, they have also stimulated new ways of looking at religion, and spiritual motivations. Conservation ideals have encouraged investigation into recycling techniques and analysis of long-term trends in climate and ecological balance, but man's adaption to these new ideals will involve a psychological revolution which will undoubtedly affect the structure of society and its future aims. The 'new nomadic lifestyle', with increased educational, medical and market facilities is an example. It may also be possible to develop new villages in dry lands as 'oasis communities'. Green belt areas can be used for stabilisation of microclimate and soils, shelter and food for human and animal populations and creating a purpose for the community's existence. The importance of green areas in cities should not be ignored; they give shade and shelter,

Top right : Sand dune reclamation in northern Libya. Indigenous plants are used to stabilise the shifting sand and interplanted with fruit and vegetables

Bottom right : Experimental plantation of saltbush (Atriplex spp.), a potentially important fodder crop, in the Negev Desert PHOTO: C. V. MALCOLM

reducing reflection and purifying the air, and enabling people to share in the visual and tactile experiences of being close to the land and its living species even though working hours may be surrounded by concrete and sterility.

The problems of changing social, economic, institutional and legislative practices will be more difficult to cope with than operating new technical procedures, and may be prohibitive in the short term. It is interesting that the UN Plan of Action to combat desertification lists law, economics, demography and sociology before natural sciences in the expertise required by land use planners. The diversity of origin and composition of dry lands will also prohibit the use of 'blanket' solutions. Each area must be appraised upon its own characteristics of climate and natural resources, land capabilities and socio-economic preferences. All these innovations will require a change in the methods of teaching. A new emphasis is already being placed on environmental sciences, understanding natural resources and how they may be used but not exhausted and training the mind to invent alternative, simple solutions to changing circumstances. With such fast rates of development as are occurring today the emphasis must be on flexibility of thought and action. The place for spiritual development must also be structured within this framework. Programmes of education in the use of land and natural resources must be instituted in schools, extension services and training centres as well as government institutions and universities.

Development with plants

Man has become unaware of the importance of plants in his everyday activities, since technology, rather than natural processes, appears to take care of our welfare. The fundamental usefulness of plants in maintaining soil fertility and stability, regulating the oxygen levels in the atmosphere and feeding the other organisms that share our planet, has only really become apparent as pollution and overcrowding have obliterated the countryside we used to take for granted. However, the most tangible uses of plants for food, shelter and fuel are still recognized, and more especially in dry lands where there is less urbanisation and a scarcity of lush vegetation.

Plants provide man with many of the comforts of modern living—and also improve his surroundings visually, by providing cool shade, shelter from wind, dust and pollution and by maintaining land in a suitable condition for future uses. When developments in both urban and rural areas are carried out using environmental appraisal and plants suited to site conditions as an integral part of the scheme, a more 'humanised' landscape results, more psychologically satisfying and with an inbuilt safeguard against site deterioration.

Long-term success depends upon a systematic understanding of dry-land ecosystems, plants and man, and a recognition of how site development will affect the existing and surrounding ecosystems. Many of the problems associated with plant establishment in dry lands arise through an incomplete understanding of site conditions. In the very variable and unpredictable climates of the arid zones every site has a unique combination of natural factors which determines the optimum methods of plant establish-

ment. To ensure that proposed developments are soundly based it is clearly essential to recognize potential planting problems at the early planning stage.

Technology can work *with* the natural ecosystem rather than against it, but only if the physical and chemical properties of site soil and water are known, together with their interactions with climate and all the site organisms living and feeding off the area. In order to bring land successfully into use, we must be fully aware of these characteristics and how they react to man's technologies. Land can be brought into use by working with the natural laws of the site, retaining soil stability and fertility using *plants* rather than expensive fencing and chemicals. Initial plant establishment in difficult areas may require artificial assistance, but once the planting is underway, fencing can be removed and the system becomes self-supporting. Artificial methods do not always assist in the natural food and water cycles or in the regulation of the tiny concentrations of plant trace elements and growth hormones, *etc.*, and we must learn to recognise and understand the processes governing these interactions. This is best accomplished by studying living, organic systems with a high efficiency of energy exchanges. In the following chapters we try to describe planning and implementation techniques that use plants and soil, water and air processes, where they are more appropriate to land and man than machinery and chemicals.

Reaction to current trends would suggest that the development of flexible settlement and cropping patterns will be the only useful answer to rapid changes in technology, ecology and climate. It is therefore essential that pilot schemes and small areas of land be developed in order to correct planning errors and faults in technique and to retain flexibility. Large-scale schemes, although successful in certain conditions, are extremely vulnerable when those conditions change. Rural development and intermediate technology will achieve better long-term successes. Increasing world populations will need more food and space in which to live and marginal lands will need to be used.

Planting can play an important part in bringing marginal land into use without destroying the balance of the rest of the region. (See Table 7.12 page 99.) Marginal land can be brought into production by techniques such as improving the microclimate (for example by providing shelter from desiccating wind and sun by planting wind breaks), increasing the efficiency of water use (for example by improving catchment areas, aquifer recharge, rain water harvesting, reducing evaporation and recycling water for different land uses and within each land use or region) and increasing the efficiency of the soil by using techniques that maintain it in a condition suitable for future and possibly different uses without the accumulation of harmful substances, pests or disease. Chapter 8 describes some of the techniques involved.

Irrigation of marginal land in this way could create more productive ecosystems by the mere addition of water. The indirect effect of water run-off from an irrigated crop might also be significant. In this manner, newly vegetated rangelands could be created for man and livestock if water conservation and water use efficiency were to be practised.

Test plots of trials to show how plant succession is altered by applying water to indigenous vegetation will give valuable results for further research. The different structures of the plant communities can be plotted as the succession evolves, and their new interactions with soil, water, microclimate, *etc.* assessed together with the changing insect and animal populations feeding on them.

However, there is not, in every new situation that man presents to himself, a plant species that precisely fits the uses required of it for the site conditions in which it is to be grown. It may be necessary to breed new plants for use in dry-land areas of limited resources, especially when concerned with factors such as salt tolerance, high water-tables and the unstable, sometimes rocky, soils often encountered in marginal land. Wherever possible, plants should be selected, bred and developed to

1 conserve natural resources
2 increase efficiency of use of resources
3 increase productivity of plants

This has been discussed in greater detail in chapter 4.

Much of the technology involved in using marginal lands to the full is not new, as can be seen by the success of such peoples as the Nabateans 2000 years ago. If man can balance his demands with the carrying capacity of the ecosystem current trends can be reversed. This means careful management of his cropping, his livestock, indeed all his community activities. Above all it means management of himself as an integral part of the ecosystem.

There is also, with new cities, a chance to encourage urban development with an ecological rather than purely material emphasis. Many master plans have been drawn up over the last decade, paying due attention to all the cultural and physical requisites of man in an urban environment, but few have registered the impact of such development on the future land use and the natural characteristics of the area. As in the past, economic expansion has progressed as a result of market enterprise with little attention paid to its interactions with surrounding land uses. We are still in the process of learning and testing new integrated approaches, relating man's needs to site conditions and interpreting and adapting to the new situations that arise as a result. A more complete approach to the relationship of all land uses to each other is required in order to maintain the resources of our planet in the most healthy condition for our future use and this is especially true for dry lands. In this way land can be maintained in a condition suitable for future planting or alternative uses. Most importantly, there will be energy reserves and flexibility of use if climate or man's aspirations and needs change.

Integrated approach to land development

Balanced developments in the future will be with plants and for plants—our primary food producers and guardians of soil, water and air quality, and the integrated approach to land use planning is developed from the three basic principles stated in the introductory chapter:

1 Match land use to site resources
2 Match plants to site resources and land use
3 Short-term benefits should not be exploited to the detriment of the long-term future of the site.

In the following chapter, these principles are translated into a plan of action showing the sequence, phasing and type of implementation techniques that can be used.

7 Techniques for development with plants: survey and masterplanning

The techniques which may be used to develop balanced environments in the dry lands are many and varied. The majority already exist, either in the technologies of traditional land use systems or in the developments of modern technology. The key to their successful application is a thorough understanding of the principles on which they are based and the effects that they will have in any given situation. It is this element which has, in most cases, been lacking in the past. Too often developments have been attempted by simple transfer of technology from one area to another with no attempt either to understand the implications or to tailor the technologies to the new situation. The techniques that follow are by no means an exhaustive list. They do however represent the main areas to which attention must be directed.

The following plan of action shows how a knowledge of site conditions can be interpreted into practical implementation techniques, testing their 'fit' with the natural site ecology using methods such as the environmental impact analysis.

SURVEY, ANALYSIS AND INTERPRETATION

There are few areas of the world which have not previously been studied. A desk study using previously collected data and reports on the area together with survey photographs can therefore often save valuable time on site: watersheds, catchment areas, changes in soil type and vegetation, direction of dune movement, for example, can be traced and delineated on maps prior to site survey. Maps can be made from aerial or satellite photographs by photogrammetry.

The intensity of the work to be carried out will depend on the scale of the job and whether a macroplanning approach is adopted, as in the formulation of master plans and land use studies, or a microplanning approach where design and cropping plans are worked out to the last detail. This will affect the numbers of people, the type of experience required in the team and the amount of survey and interpretation carried out on site. From this preliminary appraisal of the project, a job programme detailing phasing, staffing and fees can be compiled.

The team chosen to work on the project should be balanced in their various disciplines and approaches to the subject in hand, capable of working together and generating and exchanging ideas. Most importantly, and less encountered at present, they should understand the

Plan of action, from site survey to masterplan
Note: It is essential that a comprehensive plan of action be determined at this stage, before the detailed implementation that will be described in chapter 8.

Stage	Action
Site survey and resource inventory	**Determine resources** Investigate and define resources and raw materials
Site assessment and evaluation	Qualify and quantify resources, including man's effect and interactions within and without the ecosystem
Interpretation	Find site limitations, potential and land carrying capacities: **Match resources to function**
Feasibility analysis	Suggest solutions—test their reaction with other resources and overall functioning of the ecosystem
Land use planning (including assessment of resource management)	Assess how resources can be used by man efficiently but not extravagantly Allocate most appropriate land uses to regions on the site and assess how they complement adjacent settlements and resources, and how ecological balance may change over a period of time Choose alternatives if there is a predictable deterioration of ecosystem or man's living conditions
Masterplan (This may be a city, town, farm, forest, market garden, *etc.*)	Delineate and phase land use regions

interactions and interdependence of all the site criteria and how the various studies relate to each other—similar in fact to an ecologically balanced community. Each member should present an accurate, realistic study of his particular discipline and how it affects and is affected by all the other site factors.

Methods of survey
Large scale and aerial or even satellite surveys will be needed for macroplanning projects, whereas detailed, on-

site survey information, designs and planting techniques will be needed for microplanning projects. Aerial survey allows large areas to be covered quickly and provides useful data for the overall planning phases of a project. Where photographic runs are available for different years, changes in land use, in cropping patterns and in ecological conditions such as desert encroachment can be determined.

Other types of 'remote sensing' techniques that can also usefully be used are satellite photography, radar, heat sensing and photography using light within and beyond the visible spectrum. A great deal of information can be gained for example from ERTS satellite imagery—photographs derived from the U.S. LANDSAT programme. Imagery can be produced covering various bands both of the visible spectrum and beyond. This can be superimposed and computer enhanced to provide 'false colour' imagery which brings out particular features of interest such as vegetation, geology and water resources.

Dr. Musa Qutub has recently developed a technique of tracing ground water using photographs taken in space over 500 miles above the Earth's surface. This depends on recognizing 'lineaments' on the photographs—fractures in the Earth's crust which are very porous and drain water rapidly into the ground water system beneath the soil surface. An analysis of maps and overlays of these fractures, together with changes in vegetation (e.g. deep-rooting species indicating water at depth) and surface drainage, can provide useful information such as where aquifers are being recharged and locations for well drilling; in conjunction with geology, rainfall records and on-site tests, well yields can be determined. Information can also be obtained on the location of oil fields, mineral deposits, flood areas, the extent of urban growth and the siting of major structures in relation to topography and resources.

Aerial surveys and, more recently, satellite studies and other remote sensing techniques have been employed to chart factors such as land use, plant health, vegetation types and patterns, hydrology, geological land forms, animal migration patterns, dust blow, desertification and population changes. Surveys of this type, taken over a period of time and correlated with historical records, can map the changes in ecosystems. Their analysis can often pinpoint the cause of change. Improved coverage and equipment in hydrological and meteorological recording stations are charting not only every-day water and climatic data, but also changes throughout the centuries. For smaller projects, ground surveys will be more appropriate for more detailed work. All aerial or satellite photography techniques of course require ground control surveys to correlate the imagery to the actual situation.

Economic and social surveys may be carried out by questionnaires and by close contact with the population concerned. Field studies add the detail to the large scale surveys. Comparisons of ecological surveys in stable and unstable communities can identify the causes of instability. These comparisons are carried out studying on site the geological and soil characteristics, their relationships with topography and agents of erosion and deposition, the surface and underground water supplies, and the plants and animals living there, and comparing the differences between the two types of communities.

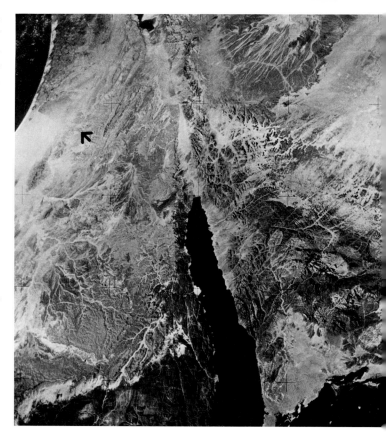

This Landsat photo from space shows a plainly visible division between grazed and ungrazed land in the Negev area of the Sinai desert (arrow). Livestock have stripped the vegetation cover in the grazed area, increasing the reflectance of the ground surface
PHOTO: DR. C. W. MITCHELL

The stability of the environment, or its instability, would indicate whether it is in climax, or whether it is in the process of degrading. The more stable the environmental elements, the more stable will be the plant communities and their constituents. Similarly, the less stable environment indicates considerable disturbance, and further research will be needed to establish which causes are relevant. These can be carried out by monitoring changing areas and setting up trials varying the possible factors involved in change.

Whatever technique is selected there is no substitute for on-site visits by as many members of the team as possible.

Elements to be surveyed
The elements to be studied when a survey is undertaken are shown in table 7.1. It must be remembered that all of the natural characteristics determine the *land capability* and interact to produce the '*carrying capacity of the land*'—i.e. its capacity to support a certain density of plants, animals and other organisms as well as man's settlements and land uses.

The key to any successfully ecologically based project is the efficient co-ordination of all this information; its presentation in a useful manner and at the correct stage for other disciplines to analyse and assess the interactions with their study; and its overall synthesis into a workable project derived from site conditions and resources.

TABLE 7.1 SITE SURVEY CHECKLIST

1 Hydrology:	Determination of underground and surface hydrology and water resources
2 Geology:	Investigation and analysis of surface and sub-surface geology
3 Topography:	Determination and analysis of topography
4 Soils:	Investigation of soil characteristics and collection of soil samples
5 Climate:	Collection and analysis of meteorological data
6 Ecology: (a) Flora and fauna:	Investigation of site ecology Determination of location and types of indigenous plant and animal communities, frequency of distribution and associated land and water factors such as indications of site characteristics and plant suitability, plant availability, breeding material. Evaluation of traditional and modern plant establishment techniques
(b) Human factors:	Examination of human factors Determination of social land use factors, including energy sources, existing infrastructure, services, traditions, culture, values and their effect on the land Assessment of socio-economic factors

Each of these survey elements will be discussed showing factors to be analysed, methods of analysis and the practical interpretation of the analysis for implementation on site.

1 Hydrology and water resources

The availability of water to supplement the very low supplies of soil moisture is usually the most critical factor controlling development options in the arid areas.

For most planting schemes it is necessary to supplement the natural moisture supplies. In only a few areas, normally mountainous, is natural rainfall sufficient for successful plant growth, and even here, choice of species may be very limited.

A fundamental starting point for a development project must therefore be to identify and evaluate the water *resources* available. On a more detailed level, the fundamental starting point for a planting project must be to identify and evaluate the water *supplies* available. It is no use completing the project designs, then calculating the water requirements, only to find that the water supplies are not adequate. This may seem an obvious point but several recent projects for Middle Eastern countries have been completed on this basis and, not surprisingly, never implemented.

The major sources of water are shown diagrammatically in Fig 16. The types of water to be analysed are
· Rain water
· Surface water
· Ground water
· Processed water.
Their quantity, quality and cost must all be tested.

Fig 16 *The major sources of water for planting projects (schematic)*

Methods of analysis

1 Rainfall

Rainfall in arid areas is generally insufficient to sustain concentrated planting. In most cases rainfall is also extremely unreliable as regards both quantity and time of occurrence.

In extremely arid climates rainfall can be ignored as a source of moisture. In less arid situations it can make a significant contribution to plant water requirements and should enter into the calculations.

Rainfall records are kept by practically all meteorological stations and often by agricultural research stations and government farms. To evaluate the contribution rainfall can make it is necessary to consider two factors—firstly the 'effective rainfall', secondly the probability of receiving a given depth of rainfall.

Various formulae have been developed for calculating effective rainfall—that portion of the actual rainfall which can be utilised by the plant. The USDA Soil Conservation Service, for example, have produced tables by which monthly effective rainfall can be computed from total monthly rainfall and monthly crop consumptive use. The figure derived then has to be corrected according to the moisture storage capacity of the plant root zone (again from USDA tables). Effective rainfall in excess of the sum of monthly consumptive use and root zone storage will not be available to the plant and must be discounted.

The amount of rainfall which may reliably be received is calculated by analysis of rainfall records. Annual rainfall is plotted against the probability of its occurrence. The amount to be relied on is then read off against the acceptable probability, normally ranging from 75% (3 years in 4) to 90% (9 years in 10). Acceptable probability depends upon the value of the crop and the likely losses in low rainfall years.

2 Surface water

This is the main traditional source of water for irrigation. Water may be abstracted from rivers or lakes, and dams may be built to create storage facilities to even out seasonal flows in relation to demand. Also included in this category is shallow sub-surface flow in the beds of wadis. Surface

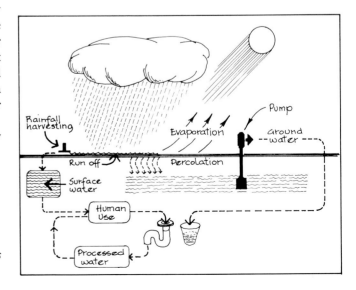

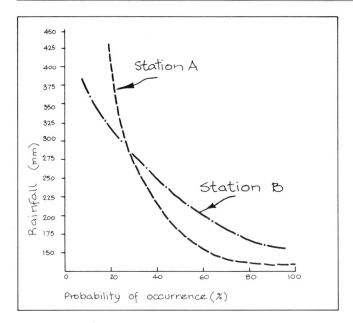

water resources are normally evaluated by delineation of catchment areas and stream gauging using weirs, flumes or current meters.

Measurements must be taken of both base (normal) flows and flood flows.

3 Ground water

Water percolating into the ground usually flows along permeable rock strata termed aquifers. Limestone, for example, is particularly porous and has many underground caverns as well as permeable layers. Evaluation of ground water resources requires test wells to be drilled for pumping tests, together with observation wells in which the level of water in the aquifer may be studied during pump testing.

The basic criterion which has to be established is the 'safe yield' of water from a well or aquifer system which will not exceed the recharge of the aquifer and cause the water flow to dry up.

4 Processed water

Considerable interest is currently being shown in the re-use of water, particularly treated sewage effluent (TSE). In countries where water is scarce (and expensive) such recycling should be encouraged. However the value of recycled water is totally dependent upon its quality. This in turn relates to the degree to which it is treated.

Processed water can also be taken to include desalinated water, water from solar stills and water from dew precipitation. The objection usually raised against their use is that of cost. However this commonly reflects a failure to establish the true costs of more conventional water supplies. Desalination can include the huge flash distillation process or reverse osmosis through membranes, or electro-dialysis and ion exchange. The latter are more efficient at lower concentrations of dissolved salts.

Criteria involved in analysis

Regardless of the actual source of the water, there are three basic criteria which must be evaluated: quantity, quality and cost.

Fig 17 *(left) Specimen rainfall probability graph*

QUANTITY The survey must establish that sufficient water is available for the proposed scheme. This means evaluation not only of the short-term availability but also of the long-term 'safe yield'. This is particularly important with ground water, where excessive depletion of the water source is less apparent. The safe yield of an aquifer system is equivalent to the quantity of recharge and seepage into the aquifer from surface run-off water, streams and rivers. Ground water surveys must therefore establish both the quantity of water stored in the aquifer and the rate of recharge, which can be complex. Considering single wells or well-fields one must also establish the permeability of the aquifer—the rate at which water abstracted in a small area is replaced from the rest of the system through the water bearing strata.

This normally requires pump testing of the wells to determine the discharge at which the water level in the well achieves a stable level.

Many aquifers in arid areas are already being over-exploited—extraction is exceeding recharge and water is effectively being 'mined'.

QUALITY Water quality can be considered under the three main headings, suspended solids, biological content and

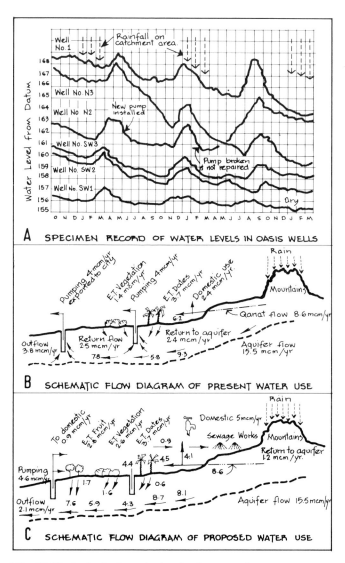

Fig 18 *Hydrological analysis of a desert oasis*

Sabkah area on the coast of Libya

The water-table varies between 10 cm and 200 cm below the ground surface. The extent of salt build-up can be seen from the excavated material

PHOTO: JOHN TOWNEND, MINSTER AGRICULTURE

dissolved solids. The significance of each is discussed below.

• Suspended solids

These range from sticks and leaves to silt and mud. Suspended solids can be removed by filtration. The degree of filtration required will be determined by the nature of suspended solids present relative to the type of irrigation systems used.

• Biological content

This includes water weed, seeds, algae and bacterial slimes. At low levels they do not present problems. At higher levels they can block irrigation canals, pipelines and sprinkler and trickle nozzles. In some cases they can be removed by filtration but more usually require chemical treatments such as chlorination of water.

With treated sewage effluent particular attention must be paid to the levels of viruses, bacteria and other organisms presenting health risks. This is essentially an engineering problem and requires treatments such as chlorination. The planner however should always satisfy himself that the levels of such organisms are with the limits prescribed by

TABLE 7.2 WATER QUALITY STANDARDS (Reference: *Saline and Alkaline Soils*, U.S. Salinity Laboratory, 1954)

The most important hazards to plant growth include excessive quantities of

> total salts
> sodium
> carbonates
> boron

1 Total salts: Measured by electrical conductivity of water samples. Destroys plant tissues and osmotic balance and water uptake

EC is electrical conductivity measured in mhos/cm at 25°C
Normally quoted as EC $\times$ 10^3 stated as millimhos/cm at 25°C
    or EC $\times$ 10^6 stated as micromhos/cm at 25°C
Critical Values are (EC $\times 10^6$)

Low salinity hazard	0–250
Med salinity hazard	250–750
High salinity hazard	750–2250
V. High salinity hazard	2250+

(for crops and non-tolerant plants, but many plants used in urban planting can survive 5000 or more)

2 Sodium salts hazard: Sodium adsorption (SAR) deflocculates soils and injures plant tissues

Measures the sodium hazard (which affects soil alkalinity) in terms of the concentration of Na^+ ions relative to other cations (Ca^{2+} & Mg^{2+} are major ones)
Where soils and water contain high concentrations of calcium or magnesium the sodium hazard (and SAR) will be lowered. Gypsum can be added to the soil to decrease sodium hazard

Formula:

$$SAR = \frac{Na^+}{\sqrt{\dfrac{Ca^{2+}+Mg^{2+}}{2}}}$$

all concentrations expressed in milliequivalents per litre

Critical values are related to total salinity as shown in Fig 19

3 Bicarbonate hazard: Residual Sodium Carbonate (RSC)

Bicarbonate ions precipitate Ca and Mg from the soil as carbonates. These can block irrigation pipes and in the soil water increase soluble Na relative to soluble Ca and Mg and potentially increase the sodium hazard
Defined as: RSC $= (CO_3^{2-} + HCO_3^-) - (Ca^{2+} + Mg^{2+})$
(all concentrations in milliequivalents/litre—a further measure of alkalinity hazard)
Critical Values

Safe	0 $-1·25$	These values are less
Marginal	1·25 $\div$ 2·5	critical in acid soils
Unsuitable	2·5 +	

4 Boron hazard: Measured in ppm

Boron dissolved in salt solution is harmful to plant growth and can be difficult to leach away. (See Appendix for relative tolerance of plants to boron)

international standards for the use he intends to make of the water.

• Dissolved solids (salinity)

Most water supplies in arid areas contain significant levels of dissolved solids. These are mineral salts which are dissolved out of rocks and soil and are commonly referred to as 'salinity'.

In some soils, such as the silty 'sabkah' flats, where the water-table is continually high and ground level is low, constant evaporation of water from the surface and capillary rise cause levels of salinity that are greater than in sea water. Boron levels in particular are often very high and toxic to plant growth. Bedrock and soils affect salt concentrations, for example ground water that has passed through granite is usually higher in the potentially hazardous sodium and potassium salts than limestone.

The sensitivity of plants to salinity is extremely varied but it can generally be said that the more exotic species have low salinity tolerances. Different plants show varying degrees of tolerance to different concentrations of mineral salts. It is therefore vitally important to establish the concentration of total dissolved salts and the levels of individual mineral salts present in the water available at the start of the design exercise. The major water quality standards are illustrated in Table 7.2.

Plants are sensitive to the salinity level in the soil water, which is a function both of the salinity of the irrigation water itself and of the irrigation management regime. Once the quality of irrigation water is known, plant species, irrigation systems and irrigation management regimes can be selected which ensure successful plant growth.

Chemical analysis of irrigation water therefore assesses total dissolved salts (TDS) measured in ppm, or, when using electrical conductivity method, in mhos/cm at 25°C. The levels of calcium, sodium, magnesium, potassium, boron, iron, carbonate and bicarbonate, sulphate, chloride and nitrate present should be determined individually. The pH, (i.e. measure of acidity or alkalinity) must also be known in order to calculate which plants will thrive.

To avoid deterioration water samples should not be kept stored for a long time prior to analysis. Storage in a dark, cool place is preferable.

It is particularly important to check the quality of treated sewage effluent (TSE). During the treatment process salts tend to be concentrated in the water and others, notably heavy metals, may be added by industrial effluents. Conductivities of 2000–4000 μmhos are typical in Middle East countries for well managed treatment plants.

Most of the work on plant salinity tolerances has been done with crop plants. Such information as is available on decorative, exotic species tends to be piecemeal and has to be hunted out of literature. It is not always relevant to different site conditions.

COST Establishing the cost of obtaining water for a planting project will involve comparison of alternative sources and their development costs. This should cover not only the actual abstraction costs but the related costs required to maintain ecological balance.

Practical interpretation of water analysis
The analysis will indicate effects in two main categories:
1 Effect on plant selection
2 Effect on soil conditions.
Plant selection in relation to total dissolved salts can be assisted by the work carried out by Firmin (1968) (see Appendix 2.3). Indications of crop tolerance to salinity are also listed.

Where pH and sodium hazard are high, only alkalinity tolerant species can be used. These can be found from ecological studies on alkaline soils. Where sodium and bicarbonate hazards are very high, calculated amounts of gypsum can be added to the soil to improve texture and aeration and to increase the soluble calcium concentrations

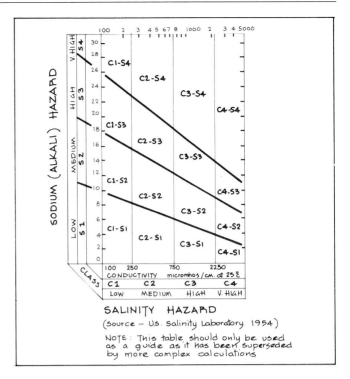

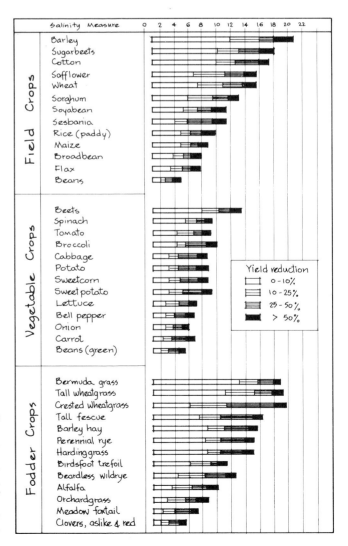

Fig 19a *(above)* and 19b *(below) Salinity hazards for various crops. (The salinity measure in Fig 19b is given in millimhos/cm at 25°C)*

TABLE 7.3 GEOLOGY CHECKLIST

Factors to be analysed	Interpretation
Presence and characteristics of geological faults	Siting of land use in relation to volcanic activity, topography
Location of porous strata	Assists in assessing location of aquifers
Parent rock orogeny, strata, minerals, whether strata igneous metamorphic, sedimentary	Minerals for extraction, minerals for soil fertility or salinity, erosion potential, suitability for foundations, support, underground sewerage, drainage natural gas, presence of water for boreholes, presence of underground mining and therefore subsidence hazard
Depth to bedrock	Soil thickness, erosion potential, whether water will drain into bedrock or remain above, suitability for cultivating
Effect of parent rock on ground water	eg. granite $$Na+K>Ca+Mg$$ $$\left.\begin{array}{l}\text{Limestone}\\\text{Dolomite}\end{array}\right\} Ca>Mg>Na+K$$ $$\text{Basalt } Na>Ca>Mg>K$$ in each example: $$HCO_3>SO_4>Cl$$

TABLE 7.4 TOPOGRAPHY CHECKLIST

Factors to be analysed	Practical interpretation
Exposure of site to adverse climatic conditions, particularly wind, frost	Site in sheltered areas or erect shelter belts, *etc.*
Ground slopes in relation to rainfall run-off and identification of possible soil erosion as a result	Assess capacity of run-off area for amount of rain-water that can be collected and stored. Assess areas of erosion hazard and improve soil structure, stabilize with plants or structures, terrace, or divert water if it does not have a substantial effect on hydrological cycle
Areas subject to landslides or soil creep	Stabilise, decrease moisture content or avoid developing
Suitability of site for farming techniques, mechanical cultivations, irrigation methods	Assess need for levelling, contour ploughing, terracing effect on water pressures due to gradient, size of field possible
Views, visual appreciation, use of land form from an aesthetic viewpoint	Siting of constructional and living elements of the landscape to form a pleasing grouping
Site suitability for construction and engineering works	Siting of buildings, roads, dams, bridges, *etc.*

and decrease sodium toxicity. As boron is difficult to leach, only boron tolerant plants can be used if concentrations are greater than 2 ppm.

Regular leaching will be required to flush potentially harmful salt concentrations out of the root zones. Leaching requirements can be calculated depending upon salinity of soils, irrigation water and soil conditions. Irrigation systems such as trickle irrigation, by applying small and frequent water applications, in effect continually leach the root zone of salt build-up, as the rooting zone is maintained in a permanently moist condition.

2 Geology
A knowledge of the geology of the site will assist in interpreting information such as where aquifers may be found, how soils have evolved, and how they will react to planting and irrigation.

The geology of a site does not normally have a direct influence on plant ecology. Its effect is usually secondary through development of soil and water resources. Only a brief knowledge of geological conditions is therefore needed to assist in ecological interpretation. Analysis is carried out using information extracted from maps, cross-sections showing strata, boreholes *etc.* and seismology readings. A checklist is given above, in table 7.3.

3 Topography
The approach to a topographical analysis is summarized in table 7.4. The method of analysis involves:
Large scale: photogrammetry (i.e. plotting contour maps from aerial photography)
Detailed work: conventional surveying of levels and distances, using a theodolite, visually, or using sound techniques. Areas should be mapped and slope percentages or gradients over the site recorded.

4 Soils
Methods of analysis for establishing soil conditions include the study of soil maps and the undertaking of field work and laboratory analysis. With field work, samples should be taken at regular intervals over the site; soil profile pits should be made and samples taken from each strata, or at regular intervals, and permeability and infiltration tests must be conducted. Laboratory analsysis involves test for physical changes by mechanical analysis, and chemical analysis is conducted by flame photometry, fractionation, distillation and titration techniques (see USDA handbook No 62 *Saline and Alkaline Soils*).

Table 7.5 (p 91) gives a checklist of factors to be analysed and interpretation of results obtained using these methods of analysis.

5 Climate
The development of climatic theory is just beginning, and historical records are still being analysed. Techniques such as radio-active carbon and tritium dating of soil and water, geological history and distribution of annual growth rings inside tree trunks are being used. (Wetter years show greater trunk growth and therefore a wider annual ring in tree cross-sections. Previous droughts can therefore be noted using very ancient trees.) Energy systems, including sunspots, are also being studied for any correlation with previous droughts.

Table 7.6 summarizes the approach to climate analysis.

TABLE 7.5 SOILS ANALYSIS CHECKLIST

Factors to be analysed	Practical interpretation

Soil types, changes in drainage, soil moisture over site and with depth presence of hard pans e.g. of clay or iron that impede cultivations and drainage	Assess basic soil characteristics, e.g. soil fertility
	  percolation rates
	  soil stability
	  salinity—possible hazards to plants
	  effect after irrigation
	  alkalinity
	  retention of structure after irrigation (e.g. loss of structure to form a heavy, solid mass of silt, if high Na in water)

Soil structure, texture	Sandy soils are liable to drift and need stabilizing; silty soils are stable but accumulate more salts and are more difficult to leach (e.g. sabkahs); organic matter provides plant nutrients but is usually low in dryland soils
pH	Assess acidity or alkalinity and select appropriate species
Electrical conductivity (EC) in mhos/cm at 25°C	Assess total salinity and select appropriate species
Gypsum Total carbonate ion content	Flocculates clay to form good crumb structure and aeration alkalinity
%Nitrogen (N) total and available phosphorus (P) soluble and exchangeable potassium (K)	Assess fertility—N & P is often low in dryland soils; high K can exacerbate Na hazard
Calcium (Ca) Magnesium (Mg)	Use only calcifuge plants; if high, buffers against sodium damage
Sodium (Na)	Increases alkalinity if with high carbonate; deflocculates clays
Iron (Fe)	If low, causes leaf chlorosis and poor growth especially citrus
Boron (B)	Toxic to all but very tolerant and indigenous plants if greater than 4 ppm
Chloride (Cl)	Toxic if high, causing leaf and root scorch
Carbonate (CO_3) Bicarbonate (HCO_3)	Alkalinity hazard if high; iron micronutrients are unavailable in alkaline soils and will need adding as sequestered iron
Nitrate (NO_3)	Toxic if high, especially if caused by seepage from septic tanks
Sulphate (SO_4)	Toxic if high; special cement must be used for construction

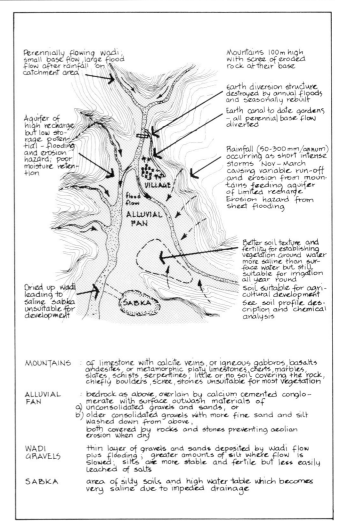

MOUNTAINS : of limestone with calcite veins, or igneous gabbros, basalts andesites, or metamorphic platy limestones, cherts, marbles, slates, schists, serpentines; little or no soil covering the rock, chiefly boulders, scree, stones unsuitable for most vegetation

ALLUVIAL FAN : bedrock as above, overlain by calcium cemented conglomerate with surface outwash materials of
a) unconsolidated gravels and sands, or
b) older consolidated gravels with more fine sand and silt washed down from above,
both covered by rocks and stones preventing aeolian erosion when dry

WADI GRAVELS : thin layer of gravels and sands deposited by wadi flow plus flooding; greater amounts of silt where flow is slowed; silts are more stable and fertile but less easily leached of salts

SABKA : area of silty soils and high water table which becomes very saline due to impeded drainage

SOIL PROFILE FROM CONSOLIDATED ALLUVIAL FAN DEPOSITS

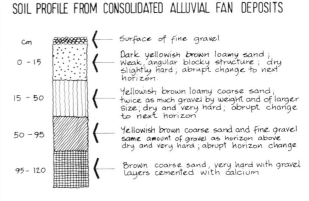

cm

0 - 15 — Surface of fine gravel; Dark yellowish brown loamy sand; Weak, angular blocky structure; dry slightly hard; abrupt change to next horizon

15 - 50 — Yellowish brown loamy coarse sand; twice as much gravel by weight and of larger size; dry and very hard; abrupt change to next horizon

50 - 95 — Yellowish brown coarse sand and fine gravel same amount of gravel as horizon above dry and very hard; abrupt horizon change

95 - 120 — Brown coarse sand, very hard with gravel layers cemented with calcium

CHEMICAL ANALYSIS

INTERPRETATION :

A loamy sand of slightly alkaline to neutral reaction and low salinity

The higher exchangeable calcium to sodium ensures that structure is retained under irrigation

There are no sodium or iron hazards

Fertility is generally low and will need additions of fertiliser and organic matter to establish vegetation and improve moisture retention

This soil would be classed as unsuitable for arable cultivation under U.S. classification of soils. However, many of these soils and more saline examples are frequently used for irrigated agriculture in dry lands and with adequate quantity and quality of water can produce vegetable, fodder and tree crops under irrigation

* SAR = Sodium Absorption Ratio

Soil Texture			
Coarse sand	Fine sand	Satur.	Dry
60%	12%	20%	3%
pH	E.C. (Electr. Conduct.) mm hos/cm	Gypsum $CaCO_3$	% $CaSO_4$
8	1.5	17.5%	0.1
Exchangeable cations me/100 g			
Ca	mg	Na	K
5.8	0.6	0.1	0.2
Soluble cations in saturation extract me/litre			
Ca	mg	Na	K
9	5	4.6	0.4
Soluble anions me/litre			
Cl	SO_4	CO_3	HCO_3
13	0.1	–	6
SAR*	N + P	B	Fe
1.76	very low	no hazard	very low

Fig 20 *Specimen soil map with notes*

Data should be collected from meteorological stations, Government bodies, agricultural research stations, airports, *etc.* and statistically analysed to determine long-term mean values (normally on a monthly or ten-day basis). In some cases (notably with rainfall) a probability analysis should be made to determine reliability.

TABLE 7.6 CLIMATE ANALYSIS

Factors to be analysed	Practical interpretation
Rainfall: min. max. mean monthly intensity (periodicity)	Necessity for irrigation Possibility of rainwater harvesting Aquifer recharge Flood flows and erosion Drainage requirements Access onto soil surface for cultivation
Temperature: min. max. mean monthly	Crop suitability Necessity for cooling for plants, livestock and human beings
Wind: prevailing direction seasonal changes velocity pollution	Shelter Cooling effects Structural design to minimize storm damage Erosion (particularly sand and dust storms)
Solar radiation: intensity, periodicity day length	Shade to reduce effects on plants, livestock and human beings Glare Crop suitability in relation to day length and cloudiness
Humidity: min. max. mean monthly	Stress on plants, livestock and human beings Crop suitability
Evaporation figures (USWB Class A pan figures are the best)	Crop water requirements Evaporation losses (hydrology)

Plant water requirements

An analysis of climatic data is essential in determining plant water requirements. These are quoted in *annual* and *seasonal* terms, and this information helps engineers establish such criteria as dam sizes but is not directly useful for irrigation design. In order to establish the required capacity of the irrigation system it is necessary to know the peak water requirement on a *daily* basis.

One can design to meet the absolute maximum daily water requirements. However, it is more usual to design to the mean monthly daily maximum, since absolute maximum evaporation is rarely sustained for more than a day or two. The cost savings effected can be considerable, since the mean monthly figure is commonly 12–13 mm/day whereas absolute maximum values often exceed 20 mm/day. To convert such figures to actual requirements for water application it is necessary of course to allow for the efficiency of water application by the irrigation system and any requirements for extra water for leaching of salts. How much water to actually apply will vary with the season and stage of growth of the plants.

In order to establish actual irrigation schedules one must consider crop water requirements over shorter periods, normally monthly or ten days. There are three principal methods of establishing plant water requirements:

1 Direct measurement
This may be achieved by isolating a volume of soil containing plants in a device called a Lysimeter. The quantities of water supplied, stored in the soil and lost through drainage are measured, and the quantity used by the plants calculated by the difference.

This technique is the most accurate available but is only practical where there is a long design period. Gravimetric techniques, involving soil sampling followed by oven drying to determine soil moisture content are an alternative but have similar disadvantages.

2 Simulation
Actual crop water requirements have been shown to be proportional to evaporation from an open water surface (Eo). Since it is impractical to measure evaporation from a lake or pond, small, specially designed evaporation pans have been developed. The most widely used is the US Weather Bureau (USWB) Class A pan, often found at meteorological stations. A Class A pan does not directly measure Eo. Strictly speaking therefore Epan needs to be related to Eo by a factor, commonly about 0·8 since pans tend to overestimate evaporation. It is more usual, however, to convert directly from Epan to ET (crop water use) by applying a crop correlation coefficient. When using such factors care must be taken to ensure they refer to Epan and not to Eo.

Most work on crop coefficients has been carried out on crop plants, and little information is available for decorative species. For many areas in the Middle East crop factors are not available. (They have to be determined by comparison of pan evaporation with Lysimeter readings.) Factors for climatically similar areas, such as Arizona, must therefore be used.

3 Correlation with climatic data
Various methods have been developed to correlate crop water requirements directly with climatic data. The most widely used are those of Penman, Blaney and Criddle and the Radiation method. Table 7.7 (p 93) compares the main characteristics of these three correlation methods together with the use of Class A pans.

Two fundamental problems exist with correlation methods. Firstly, different methods produce results in different forms which then have to be converted to crop water requirements by the use of crop factors. Each method requires its own set of factors. Ideally these must be determined empirically for the area concerned, but in practice they are normally taken from similar areas elsewhere. Secondly they take account of only a limited number of the factors affecting crop water use.

A recent report produced by the FAO Consultative Group on Crop Water Requirements simplifies this situation. The report presents modifications which allow the methods presented above to generate the water requirements of a reference crop. The modifications

TABLE 7.7 METHODS FOR DETERMINATION OF CROP WATER REQUIREMENTS

Method	Blaney and Criddle formula	Radiation formula	Penman formula	Pan
Formula	$f = p(0.46t - 8.13)$ p = percentage of annual daylight hours occurring during the period—from tables according to latitude t = mean monthly temp (°C)	$ET_p = W\,R_s$ W = Weighting factor for temperature and altitude R_s = Solar radiation expressed as mm/day equivalent evaporation	$E_0 = \dfrac{\Delta/\gamma\,H + Ea}{\Delta/\gamma + 1}$ Δ = relationship between water vapour pressure and temperature γ = constant related to air temperature H = Net available energy (Heat budget) $E_a = 0.35\,(e_a - e_d)$ $(0.5 + 0.01 U_2)$ in mm/day U_2 = windspeed in miles/day at height of 2m. $(e_a - e_d)$ = saturation deficit	Direct measurement of pan evaporation in mm/day
Data required	Temperature	Temperature Sunshine (Radiation)	Temperature Humidity Wind Sunshine (Radiation)	Evaporation
Form of Result	f = consumptive use factor Multiply by empirical crop factor to get consumptive use U	ET_p = Potential evapotranspiration for grass Multiply by empirical crop factor to get crop potential evapotranspiration ET crop	E_0—evaporation from open water, or ET_0—evaporation from reference crop, depends on constants used in equation. Multiply by empirical crop coefficient to get crop potential evapotranspiration ET crop	E pan = evaporation from pan Multiply by Pan coefficient (K pan) to get Eo or by empirical crop coefficient to get directly to crop evapotranspiration ET crop
Assessment	Theoretically least accurate as depends on single climatic factor only	Theoretically most accurate methods for predicting evapotranspiration over short periods (10 days)		Second best method in general. Siting of pan is critical to accuracy. Well sited pans can give better results than Penman or Radiation methods
	Gives good results in arid areas where temperature is major factor—fails to allow for wind and relative humidity	Similar to Blaney and Criddle	Considers all relevant factors so potentially most accurate	Similar to Penman if well sited
	Most widely used, as temp. data normally widely available and reliable	Sunshine or radiation data not always available	Complete data rarely available and, due to greater complexity of instrumentation, less reliable	Pans often badly sited and managed. Assessment of these conditions essential

incorporate consideration of other climatic factors not included directly in the formulae. A single set of crop factors may then be used for all methods, which take account only of the condition of the crop itself.

6 Ecology

For the analysis of ecological conditions a survey of the existing classifications must be made, a checklist for which is given in table 7.8. The following fieldwork must be undertaken and records made:

1 Transect across a site and record all species along the line—this is good for showing succession e.g. from high salinity to low

2 Throw quadrant at random and count numbers of different species in them to calculate density, % frequency

3 Generally record all plant and animal species seen and correlate with soil, water, climate, land form, season, etc.

4 Represent the information in a dynamic way which evaluates the constantly changing situation and maps the direction and character of change

5 Visit and record data from research stations, nurseries and trial plots, and experiment using planting under similar conditions to those of the site.

TABLE 7.8 ECOLOGY CHECKLIST 1

Factors to be analysed	Practical interpretation
1 FLORA AND FAUNA Identify and map: community types	Determine the best species to use and possibly introduce to the site following assessment of site
density frequency location interdependence of species feeding niches shelter breeding places time of day for feeding *etc.* incidence of pests and diseases	conditions, indigenous species and phytogeographical zone Determine site amelioration techniques, e.g. irrigation, in order to increase efficiency of man's use of site and assess how this will affect the existing conditions in the short and long term
2 PLANTS Identify key species and zonal type e.g. Sahelian, Sudanian, Mediterranean	Assess likely build-up of pests and disease if the diversity of the natural ecology is narrowed. e.g. by monocropping *etc.*
Identify and map communities and stages in ecological climax related to different site conditions	Determine the type of protection needed to prevent excessive grazing of new plantations
Identify and map indicator species e.g. demarcating areas of high water-tables, unstable soils, fertility, salinity, overgrazing, trampling, waterlogging, *etc.*	Adapt traditional techniques of plant establishment and site amelioration to suit ecological status.
Assess nutrient cycles and their dependence on certain species	MATCH PLANTS TO USES, SITE RESOURCES AND ECOLOGICAL BALANCE
Assess usefulness of traditional and modern propagating and planting techniques in relation to site ecology	

MOUNTAIN VEGETATION: *Zizyphus nummularia*, *Zygophyllum* spp. *Salvadora persica*

ALLUVIAL FAN : occasional *Acacia tortilis*, xerophytic shrubs and ephemerals after flooding

CONSOLIDATED SOILS (Higher water table) : greater density of *Acacia tortilis* on drier silty soils. *Prosopis spicigera* on deeper groundwater

WADI VEGETATION : Xerophytes :- *Haloxylon salicornicum*, *Anabasis articulata*, *Salsola* spp., *Artemisia* spp. Grasses - *Panicum turgidum*; *Agropyron* spp. Ephemerals :- *Salsola inermis*; *Aristida*, *Poa*, *Stipa* spp. of grass. Trees - *Prosopis spicigera*; *Zizyphus spina christi*; *Acacia nilotica* Shrubs :- *Nerium oleander*, *Salsola* species on sands, *Fagonia* spp., *Zilla spinosa*

SABKA HALOPHYTES : *Tamarix* spp., *Suaeda* spp., *Halocnemon* spp. *Arthrocnemum* spp., *Nitraria retusa*; *Atriplex* spp.

For the ecological study to be complete, a study of man and his effects on the environment must also be made. The approach to such a study is summarized in checklist 2 (table 7.9, p95).

Man's effect must be surveyed by collecting data on population size, structure and pressures, socio-economic goals, cultural and behavioural patterns and health conditions. The aim is to express the dynamic situation, compiling a dynamic model of the survey data and how it is interrelated. The direction and character of change must be recognized and evaluated. On a large scale this is often only possible using computers as the data is so complex and varied.

MASTERPLAN DEVELOPMENT: LAND USE STUDY

Equilibrium within any natural system is usually maintained by feed-back systems, one factor relying on the level of others to retain optimum balance. A diagram showing the ecological interactions of each factor is complex but will show any short-falls in the planning process. Man's effect on an ecosystem can therefore be determined by analysis of the survey data and the components and feed-back mechanisms of the ecosystem. Guidelines can then be proposed for developing the site without disturbing ecological balance.

A resource inventory and compilation map overlaying geological information with information about soils,

hydrology, flora and fauna *etc.* will assist in determining the combination of factors resulting in a particular site ecology. For example there may be dry, shifting sands and low water-table in one area, and high water-table, silty, saline soils with a different site ecology in another, and many other combinations. These land types have different potentials for development. Some are more easily degraded and their resources exhausted more quickly than others. It is therefore necessary to delineate these areas so that they can be developed with greater attention to recycling of resources and a strict monitoring of land use capacity. They may be visually delineated on the compilation map, fig 22.

Each land type potential has a most appropriate land use which can be determined by using land use criteria. The criteria are based on natural resources, ecological characteristics and the requirements of each land use, e.g. moist, flat, deep, fertile, sheltered soils for agriculture. In dry lands, where a misuse of resources can result in devastation, it is vital that the land types and their potential are directly matched to land use, rather than a land use being imposed upon a site that may not have the resources to maintain the development in the long term. *Remember to match land use to resources.* The best 'fit' will determine the most appropriate land use for a particular land type.

The survey data is also used to calculate land carrying capacity i.e. *intensity* of use. The number of plants that can grow on the site will be determined by the quantity and

TABLE 7.9 ECOLOGY CHECKLIST 2: THE STUDY OF MAN'S EFFECT ON THE ECOLOGY

Factors to be analysed	Methods of analysis	Practical interpretation
HUMAN FACTORS: Population, settlement patterns density, location, community type, structure, population changes, migration, racial and ethnic composition, age-breakdown, education, lifestyle, employment, income, standard of living, housing composition, community history, political changes—all placed in their regional context, educational level, literacy rate Culture history, scenic, traditions, religions, aesthetics Food availability, eating habits, taboos, status, nutrition education Health disease, pollution, famine, economic situation, policy, markets Land use open country, agriculture, forestry, horticulture, residential, commercial, industrial Infrastructure services, power, fuel, sewerage, drinking water, community facilities, e.g. schools, hospitals, recreation, social welfare service	Survey existing data, questionnaire of people living in area Obtain statistics and map and analyse them to find how new land uses may improve conditions for man whilst maintaining ecological balance to prevent adverse effects in the long term building up Analyse how development will affect the patterns of behaviour of indigenous plants, animals, soil organisms, water wildlife, insects, *etc.*, water pollution, air pollution, fire hazards, severance of existing land uses, including recreation and landscape scenery Analyse future economic forecasts to predict possible trend in market trading, growth of project financially, calculation of least cost, maximum benefit analyses including the difficult evaluation of landscape beauty and damage to the ecosystem Does the project affect any legalities, local, state or federal agencies, *etc.*	Dense populations in urban situations will require different land use development policies and plant establishment techniques to those in rural areas Establish land carrying capacity and land use potential from a summation and correlation of all the ecological data Identify pressure zones where man is over-using, polluting and over-extracting resources and revise management patterns and techniques Establish the relationships between man, his crops, his domesticated animals and the indigenous flora and fauna, i.e. are they in balance with the land are soils eroding, pests and diseases increasing, is fertility being lost? Establish policies for water use in different areas, as one area may rely upon another for its water

Fig 21 *(facing page) Specimen ecological map with notes*

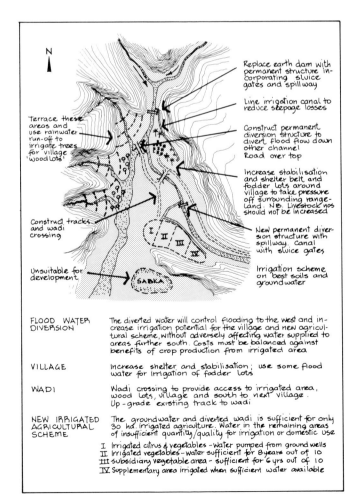

Fig 22 *Compilation map for a rural development project*

quality of water available, by soil–water relationships and by the incidence of pests and disease. The stocking rate of domestic animals can be established for most areas. Planning procedures and the results of these calculations will determine the optimum number of people or families that can use the area. Any limitations to site development are listed and mapped, e.g. high water-table, salinity, whether liable to erosion. The resource base of the site's natural and cultural factors and the land carrying capacity can then be analysed for land use capability, management options selected, and the most appropriate land use or multiple use chosen. An example of the procedures and decisions that may need to be taken to formulate a land use plan is shown in fig 23 (overleaf).

The major land use types are listed in table 7.10 (p. 96) in order of increasing intensity of use and are often parallelled with a decreasing survival of natural ecology and significant amounts of planting.

Each land use has a most suitable combination of natural resources. These land use criteria are based on factors such as those listed in table 7.11 (p. 97). The suitability of a certain site and its resources can be assessed by scoring the 'fit' of the site conditions with the land use criteria.

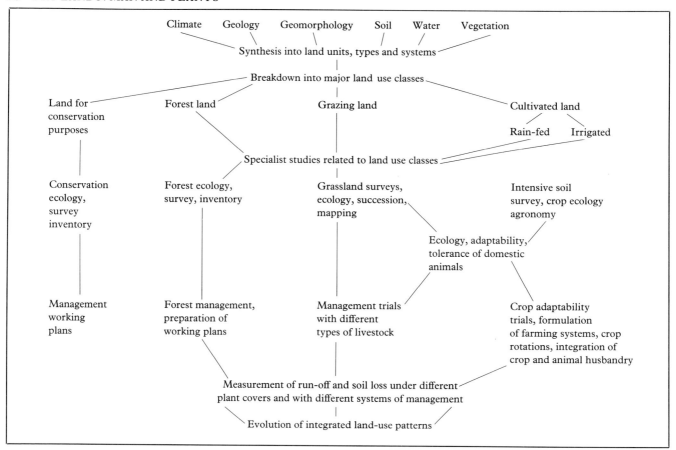

Climate Geology Geomorphology Soil Water Vegetation

Synthesis into land units, types and systems

Breakdown into major land use classes

Land for conservation purposes   Forest land   Grazing land   Cultivated land

Rain-fed   Irrigated

Specialist studies related to land use classes

Conservation ecology, survey inventory

Forest ecology, survey, inventory

Grassland surveys, ecology, succession, mapping

Intensive soil survey, crop ecology agronomy

Ecology, adaptability, tolerance of domestic animals

Management working plans

Forest management, preparation of working plans

Management trials with different types of livestock

Crop adaptability trials, formulation of farming systems, crop rotations, integration of crop and animal husbandry

Measurement of run-off and soil loss under different plant covers and with different systems of management

Evolution of integrated land-use patterns

TABLE 7.10 LAND USE TYPE

Land use	Function
Wild areas	Waste areas and areas of indigenous flora and fauna for conservation or amenity purposes
Water areas	Natural rivers, lakes, artificial reservoirs for drinking water, irrigation, recreation, landscape beauty, wildlife reserves, fish farming, wells, storage tanks, extraction of salt from salt pans, water catchment areas
Afforestation	Timber, pulp, shelter, soil stabilisation and desert reclamation, rubber, medicines, dyes, nuts, fruit, recreation; the amount of wildlife depends on the species chosen
Agriculture	Food crops, livestock, fish, fodder, rangeland and grassland for grazing
Horticulture	Tree crops, fruit, intensive vegetable growing, nurseries; trees, shrubs for decorative planting
Amenity	Playing areas, sports racing, public areas, e.g. art centres, meeting places
Transport and services	Communications, road networks, water, electricity, gas, roadside landscaping
Residential	Housing, gardens, smaller open spaces for playing, relaxing, meeting, aesthetic settings, landscape planting
Commercial	Working areas, shops, offices, workshops precincts and landscaped areas
Industry	Machinery, factories, extraction—mining, quarrying, fuel, power-stations, desalination plants, screen planting, landscaped offices

Fig 23 *Procedures used in land use planning (after E. S. Hills, 'Arid Lands', Unesco 1966)*

In summary:

Survey
↓
Resource inventory
↓
Land type compilation map
↓
Land potential
↓
Land use criteria
↓
Appropriate land use

From these results, a complete study area can be allocated different land uses relating to different site conditions and a land use master plan compiled.

Similarly, for a city, farm, horticultural holding or recreation centre, different uses will be derived for different site conditions, e.g. shelter belt planting where shelter is required, decorative planting where visual attractiveness is important and soils are not too saline, cropping rotations on the best suited agricultural soils. The master plan layout devised from these studies will also set out guidelines for implementation concerning site amelioration and monitoring of conditions, and criteria affecting irrigation, choice of plants and cultivation and maintenance techniques. Initial plans will be revised, acting on data from pilot schemes, impact studies and reactions of the people concerned.

Using these procedures the planning phase will have been considered from practical site details ensuring that solutions are in keeping with the site and its proposed functions.

TABLE 7.11 LAND USE CRITERIA

Land use type	Hydrological requirements	Ecological requirements	Climatic requirements	Topographical requirements	Geological and soil requirements	Economic requirements
Wild areas[1]	Often too wet or too dry for other land uses, e.g. desert interior, saline, sabkahs	Special area for conservation of wild species, 'gene banks' or nearly extinct species	Not critical	Often too steep for other land use e.g. wadi sides, mountains, hammadas, sand dunes	Often too difficult and liable to erosion to be disturbed by other land uses	Not critical
Afforestation for shelter fodder crops fruit trees	Not as critical as for agriculture but low water availability will support only shelter species. Salt tolerant species can be established on saline high water-tables, e.g. date palms, although fruit is poor	Not critical as afforestation. Can improve soil stability in water catchment areas, and improve shelter and microclimate for other land uses and increases efficiency of use of water-tables at depths too great for shrubs or crops	Low rainfall will support shelter rather than fruit species	Steep slopes can be utilized when this is not economical for other land uses. e.g. wadi sides, mountains, hammadas, sand dunes	Less fertile, rockier, thinner soils can be used than for agriculture, and trees grown for shelter and fodder rather than fruit	Return on timber or shelter must be greater than cost of establishment and maintenance— needs accessibility to mills, factories, markets, *etc.*
Water areas	Too much surface water for other uses except wild areas or areas essential to the adequate functioning of the hydrological cycle which should remain untouched to function efficiently, e.g. watersheds, catchment areas, springs	Ecology of wadis, streams, springs, waterfalls, high water-tables, coast lines, lagoons. Planting to stabilise slopes and improve catchment should be encouraged	Not critical except as recharge for the hydrological cycle	Not critical except where rainwater run-off is to be channelled to more fertile plains below	Not critical; run-off from mountains can be collected in underground or surface reservoirs if impermeable bedrock exists	Should not be developed even if economically feasible if there will be adverse interference to the hydrological cycle
Agriculture cereals root crops pulses pasture for dairy beef, poultry, fish	Regular supply of soil moisture either from non-saline water-table or using storage or pumping and irrigation (where water source is saline choose salt tolerant crops); avoid plains where flooding occurs frequently unless rice is to be grown	Fertile alluvial or sandy plain flora and fauna more prolific, especially if water-table is not too low, than other land types. Retain scrubland and trees as shelter and soil stabilisers. Maintain soil fertility by crop rotation, green manuring, retention of trees, addition of organic matter, fallows and return to scrubland when required. Use fodder scrub and lucerne for livestock where grassland cannot establish	Shelter from wind and some shade is necessary; sowing and harvesting can be timed with wet and dry seasons; crops suited to correct day length must be chosen	Flat or gentle slopes, e.g. alluvial plains; contour ploughing is needed on slope to prevent soil erosion due to heavy rains, irrigation, or sand blow	Stable sandy or clay loams, thick, fertile soils with a mimimum of rocks or gravel, moist but not water-logged or excessively saline, good percolation rates and no impeded drainage unless well below the rooting zone; fertile soils, e.g. on alluvial plains and playas or sandy stabilised soils with irrigation and organic matter to maintain fertility and soil moisture. Silty soils should be avoided if irrigation water is saline	Good infrastructure and accessibility to markets necessary; irrigation spreads the seasonality of cropping and labour peaks

[1] i.e. areas large enough to sustain natural ecological balance without interference from man—areas showing free expression of site ecology, its pattern of growth and the species it supports depending on the intrinsic properties of the water, soils and topography

Land use type	Hydrological requirements	Ecological requirements	Climatic requirements	Topographical requirements	Geological and soil requirements	Economic requirements
Horticulture fruit vegetables tree crops	Essentially as for agriculture but as crops are more intensively grown, even better conditions of stability, fertility and good quality water are needed Water quality ideally less than 5,000 ppm. Treated sewage effluent can be used if treated against health hazards; desalinated water needs fertiliser adding		Many vegetables prefer the cooler season, e.g. tomatoes, potatoes, beans; these can be grown with some shade to reduce temperatures; pollen is killed at too high temperatures and some fruit trees cannot bear fruit, e.g. apples, apricots	As for agriculture; higher altitudes better, as cooler for tree fruits and exotic vegetables	Fertile alluvial or sandy plains, or controlled-environment polythene houses on these soils, or hydroponics	As for agriculture; economic returns on controlled-environment cropping compared with the cost of importing is marginal; however it is useful where self sufficiency is necessary and exotic vegetables are required
Amenity	Not critical unless large areas of trees, grass, or vast displays of exotic vegetation are required	Wild areas, forestry, and some water areas for boating and fishing are compatible land uses depending on resources available and their robustness. 'Tougher' species are required in civic, urban and industrial areas	Suitable for humans, i.e. cool, low humidity, shaded, sheltered from winds and dust storms	Not critical, except for large flat areas needed for football pitches, race courses, etc.	Not critical for wild areas but essential if gardens of exotics are to be established	Planned recreation, e.g. football, race courses, must cover costs of establishment and maintenance or be subsidised by government; land with a high potential for other more economic uses should not be used unless no other areas are available
Residential	Water for domestic use primarily, poorer quality for planting; avoid flood plains	The less vegetated areas can be used although the retention of existing trees and planting of new vegetation will greatly enhance living conditions	As for amenity; shelter belts will be essential	Gentle slopes can be used for housing; steeper slopes can be made into play areas or shelter belts	Stable for foundations to houses—avoid unstable or waterlogged soils e.g. sabkahs; leave fertile soils for agriculture; if necessary import limited amounts of good soil to establish vegetation around houses	Near to markets, education facilities, water, electricity, etc.
Commercial	Water for domestic use only	As for residential, other poorer quality areas can be used	As for amenity	As for residential; steeper slopes can be used as garden focal points and shelter belts	As for residential although sabkahs can be used if they can be drained and/or stabilised	High economic returns available if sited in cities near markets, ports, harbour, airports, roads, residential areas
Industrial	Water needed for power and in processing should be recycled	Least vegetated areas can be used. Pollution should be controlled. Focal points of vegetation and green trees belts will be psychologically necessary	Not critical if buildings are air-conditioned	Needs visual screening; flat areas for buildings	Worst soils can be used providing stability is good for foundations	Adjacent to energy source, harbour, airports, roads, etc.

The development of marginal land

The Earth's human populations are increasing, and more marginal land is being put into productivity. The land use criteria can also be used to draw up ways in which marginal land may be used. Some examples are given in the following table. It may be necessary to breed new plants and livestock to improve productivity in marginal conditions.

TABLE 7.12 THE USE OF PLANTS IN RECLAIMING MARGINAL LAND

Land type	Function	Techniques
Rocky uplands	Afforestation	Terrace, channel water to decrease erosion, increase shelter, regulate wadi water flow
Rocky plains	Tree crops/fodder	Use run-off leading to micro-catchment areas, make a shelter belt
Sandy plains	Tree/field crops	Shelter belts, stabilise with plants, harvest rainwater, recharge aquifers, *etc.*, use water conservation techniques, hydroponics
Dune fields	Tree crops/fodder on dunes, field crops in depressions	Shelter, stabilise with plants, recharge parched aquifers, water conservation
Dry silts and clays	Crops	Shelter with plants, add sand and calcium to soil to give flocculated soils when irrigated and therefore good texture and aeration; leach
Wet silts and clays	Crops	Drain, use phreatophytes that live on high moisture/water-table and transpire water heavily and so beneficially lower the water-table, add calcium before irrigating and leach
Sabkhas (high water-table) (high salinity)	Afforestation, shelter belts	Drain if possible, leach, use phreatophytes
Brackish water/saline soils	General crops	Leach, use small and frequent irrigations to maintain salinity out of wetting/rooting pattern; use salt tolerant plants

NOTE

1 McHarg, I. *Design with Nature*. Natural History Press: New York 1969

8 Techniques for development with plants: detailed planning and implementation

This chapter is concerned with the detailed planning procedures needed to ensure that site development and implementation techniques are suited to site conditions. It later describes the different planting techniques that are used in dry lands.

DETAILED PLANNING

Unfortunately many development projects have not originated from careful matching of land use to site resources as set out in the previous chapter. It is vital in

these cases, and for all new projects, to carry out a study to show that the development will be in harmony with site ecology and existing and long-term uses of resources. We therefore make no excuse for repeating here the plan of action for formulating the master plan, as a reminder that detailed planning is useless unless the overall conditions are taken into account. All projects will require a checking procedure to ensure that implementation and maintenance techniques do not have adverse environmental implications. This can be achieved using environmental impact techniques.

PLAN OF ACTION FROM SITE SURVEY TO MASTER PLAN

Stage	Action
Site survey and resource inventory	**Determine resources** Investigate and define resources and raw materials
Site assessment and evaluation	Qualify and quantify resources, including man's effect and interactions within and without the ecosystem
Interpretation	Find site limitations, potential and land carrying capacities **Match resources to function**
Feasibility analysis	Suggest solutions—test their reaction with other resources and overall functioning of the ecosystem
Land use planning (including assessment of resource management)	Assess how resources can be used by man efficiently but not extravagantly Allocate most appropriate land uses to regions on the site and assess how they complement adjacent settlements and resources, and how ecological balance may change over a period of time Choose alternatives if there is a predictable deterioration of ecosystem or man's living conditions
Masterplan (This may be of a city, town, farm, forest, market garden, *etc.*)	Delineate and phase land use regions

DETAILED PLANNING AND IMPLEMENTATION

| Detailed planning including **environmental impact analysis** choice of water source choice of irrigation system choice of plants choice of soil amelioration financial assessment for each area of useage and land type | Conserve resources selecting **appropriate implementation techniques** Test 'fit' of land use development on a specific site Feed back to resource management to establish irreversible adverse impacts and choose alternatives to avoid exhaustion of resources, massive inputs for implementation and maintenance, adverse effects on the ecosystem. Detail implementation and maintenance techniques and final layout plans |
| **Implementation** Trials, nursery, earthworks, irrigation installation, planting, maintenance | Carry out the work and maintain |

This chapter will outline the techniques required to carry out each of these stages of the detailed planning and implementation, giving special reference to the role of plants in dry-land development. The broader issues of urban planning, industrial applications and architectural design will be discussed only with regard to plants and their uses in these situations.

Environmental impact studies
The 'fit' of a proposed project brief to land type and resources can be tested using ecological models and environmental impact studies. Impact studies are simpler and more commonly used at present. Although a relatively new approach to site development procedure, they are now statutory in American and World Bank projects and are

PROPOSED DEVELOPMENTS WHICH MAY CAUSE ENVIRONMENTAL IMPACT

Impacts Scale: 1 = low 5 = high

NATURAL & CULTURAL RESOURCES

		WATER DIVERSION	IRRIGATION	INTRODUCTION OF EXOTIC FLORA & FAUNA	ALTERATION OF GROUND LEVELS	CLEARANCE	CONSTRUCTION (BRIDGES & SPILLWAYS)	IMPROVEMENT OF ACCESS (ROADS)
HYDROLOGY	Surface Water Quality	-1			-1		-1	
	Quantity	4	-1	-2	2		2	
	Groundwater Quality	2	2					
	Quantity	3	2	-2				
	Flooding/Erosion Silting Up	4	2		2	4	-2	4
GEOLOGY SOILS	Strength for Foundations Engineering/Construction						1	1
	Topography	1		-1	2			
	Erosion	4	1	3	2	-3	4	1
	Compaction	1	1	1	2		-1	-1
	Soil Quality	2	1	1	2	-3	-2	-2
MICRO-CLIMATE	Soil Moisture/Evaporation	2	4		-1	-2		
	Wind			2		-2		
	Temperature			2		-1		
	Humidity	1	2			-1		
	Solar Radiation					-2		
FLORA & FAUNA	Community Quality	1	2	-1	-2		-2	-2
	Breeding Niches	-1	2	2	-2		-2	-2
	Individual Species	1	2	-1	-1	2	-2	-2
	Pests & Diseases	1	-2	-3		1		-1
MAN	Population, Size & Pattern	2	2					
	Culture & Social Organisation	2	2				2	3
	Food	4	4	4	1	1	2	3
	Health	1	1	1				
LAND USE	Wetlands	-2	-1	-1	-2	-2	-2	
	Wild Areas	-2		-1		3	-2	-3
	Agriculture Arable	4	4	4	2		3	3
	Grazing	2	2			-1	1	
	Horticulture	4	1	4	2	3	3	3
	Residential	1		1			2	3
	Commercial	3	3	3	1			
	Industry							
	Forestry	3	3	3	4	-1		
	Recreation			2				
ECOLOGY	Infrastructure	1	2		1	1	3	3
	Ownership Patterns	2	2				1	1
	Aesthetics, Views etc.	-1	-1	2	1	-2	-2	-2
	Employment	3	3	3	1	1	3	3
	Income Generation & Distribution	3	3	3	1	1	3	3

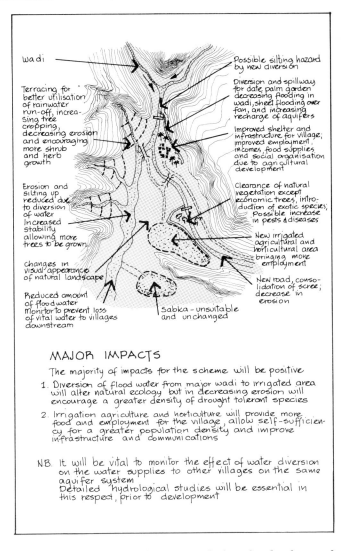

wadi

Terracing for better utilisation of rainwater run-off, increasing tree cropping, decreasing erosion and encouraging more shrub and herb growth

Erosion and silting up reduced due to diversion of water. Increased stability allowing more trees to be grown

changes in visual appearance of natural landscape

Reduced amount of floodwater. Monitor to prevent loss of vital water to villages downstream

Possible silting hazard by new diversion

Diversion and spillway for date palm garden decreasing flooding in wadi, sheet flooding over fan, and increasing recharge of aquifers

Improved shelter and infrastructure for village; improved employment, incomes, food supplies and social organisation due to agricultural development

Clearance of natural vegetation except economic trees, introduction of exotic species; Possible increase in pests & diseases

New irrigated agricultural and horticultural area bringing more employment

New road, consolidation of scree; decrease in erosion

Sabka – unsuitable and unchanged

MAJOR IMPACTS

The majority of impacts for the scheme will be positive

1. Diversion of flood water from major wadi to irrigated area will alter natural ecology but in decreasing erosion will encourage a greater density of drought tolerant species

2. Irrigation agriculture and horticulture will provide more food and employment for the village, allow self-sufficiency for a greater population density and improve infrastructure and communications

N.B. It will be vital to monitor the effect of water diversion on the water supplies to other villages on the same aquifer system. Detailed hydrological studies will be essential in this respect, prior to development

Fig 24 *Environmental impact analysis: sketch plan and matrix*

used in some parts of Australia and Great Britain. New methods of interpreting and evaluating impacts are being continually devised as more and more of these studies are carried out. It is also hoped that simpler methods of analysing and interpreting ecological models into practical on-site solutions will soon be developed. The aim of these environmental studies is to assess the impact of the proposed land use or site development on the particular land chosen and to alert the developer to any short- and long-term effects that may be harmful to the site.

Procedure

The various phases and techniques used in the proposed land use developments, constructional operations and short- and long-term operating techniques are listed against the site characteristics. Every time there is interference with the site's present physical and cultural situation, the magnitude of the impact is scored. These impacts may be beneficial as well as detrimental.

Where adverse effects are noted, alternatives are then considered, in the form of alternative sites if the use is to be fixed, a more appropriate use if the site is fixed, alternative

designs to accommodate different uses over the most suitable areas of the site and site amelioration and alternative techniques and operating procedures if site conditions are impaired by the original proposals.

Special attention is paid to any irreversible impacts, and where these are of a substantial nature, new uses are considered for the land in question.

In this manner any adverse effects on site conditions will be recognized and either avoided at the planning stage or monitored to ensure they are kept within reasonable limits during project functioning.

Input data

The procedures taken for an environmental impact assessment usually include:

1 A description of the present conditions, i.e. survey data and resource inventory
2 A description of the proposed actions
3 An assessment of the probable impact of the proposed actions on natural and cultural resources
4 An assessment of any unavoidable, adverse impacts
5 Generation of alternatives to avoid adverse impacts
6 Assessment of short-term versus long-term actions and impacts

7 Assessment of irretrievable and irreversible impacts

8 Assessment of what environmental monitoring processes are needed, e.g. to monitor salinity, water qualities, erosion, density of vegetation, air quality, wildlife.

These studies require inputs from multi-disciplinary teams in order to recognize all the interactions between projects and site conditions and to suggest solutions.

All of these characteristics are linked to man's settlement patterns, population size, incentives to live and work in various places, economy, cultural traditions, and politics. The above checklist and the checklist on p.86 for collecting survey data on these physical and cultural characteristics can also act as a basis for environmental impact statements and resource management programmes (*viz.* data on hydrology, geology and soils, topography, climate, biology, including human factors, will be required).

Courses of action suggested by results of study

In planting projects in dry lands, the type of adverse impacts most commonly encountered include exhaustion of water resources, interruption of the hydrological cycle, salinisation of soils and ground water, increases of grazing intensity where fodder is more available and subsequent decreases in regeneration of vegetation, loss of soil structure through trampling and decreases in soil fertility and soil erosion due to overcropping and bare fallows (see chapter 6).

These adverse impacts can often be avoided by changing the siting of buildings, recycling any water required and, if necessary, purifying waste water and recharging aquifers. The numbers of animals to be raised can be reduced or a more highly vegetated site chosen. Using plants suited to site conditions will avoid loss of fertility.

Beneficial impacts include soil stabilisation, increases in fertility, visual screening, shelter, improved microclimate, lowering of a high water-table, provision of food and fodder and any improvements to man's lifestyle. These can be used to compensate for, or replenish, loss of other resources, providing the loss is not irretrievable. The

unsightly views, smell, pollution and noise of many industrial buildings have stimulated many planning departments to ask for an impact analysis of likely hazards of construction and operating procedures of industrial areas and mining and quarrying sites. Most planning applications for urban and industrial developments must now be accompanied by landscape earth moving and planting, to improve microclimate, to sustain ecological balance in the surrounding areas and to maintain visual attractiveness, significant views and focal points and to highlight areas or buildings of interest.

DESIGN AND IMPLEMENTATION

The following design/cropping criteria should be borne in mind at the detailed design stage:

1 The basic criteria for site development will have been previously determined at the survey and interpretation phase, when site limitations such as salinity, high water-tables and wind will have been assessed, and a plant list compiled of suitable plants to use in such circumstances. Using this information, the detailed planning phase will determine the best way of using the site and the techniques to be employed. These will be in accord with the natural resources available and the recommendations of any environmental impact statements.

2 The use of the site and the plants to be grown must therefore be planned in conjunction with the client's wishes and the resources available. The layout of buildings and planting area must be determined in relation to site logistics, the yields required, the machinery and equipment to be used and water and soil characteristics. Visual impact should also be considered from both within and without the site. For an agricultural project, criteria such as the following are important:

Fig 25 *Sketch plan for a farm development*

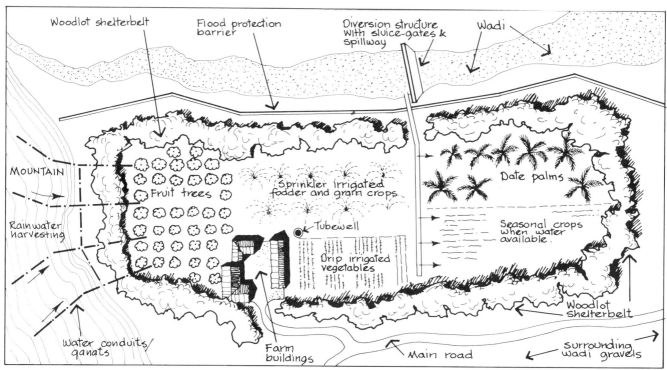

- market demand for potential crops
- crop output/input ratios
  (i.e. yield under site conditions/inputs necessary to achieve yield)
- crop rotations in relation to soil fertility and pests and diseases
- possible integration of livestock enterprises
- processing of crop products and utilisation of by-products
- integration of project with existing agricultural activities. Effect on rural income levels and employment creation.

For decorative planting and landscaping, the function of the site, the visual and spatial effects required, existing land forms and the size and shape of the areas to be planted, the amount and manner in which the site will be used and viewed, its relationship to buildings and other sites are examples of the criteria involved. As water is such a precious commodity, decorative planting wherever possible can include some productive trees, e.g. fodder or tree crops for fruit, nuts, berries.

3 The amount of labour available and the cost of maintenance will also influence design. Similarly with farming techniques, where resources are adequate, tree crops can be under-planted with row crops or fruit bushes, or the ground beneath can be grazed by livestock, in order to maximise production and multiple use of sites.

4 At this detailed design stage it will be seen that not every site will present optimum conditions for plant growth. Many sites will need initial encouragement, such as the provision of shelter or soil stabilisation, to accept their new land use and to realise their potential for plant growth. Where an ecological policy is adopted for site development deriving plants and planting techniques from site ecology and traditional techniques, the planting, once established, will continue to ameliorate site conditions with a minimum of assistance. The use of modern materials is advocated where they improve the efficiency of utilisation of site resources and stimulate and perpetuate natural ecological processes.

SITE AMELIORATION TECHNIQUES

Prior to planting, the site may need grading or terracing, construction of shelter, installation of irrigation and soil improvement. These techniques will be considered under the headings of improving
1 topography
2 microclimate
3 soil—water relationships
4 soils.

1 Improving topography

- Techniques include ground shaping to prevent erosion, and to improve stabilisation and rooting conditions for planting and gradients for irrigation.
- A saline water-table can be held away from the root zone in some areas if an interception layer of coarse rubble is placed above the water-table's maximum level in order to break capillary rise. Clean, sweet soil can then be placed on top, for the rooting zone.
- It is important that any fill imported from another site be free from contaminants of salts, pests or chemical wastes. Where irrigation water is saline, soils that are as free from silt as possible should be used, as silt is quickly de-structured by sodium salts.
- Consolidation of sandy soils is often impossible and stabilisation of new earthworks is best achieved using live plant material, providing there is sufficient irrigation water available.

2 Improving microclimate

Many dry-land sites are exposed to wind, intense solar radiation, extremes of temperature and shifting sands. Young plants will initially need protection until they are well adapted to site conditions. Techniques to ameliorate these conditions will be discussed under headings of wind, solar radiation and temperature, relative humidity and evaporation and rainfall.

Wind

The techniques for combating wind can best be expressed in table form, as follows (table 8.2).

Wherever possible, the wind break should be of fast growing species planted prior to the rest of the project in order to provide a more mature barrier and to improve microclimate prior to execution of the main body of planting.

The U.S.S.R. has recorded increases in yield of grain crops by 20–30% and by 100–200% for grasses, due to shelter belts. They can also trap snow in the cold deserts and release it as water in spring as the snows melt and irrigate spring crops.

Fig 26 *Sketch plan for landscape design*

TABLE 8.1 IMPROVING TOPOGRAPHY

Topographical type	Earth shaping	Plant species	Planting scheme
Steep slopes of wadis, mountains *etc.*	Make narrow, flattened ridges on steepest slopes to permit irrigation and rainwater harvesting without soil erosion. Uniformity of irrigation distribution is affected by slope	*Acacia* spp. *Prosopis* spp. *Zizyphus* spp. *Calligonum* spp. *Atriplex* spp. Citrus fruits, avocados; vegetable crops on large flat terraces	Usually >25% slope afforestation with fodder crops, shelter or stabilising species; tree crops e.g. fruit on 10–25% slopes; larger terraces for agricultural crops—10% slope
Gentler slopes on deeper soils	Contour plough to prevent soil erosion by wind blow or heavy rainfall in fallow season especially	Dry land crops or irrigated crops. Field size depends on steepness of slopes and where mechanisation is needed, field crops will only be grown on flat areas, with vegetables of non mech. crops on gentle slopes	Dryland farming
Shifting dunes	Do *not* disturb by earth moving of any description or plants will be covered in sand or uprooted at the first wind blow as the dune moves	*Calligonum* spp, grasses, *Atriplex* spp. *Nitraria* spp. *Eucalyptus* spp. *Tamarix* spp. *Casuarina* spp. *Prosopis* spp.	Stabilising shelter belt trees and shrubs. Irrigation will be necessary initially; thereafter plants can survive on any perched water-tables in the dunes
Flat, low areas with high water-table	Grades should not be lowered in these areas or plants will become waterlogged. Raising levels is beneficial providing the water-table does not become out of reach of plant roots	Phreatophytes if water-table is very near the surface, e.g. *Tamarix* spp. *Eucalyptus* spp. *Atriplex* spp *Arthrocnemum* Any species suited to site if soil is built up and water is not saline	If water is good quality any species tolerant to waterlogging for afforestation; agriculture using large field crops; urban planting, where the soil is built up to prevent waterlogging

TABLE 8.2 IMPROVING MICROCLIMATE: WIND

Requirement	Techniques	Plant species—or materials used
Shelter for individual plants	Tree guards placed in a circle around newly planted trees and shrubs or in the direction of the prevailing wind. Care should be taken to avoid overshading	Dead palm fronds Plastic mesh Hessian
	Planting leewards of existing plants	
	Anti-transpirants—chemicals which slow or prevent transpiration for 10–14 days and allow root uptake of water to become established prior to excessive loss through transpiration	Seaweed based alginates, 'S60'
Shelter for larger areas—must have 33% permeability to prevent scour and eddying effects on the leeward side, and consequent soil erosion and uprooting of plants	Shelter belts will provide shelter for 5 × own height, at 33% permeability, on windward side and 30 × h to leeward. Maximum decreases in velocity occur at 10 × h. The shelter belt profile should be rounded, with no sudden changes in height in order to direct the wind smoothly above the belt. Shrubs should be planted on the outside edges to complete the profile	Tough wind tolerant spp. on outside e.g. *Zizyphus, Tamarix, Prosopis, Acacia, Azadirachta* to 'nurse' less tolerant, slower growing species inside shelter belt e.g. *Ficus* spp. *Terminalia,* mangoes, guava
	Windbreaks, screens—these can be portable	Palm leaves, bamboo, coconut, banana, timber or plastic sheeting, hessian staked firmly into the ground; perforated brickwork
	Earth shaping is not usually useful in dry lands due to the possibility of wind erosion of dry soils and sand abrasion and burial of plants	Use stabilising spp. e.g. *Calligonum* spp. grasses, *Acacias* and chemical sprays such as asphalt initially only

Right: Hessian tree guards used to protect young trees on a desert afforestation scheme from windblown sand. Plastic mesh is more satisfactory in some situations but tends to fill up with sand and is considerably more expensive

Left: Shelterbelt alongside a main road. Part of a scheme to reduce desertification in northern Nigeria
PHOTO: MINSTER AGRICULTURE

Solar radiation and temperature

Solar radiation can often be over 85% of the theoretical maximum and can be double that found in humid areas of comparable latitude. The high light intensities increase growth rate and size of plants where water is not limiting. Some eucalypts have been known to grow more than one metre per year. Leaf size under bright light is small, an adaption which assists in decreasing water losses through transpiration. Many young plants raised in shade in nurseries have a much larger leaf size because of the shade and when transplanted on site may even lose their leaves initially, the new leaf growth being much smaller and closer, e.g. *Zizyphus* spp. and *Lantana* spp.

The high surface temperatures resulting from solar radiation can cause death of unsuitable plant species, either by damage to the leaf photosynthetic material or by heating soil temperatures and soil moisture to unacceptable levels. Unshaded soil surfaces can be heated to more than double that of the air temperature which, in areas where air temperatures are often over 40°C, can be devastating to all but extremely heat tolerant plants. (20–30°C is an optimum for temperate plants and 30–40°C for tropical plants.) In the centres of large deserts such as the Sahara, night temperatures can also fall by 30 degrees or more, subjecting plants to different extremes at midday and midnight. The Asian deserts have extremely cold winters, and plants must also be frost tolerant as in the higher altitude dry lands in Iran and Saudi Arabia. Coastal areas show less diurnal variation, due to the intermediary effect of the oceans and greater cloud cover.

TABLE 8.3 IMPROVING MICROCLIMATE: SOLAR RADIATION AND TEMPERATURE

Requirement	Techniques	Plant species or materials used
Shade Reduction of glare Coolness Air movement	Tree guards, shelter belts, screens, anti-transpirants to interrupt the direct pathway of the sun's rays, dispersing light and heat. Where solar radiation is reduced temperatures will be cooler	See wind table—shelter belts *etc.*
Reduce temperature extremes in urban areas	Shelter and evaporation from water areas to even out diurnal temperature extremes	Shelter belts and pools, water cascades
	Select frost tolerant plants where frosts are a possible occurrence	e.g. *Haloxylon aphyllum* for cold deserts as *H. persicum* is not frost tolerant
Provide cool buildings	Use reflective textures and colours outside buildings to cool inside, and cool colours indoors or under shelter. Do not use black, which absorbs light and heat more than any other colour Air movements using fans, air conditioners, wind towers, perforated screens	e.g. Paint building white; use blues, turquoises inside; also mirror glass, double-skinned buildings injected with liquid which turns white if hot (a newly developed product)

Requirement	Techniques	Plant species or materials used
Controlled environment houses for man and crop production	The evaporative effect of dry moving air causing a cooling sensation has been utilised in the design of desert coolers where air is blown through a screen of trickling water, the evaporation of the water cooling the air	
Cool soil temperatures for plants	Soil mulches cool soil temperatures and reduce loss of water through evaporation. Hoeing and wetting will marginally reduce temperatures	Chippings, gravel, decayed plants, chemicals, aluminium foil for vegetable produce, mirror glass
Reduce temperature extremes for productive crops	For productive tree crops, misters and foggers have been employed to keep a thin layer of moisture on tree canopies to prevent frost forming, (the latent heat of fusion maintaining the water immediately next to the leaves as liquid rather than ice). Brackish water can also be used in misters and foggers, in mist propagation units and for cooling systems	Underground pipework or hoses as for sprinkler irrigation but using misters or foggers

Polythene mulch for vegetable crop in Jordan. Drip irrigation lines are laid under the mulch, adjacent to each plant row

PHOTO: REED IRRIGATION SYSTEMS

Relative humidity and evaporation

Relative humidity varies considerably from 30% in the arid interiors of dry lands to 100% on the humid coasts. Site humidity can rarely be altered to any great degree unless enclosed conditions exist such as in greenhouses, factories or houses.

INCREASE HUMIDITY by desert coolers, any evaporation of open expanses of water or humidifiers, foggers and misters.

DECREASE HUMIDITY by condensing the water in the air against cool surfaces and re-using the liquid for irrigation or cooling purposes. Complete recycling systems can be devised.

Many of the more decorative species used in urban landscaping are unable to survive without a certain degree of humidity, e.g. *Terminalia catappa, Jacaranda acutifolia, Lagerstroemia indica*. This can be increased by the presence of lakes and ponds, provided their attraction for mosquitoes is low. *Evaporation* can be reduced to conserve soil moisture by the use of plant cover, shade, soil mulches, protection of open water, underground irrigation, chemical anti-transpirants and anti-evaporants, foggers and misters and reducing the temperature. (See Table 8.3, Solar radiation and temperature.) Mist and dew can be harvested and used for irrigation.

Rainfall

TABLE 8.4 IMPROVING MICROCLIMATE: RAINFALL

Requirement	Techniques	Plants and materials used
Rain water conservation	Store water on large scale or in roof tanks on houses; decrease losses through coverings or waterproof sprays	Dams, reservoirs, flood regulation, decreasing evaporation Use xerophytic plants
Efficiency of use	Improve catchment areas make microcatchments using chemicals and stabilisers to increase run-off and decrease seeping losses. Use irrigation systems that prevent unnecessary water loss e.g. trickle; hoe soils and decrease surface crusts where water percolation is required	Rain water harvesting Soil mulches Trickle and subsurface irrigation Cultivation techniques to decrease evaporation and drainage losses. Use plants with low transpiration rates and low water demands.
Flood regulation	In heavy rainfall prevent flooding and soil erosion	By-pass channels, weirs, storage areas

Cloud seeding

Cloud seeding with silver iodide causes the fine water droplets in the air to conglomerate around the silver iodide and fall as rain. This is only successful where there are clouds and is less useful in the extremely arid areas where clouds are rarely seen. Care must be taken that rain does not fall in one area to the detriment of another important area.

Clouds have been seeded in the Rockies in North America and have increased the water available in the Colorado River for use in California and Arizona, for fruit and vegetable irrigation. Seeding in the humid Ethiopian highlands has increased water availability in the Nile. Howell, in 1965, reported that seeding in the Andes has provided irrigation water for the Peruvian desert, increasing run-off by 10–15%. These indirect effects often seem greater than the direct rain production which usually has a low economic return. However, seeding is used occasionally in America, Australia (the humid west), China, U.S.S.R., India, Israel (the sub-humid north). Successful experiments to increase cloud formation over the Rajputana desert have been reported by Bryson. The desert was sprayed with asphalt in order to decrease the dust in the air immediately above. This encouraged air circulation by convection, hot air rose and cooled, and subsequently clouds formed and rain fell.

3 Improving soil/water relationships

Analysis and interpretation of the survey data and proposed land use will have established the extent to which naturally available soil moisture requires supplementing. It will also indicate the most suitable type of moisture supplement depending upon the quantity and quality of water available, the type of plants to be grown and the system of management to be used.

There are many techniques of supplementing natural soil moisture. The following will be discussed in this section following a survey of irrigation selection criteria:

1 Rainwater harvesting   2 Irrigation:
- surface
- sprinkler
- drip
- sub-irrigation.

Soil moisture conservation will be discussed under the section on soils.

Irrigation selection criteria

The purpose of irrigation is to create and maintain the optimum moisture regime for plant growth.

In selecting an irrigation system for a particular planting project several major criteria may be applied, namely plant growth, control, efficiency, limiting factors, usual qualities and cost effectiveness. Each is considered separately below.

1 PLANT GROWTH Water is being continually removed from the plant root zone through diffusion, percolation and uptake by the plant. Thus the soil moisture tension (the force against which plants have to operate to obtain water) is normally continually increasing. In order to minimise the stress on the plant by holding the soil moisture tension as low as possible, the ideal irrigation system would therefore continually supply water to the root zone at the same rate as it was being depleted. This is particularly important in relation to the use of saline water. The lower the physical component can be held the greater the osmotic component that can be accommodated. This is shown in fig 27. To put this in practical terms, systems that can maintain the root zone at, or near, field capacity can utilise considerably more saline water than systems which allow the soil to dry out. The most important criterion for

evaluation and classification is therefore how low a soil moisture tension it can maintain on a continual basis.

A secondary aspect of this criterion is whether the system can feed soluble fertilizer on the same basis.

2 CONTROL Although the normal aim is to maintain the soil moisture tension as low as possible, it may be necessary, in order to exercise control over the development of the plant (e.g. to induce flowering or promote fruit set), to maintain a different moisture regime. The second criterion is therefore how well the irrigator can control the soil moisture regime using the system.

3 EFFICIENCY The third criterion is the efficiency of water use. Irrigation efficiency is defined as the percentage of total irrigation water supplied to a given area which is made available within the root zone for beneficial use by plants. Apart from wasting water, low-efficiency systems can create considerable problems of waterlogging and salinity build-up and may require expensive drainage systems to rectify these faults. From an overall viewpoint this is rapidly becoming the most important factor in irrigation agriculture. Just as pressure on the world's energy supplies is pushing up the cost of energy, so it is being realized that the world is rapidly running out of fresh water. Obviously the significance of this increases as the cost of water increases, so that for some arid countries this is already a primary criterion, and it will rapidly become so for the rest of the world.

4 LIMITING FACTORS The fourth major criterion concerns the determination of factors which may limit the use of the system. These include how well it can cope with variations of topography, how much it is affected by climate, notably wind, how well it can handle saline water and what leaching of salts is required and whether it causes any damage to the plant.

Any one of these factors may preclude the use of a system in a particular situation.

5 VISUAL QUALITIES A fifth criterion for landscape work is the visual appearance of the system and its components.

6 COST EFFECTIVENESS The final criterion inevitably must be financial. However it should be noted that the cost effectiveness or benefit/cost ratio of an irrigation system is generally more significant than the actual cost itself. Irrigation costs need to be considered over a reasonable time period—normally 5–20 years—to establish realistic operating costs, since for many schemes these are much more significant, over the project's life, than are the initial capital costs.

Although these criteria have been considered separately for the purpose of this discussion, it should be realized that in practice they interact closely.

Rainwater harvesting
The simplest means of supplementing moisture supplies is rainwater harvesting. This system mimics the manner in which some indigenous desert plants obtain moisture. The plants appear on the soil surface to be widely spaced, yet in reality their root systems extend for a considerable distance, collecting moisture from a relatively large volume of soil. Where introduced plants have smaller root systems than desert species, water can be supplemented artificially by treating the soil surface so that rain falling on areas

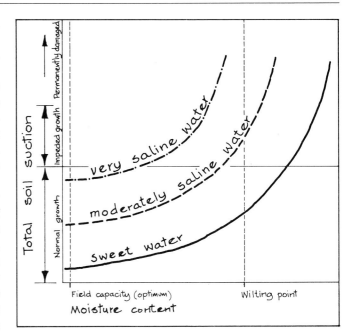

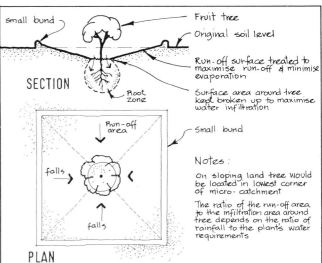

Fig 27 *(top) The effect of soil salinity on the soil suction force*

Fig 28 *(above) Schematic plan and section of a micro-catchment for rainwater harvesting*

outside the root zone runs off that surface onto the area underlain by plant roots. Traditionally this is achieved by compacting the ground surface and levelling. Modern techniques include the use of plastics and oil-based products to seal the soil surface. The size of the 'collection' area relative to the planted area must be in inverse proportion to the ratio of rainfall to plant water requirements. Allowance must be made for the efficiency of collection, which is never 100%. Small micro-catchments can feed individual plants or large macro-catchments can feed massed planting. This system is relatively low-cost, cheap to install, has very low maintenance requirements and requires no labour to operate. Although limited in application, it deserves more attention. It has been developed from the traditional methods of the Nabateans (see chapter 6—Jordan), who are reputed to have lined large areas of their mountain slopes with mounds of rock in order to collect dew as a dry season supplement. The dew was then channelled, as was the rainfall, down the slopes to the fertile plains beneath.

The value of rainwater harvesting is however related to the probability of achieving the appropriate rainfall, and rainfall can be highly variable in the arid zones.

Surface irrigation

The traditional form of irrigation in the arid zones is surface irrigation. Whether the method used is basin, furrow or simple flood irrigation, the basic principle is the same. Water is applied to the surface of the soil at some distance from the crop plants, and the characteristics of the soil surface—slope and permeability—are relied upon to control the supply of water to the plant root zone.

The simplest system is a man with a hose. This is often used in Middle East with small basins around each tree or shrub, or to flood grass areas.

Various forms of surface irrigation are illustrated overleaf.

Rainwater harvesting

Right : Fruit tree planted in a small micro-catchment, Negev desert

Below : Eucalyptus on terraced fields fed by run-off channels

PHOTOS: C. V. MALCOLM

1

2

Surface irrigation

1 Traditional surface irrigation using small basins around each fruit tree—Zerqa, Jordan

2 Basin irrigation of fruit trees, Tabouk, Saudi Arabia. In this case the basin is flooded but the area immediately around each tree is kept dry

3 Traditional irrigation for vegetables. Various shapes, sizes and layouts are used, with the plants, in this case aubergines, growing on the raised sides of the channels. Tehran, Iran

4 Pre-irrigation of a cotton field using furrow irrigation, Tehran, Iran

5 and 6 Border strip irrigation of Rhodes grass at Hofuf, Saudi Arabia. Syphon tubes lift water from the canal into the field

PHOTOS: BRUCE MACNALLY

3

Salinity build-up in the plant root zone caused by impeded drainage and over-irrigation, Jordan Valley
PHOTO: MINSTER AGRICULTURE

It is normally impractical to maintain low soil moisture tensions using surface systems, although basin irrigation can perform reasonably well if water is piped to small basins. This is primarily related to the low efficiency of such systems due to the fact that they have to use soil surfaces for conducting the water and water is lost through seepage from the point of supply along the route. In general, the level at which soil moisture tension can be maintained increases as the area under irrigation increases.

It is normally only practical to bring the soil to field capacity by applying surface irrigation. The reason for this is again related to using the soil surface to transport water. In order to ensure that the crop plants furthest from the point of water application receive adequate water, the plants closest to the application point have to be over-irrigated. The extent of this over-irrigation depends on the soil permeability—a greater proportion of the water will run laterally on silts or clay soils than on sand or gravel. It is therefore normal practice when using such systems to irrigate to field capacity and then wait until the permissible soil moisture tension builds up before irrigating again. Thus the actual soil moisture tension fluctuates considerably.

Surface systems have the lowest water use efficiency. With lined irrigation channels and small basins, irrigation efficiencies can be as high as 70%. However most systems achieve much lower efficiencies, commonly below 50%.

Considerable percolation losses occur due to over-irrigation, and in arid climates a substantial proportion of the applied water is lost in evaporation. This can cause considerable problems of waterlogging and salinity build-up if sub-soil drainage is poor, and drainage systems are often required to counteract this. A classic example of this is found in the Indus Valley, and other examples can be found in almost every country. As a result of this low

efficiency it is not normally practical to feed soluble nutrients via such irrigation systems.

The principal limitation on the use of surface systems is topography. Because the soil surface is used for water transport the systems will only function on gently sloping land. The systems are also limited in their ability to handle saline water. This relates to their ability to maintain low soil moisture tensions. Although surface systems typically have good leaching characteristics due to the normally high deep percolation losses, the relatively high moisture tensions which can build up between irrigations limit the osmotic tension which can be accommodated. These systems designed around small irrigation modules, such as small basins, have the highest ability to utilize saline water. Particular care has to be exercised with surface irrigation systems using treated sewage effluent, and primary water conveyancing is normally restricted to closed pipes because of potential health hazards. Other health problems may arise with surface systems, notably bilharzia, which is a major objection to surface irrigation in some parts of the world. The various canals and channels required for surface irrigation normally intrude into landscape design. However by incorporating them into the design exercise they can be used to form patterns of hard landscape.

Surface irrigation can be very cheap to develop, requiring in its simplest form only the construction of earth banks and channels. However, in general, efficiency is proportional to cost. Unlined canals have high percolation losses which can only be reduced by linings. Piped conveyancing is even more efficient but equally more expensive. At the same time, however, increased efficiency means reduced operating costs.

Sprinkler irrigation

Above: Sprinklers used for pre-irrigation of cotton, Gasvin, Iran

PHOTO: WRIGHT RAIN LTD

Right: Wheel-roll sprinkler line irrigating alfalfa, Karaj, Iran

PHOTO: BRUCE MACNALLY

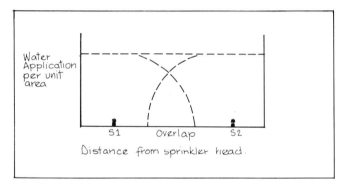

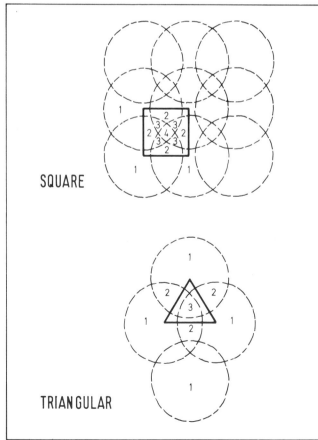

Sprinkler irrigation

The second most widely used irrigation system is sprinkler or overhead irrigation. The equipment used ranges from the very large centre pivot units which irrigate areas up to 100 hectares with a single unit, to small, closely-spaced sprinklers for nursery or decorative work. The wide availability of lightweight aluminium tube has resulted in considerable use of portable and semi-portable systems which have relatively low costs.

The characteristic of this type of system is that water is piped to distribution points from which it is sprayed onto the crop or the soil below the crop. Sprinkler irrigation is in a sense the most natural form of irrigation since it essentially simulates rain. As a result its advantages and disadvantages closely parallel those of natural rainfall.

The ability of sprinkler systems to maintain low soil moisture tensions varies with the configuration and with the standard of engineering involved. Small, closely-spaced sprinklers can achieve this reasonably well by giving light, frequent irrigations, whereas the large units often have to apply fairly heavy irrigations in order to ensure even coverage and are consequently subject to the same limitations as surface systems. With the centre pivot type the frequency of irrigation depends on how rapidly the unit can recycle.

Good distribution and hence high irrigation efficiency can only be achieved by ensuring the individual sprinkler patterns overlap to avoid 'edge effects' of alternate areas of wet and dry soil.

The same factors determine the degree to which an alternative moisture regime can be maintained. Subject to this the systems are easy to control and can be fully automated.

Sprinkler systems are considerably more efficient than surface systems. Although evaporation losses are still a major factor, percolation losses are considerably reduced, provided that the system gives uniform cover. Sprinkler systems are less affected by topography than surface

Fig 29a (top left) and 29b (bottom left) Sprinkler patterns Ideal sprinkler patterns—the sum of the output from individual sprinklers in the overlap area—combine to maintain the overall water application level. Although possible to approximate in two dimensions as shown in fig 29a, this is virtually impossible to achieve in three dimensions since most sprinkler patterns are circular and interact as shown in fig 29b

systems, although this is still a factor to consider. Centre pivot types in particular require flat land. Sprinkler systems cannot handle saline water as it causes scorch on the crop foliage. For the same reason soluble nutrients cannot be used except in low-angle orchard systems, and the system may be severely limited in areas subject to high temperature and strong sunlight which can also produce scorch. The efficiency of sprinkler systems can be dramatically reduced in areas subject to strong winds, which distort the distribution patterns.

These systems are not generally acceptable with treated sewage effluent (TSE) due to health risks involved in spraying TSE into the atmosphere and onto plant foliage.

Sprinklers often have to be operated at night in landscape schemes to avoid spraying passers-by. They are not generally regarded as obtrusive and can contribute significantly to the visual effectiveness of a scheme, especially if operated in the evening along with flood lighting.

Sprinkler systems are available as portable, semi-permanent (in place on the ground surface for the life of the crop) or permanent (solid-set—permanent underground pipes) installations. Portable systems are normally the least costly on a per hectare basis. However, the area which can be covered by one unit of a portable system is generally much more limited in arid areas than in temperate ones. Thus this cost advantage is considerably reduced.

In general, cost per hectare is inversely related to the size of the unit. Thus large centre pivot units are cheapest, followed by large travelling irrigators. Solid-set systems, using small closely spaced sprinklers, (the most efficient systems) are most expensive. Current design trends are generally aimed at reducing labour requirements. With continually rising labour costs, sprinkler systems are now often cheaper than surface systems when operating costs are considered over the life of the project.

Drip irrigation

The use of drip irrigation on a wide scale is a relatively recent development. Drip (or trickle) irrigation delivers water in controlled quantities to individual plants or groups of plants. The system uses a network of small bore plastic tubes laid on the ground surface. Adjacent to each plant, a dripper—a specially constructed calibrated orifice—delivers water at a rate normally between 2–12 litres per hour. By delivering exactly the amount of water the plant requires and applying it directly to the soil adjacent to the plant, trickle systems achieve high irrigation efficiencies. This high degree of control means that losses from evaporation and deep percolation are minimal. In many cases it is not necessary to wet the whole volume of soil in the planted area, but only that in which the plant roots are growing (this is also true of some surface irrigation systems). Drip irrigation commonly requires considerably less water than even well-designed flood and sprinkler systems.

Sprinkler irrigation

Top right : Portable raingun and riser being moved to next irrigation position on sugar cane in Africa
PHOTO: WRIGHT RAIN LTD

Middle : Travelling irrigator, Al Kharj, Saudi Arabia
Above : Centre pivot irrigation unit at Kufra, Libya
PHOTO: SPP SYSTEMS LTD

Since drip systems apply water at a very low rate, they can be set up to supply water on a daily basis. As a result they can feed soluble nutrients very efficiently and have even been used to carry systemic insecticides. Continuous irrigation has been tried but was found to restrict oxygen uptake by plant roots. In practice they are normally used on a semi-continuous basis and can maintain very low moisture tensions. Drip systems can therefore accommodate much higher osmotic tensions in the soil and hence utilize much more saline water than other irrigation systems. Indeed it has been found that many of the accepted values for the salt tolerance of crops need to be revised upwards since they were determined using less efficient surface or sprinkler systems.

A further advantage in respect of salinity is that while the systems are operating they are effectively self-leaching. This is because salts present in the irrigation water are continually moved outwards to the fringes of the wetting pattern where they are deposited.

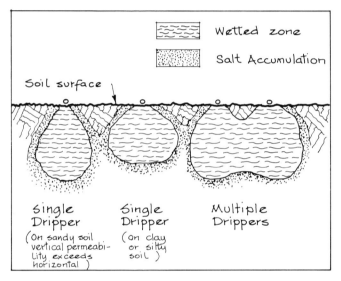

Fig 30 *Soil wetting patterns under drip irrigation*

However it must be noted that periodic leaching using sprinklers or flooding is still necessary unless annual rainfall is sufficient to wash the salts out of the root zone. With permanent crops such leaching will only be required when replanting. With annual crops, annual leaching will be required unless plants can be replanted in exactly the same positions relative to the salt patterns. This is often restricted by practicability and by build-up of soil pests and diseases. Occasional light rain washes salts accumulated at the top of the wetting pattern into the root zone, and in such cases irrigation must be carried out during periods of rainfall to prevent salt damage to the plants.

Row crops such as vegetables and sugar cane may be irrigated economically using lightweight pre-formed drip systems (bi-wall or porous tubing) but drip irrigation is not generally economic for grass or field crops.

A considerable range of monitoring and controlling devices has been developed for drip systems. As a result it is possible to maintain almost any required moisture regime. These systems are extremely efficient in terms of water use; it has been estimated that a drip system will use approximately 33% of the amount of water that a sprinkler

system will use and only 10% of the water required by a surface irrigation system.

Drip systems require high standards of filtration to avoid blockages. Algae can be a particular problem, and they are therefore less suitable for use where the water source is a small reservoir or slowly flooding river. But since these systems do not wet plant foliage and do not involve large quantities of free water on the soil surface, they are the most suitable system for handling recycled water such as treated sewage effluent, and this particularly applies when the system is buried just below the soil surface. This is often recommended to reduce the effects of direct sunlight and high temperature on the plastic materials used, but it must be remembered that any such burying implies particular attention to filtration, since blockages are less easily detected and more trouble to rectify when the pipes are below the surface.

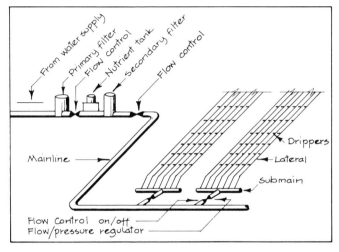

Fig 31 *(above) Basic elements of a drip irrigation system*

Below and facing page : **Drip irrigation**
1 Spiral dripper on planting of indigenous trees, Abu Dhabi, UAE
2 Desert planting of palm trees under drip irrigation, Al Ain, UAE
PHOTO: REED IRRIGATION SYSTEMS
3 Biwall tubing on tomatoes, Al Ain, UAE
PHOTO: BRUCE MACNALLY
4 Water oozes out along the entire length of seep hose tubing
PHOTO: E. I. DUPONT DE NEMOURS & CO
5 Seep hose (Viaflo tubing) on strawberries grown under plastic mulch, Spain
6 Biwall tubing on bananas, Hawaii
PHOTO: REED IRRIGATION SYSTEMS

4

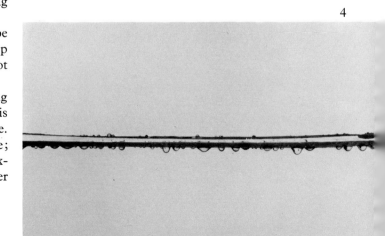

1

2

5 6

3

Drip systems are in general visually relatively un-obtrusive. In pedestrian areas they can however present a safety hazard and are themselves subject to mechanical damage. In such cases it may be preferable to use buried PVC laterals with drippers mounted on risers adjacent to individual plants.

Systems using drippers are generally comparable in terms of capital cost to equivalent solid set (permanent) sprinkler systems. However, due to lower water use and lower pressure requirements, operating costs are lower. Systems using bi-wall or porous tubing are at present rapidly declining in cost due to increased volume of sales and improved manufacturing technology. Costs are now approaching those of portable sprinkler systems.

Sub-irrigation

The fourth major type of irrigation system is sub-irrigation. This is normally achieved either by creating an artificial water-table just below the ground surface or by burying a drip irrigation system or a network of perforated pipes. When water is supplied at a depth of about 30–75 cm, moisture rises by capillary action into the root zone. The system normally requires an impermeable layer below the level at which water is supplied, to prevent excessive losses to deep percolation. This may be a natural soil feature or an artificial barrier, typically asphalt or plastic sheet. Sub-surface systems can maintain very low soil moisture tensions at levels comparable to those produced by above-ground drip systems.

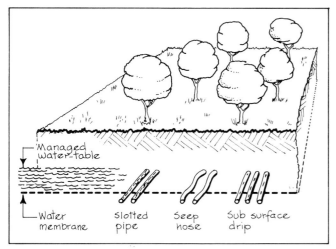

Fig 32 *Schematic illustration of various types of sub-irrigation*

Underground drip systems are comparable to above-ground trickle systems in the degree of control which can be achieved, and while the management of water-tables can produce equally good results, it can be considerably more difficult since they can be affected by factors outside the control of the irrigator. Furthermore underground drip is extremely efficient in terms of water use, whereas managed water-tables show a wide range of efficiencies depending on the subsoil conditions. Blockages are still unfortunately a major problem with underground drip systems, despite considerable research; but managed water-tables are only practical within a relatively narrow range of topographic and subsoil conditions.

Visually these systems are not observable at all. They have considerable advantages on grass areas, e.g. sports fields, where they do not wet the ground surface. This allows the areas to be used even while irrigation is being carried out.

Costs are very variable. Where naturally impervious sub-soils are present, capital costs can be very low. However the costs of installing artificial impermeable layers are generally high. Operating costs are comparable to those of drip systems.

Whichever irrigation system is used it must be designed to be able to meet the peak water requirements of plants during the hottest part of the year. The actual scheduling of irrigation can be determined by monitoring soil moisture, evaporation or by practical experience of plant requirements.

4 Improving soil conditions

The techniques for improving soil conditions can be expressed in tabular form (table 8.5).

PLANT ESTABLISHMENT

Planning

Any problems regarding traditional grazing routes and settlements of local peoples should be overcome before the project begins. The planning of operations, timing and phasing of planting with the main project, and liaison with the local people, must be co-ordinated from a site office. Delivery of equipment, clearing and forwarding materials from the docks, transport to site and hiring of labour can be extremely time consuming and erratic in countries where infrastructure is new or non-existent, and the unpredictability of the harsh climate can easily affect schedules. Many sites are in the middle of a desert plain, away from towns or city facilities, and accommodation can best be provided by tents and temporary huts.

Site preparation and timing of planting

The project must be timed to fit in with the cooler planting season, often before the rains—fencing, irrigation installations and testing, and construction work being finished and functioning before planting begins. A holding nursery can be constructed on site to allow containersed plants to be hardened off gradually to site conditions, which differ greatly from nursery conditions.

Dune stabilisation and breaking up of crusted, consolidated silt soils must be carried out. Irrigation for several days prior to planting will thoroughly wet and leach soils.

Planting techniques

For trees and shrubs to be planted in sandy soils, holes must be dug immediately before planting, as the sand will quickly fall back and refill the plant pit. In siltier or clay soils, holes may be dug earlier and, on very heavy ground, machinery such as post hole borers, may need to be used. Initial irrigations before planting can then moisten the plant pit and the back-fill. Some concreted soils may need irrigating to soften them.

Manure is placed in the bottom of each pit and dug into the soil so that young plant roots are not scorched by direct

TABLE 8.5 IMPROVING SOIL CONDITIONS

Soil condition	Techniques	Plant species and materials
Lack of stability Live materials	Plant with live, indigenous plants whose matted roots quickly hold the soil surface together and also act as shelter from wind. Experiments in Saudi Arabia, Israel and China have used low hedges planted on a grid system, filling grids with soil, broken branches, pebbles, with a sapling centrally planted to grow on as a tree crop	*Prosopis* spp. *Tamarix* spp. *Calligonum* spp. grasses, *Suaeda* spp. *Dodonea* spp. *Salsola* spp. *Calotropis* spp. *Nitraria* spp. *Atriplex* spp. *Kochia* spp.
Inert Materials	Meshes of live and dead plant materials, latex, asphalt or bitumen sprays stabilise and decrease evaporation as long as no one walks across them. Seeds can also be sown in stabilising mixtures. Mulches for surface stabilisation	Latex, asphalt, bitumen sprays; pegged polythene, plastic mesh, fences, retaining walls, gabions Gravel, silt, polythene, vegetation
Poor water retention e.g. in sandy soils	Add water-retaining substances and improve texture Mulch surface Where the water is saline, use soil conditioners with a buffering capacity (e.g. seaweed-based compounds) to prevent soil damage to plants, and deflocculation of silts and clays to structureless soils, heavy when wet, dusty when dry	Clay, organic matter, soil conditioners; gravel silt, polythene, vegetation mulches
Salinity	Leach in irrigated areas with adequate drainage Small and frequent irrigation applications maintaining moisture in the rooting zone will prevent salt build up close to the roots	Irrigation and drainage e.g. drip irrigation
	Graded rubble interception zone above a saline water table will prevent capillary rise and salt deposition above the interception zone	Interception layer with sweet soil layer on top for plant growth
	Extremely saline soils may need to be isolated from plants in urban areas	Use containers
	Replacement of soil (Artificial soils are generally too expensive and often difficult to wet once they have dried out e.g. peat, vermiculite, industrial aggregate)	Use wadi, alluvium or sweet sandy soils
	Use salt tolerant species	e.g. *Casuarina* spp. *Nitraria* spp. *Phoenix dactylifera, Atriplex* spp. *Suaeda* spp.

Soil condition	Techniques	Plant species and materials
Poor drainage	Soil conditioners can prevent sodium flocculated soils and loss of soil structure but many rely on the initial presence of clay to improve crumb structure	HPAN—Sodium polyacrylate VAMA—polymer IBMA—water soluble poly-electrolyte
	Mix silty or clay soils with sand to improve texture, aeration and drainage	Add sand
	Break up pans, e.g. of iron or clay	Plough and rip
	Organic matter improves texture and drainage as well as providing plant nutrients and buffering saline conditions	Organic matter
Poor fertility	Add organic matter, decayed plant and animal residues. These are usually in high demand and low supply in arid areas where they decompose very quickly. The lack of moisture results in there being few soil organisms to decompose the residues efficiently to available plant nutrients	Organic matter
	Nitrogen and phosphates are usually low, especially if clay is low. In alkaline soils, iron becomes unavailable and must be applied as foliar or ground feeds as sequestered iron	Nitrogen from N-fixing bacteria in roots of *Acacia Prosopis* spp.; phosphates from forest species or fertilizers applied to soil
	Soluble fertilisers can be applied through the irrigation system	
	After initial establishment adapted species should survive with little need for artificial fertilizers if organic processes and residues are used	

contact with it. For species requiring higher fertility, fertilisers or forest starter tablets may be mixed with the back-fill. These tablets are slow-release forms of fertiliser. In hot conditions, slow-release fertilisers are essential, and will give the plants a good initial start. Pots can be cut off the root ball in order to give a minimum of disturbance to the roots.

Alginate root dips have proved beneficial in decreasing root disturbance at planting time and stimulating rapid root growth after planting by coating the roots in a thin film of water so that desiccation in the initial phases is unlikely.

Where sites are exposed and windy and temperatures less cool, foliage can be sprayed with anti-transpirant the evening before planting in order to decrease transpiration for the first few days of establishment. Tree guards should also be fixed around each plant immediately after planting before the heat of midday in order to decrease desiccation due to wind and sunshine. They can also assist in preventing sand piling on top of young plants. Planting must always be carried out in the early morning cool of the day or early evening, into moist soils, and regular, frequent irrigations given until the plants establish.

Agricultural crops may germinate *in situ*, or small plants 50–100 mm high may be transplanted into open fields. These are usually planted in rows to facilitate weeding, hoeing and harvesting. Irrigation may be furrow, sprinkler, bi-wall or gated pipe, depending on the degree of water conservation required and the finance available. Crops may be planted on the edge of ridges to allow salts to rise to the top of the ridge and keep away from the plants just below. Areas between the rows may be consolidated to increase run-off of more predictable rain supplies to the planted furrows.

Above: Planting a young Zizyphus spina-christi *in pre-irrigated, unstable sand on a desert afforestation scheme. Abu Dhabi, UAE*

Fig 33 *(below) Principles of cropping on ridges*

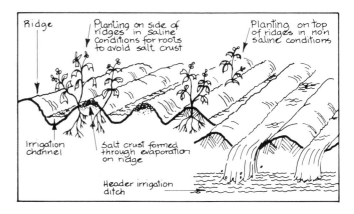

Plant propagation

Nursery requirements
Where a new nursery is to be set up for propagating plants for a specific project or to supply plants for local farmers or market gardeners, the size of land required will depend upon the number of plants to be produced, the annual turn-over of plants required for planting up, and the size and age to which they must be grown prior to planting out; the older the plants the larger the pots, and the more space is required.

A piece of land with a good, reliable water source is essential. Soils should also be suitable for potting mixes

Nursery in Northern Nigeria raising trees for shelter belt schemes. Each bed is equipped with polythene covers, and fertiliser can be fed through the irrigation water using the tank in the foreground

PHOTO: WRIGHT RAIN LTD

wherever possible to save the expense of importing and transporting soils or composts from elsewhere.

Shelter and a readily available source of sweet water and soils are essential. Windbreaks must first be planted around any new nursery site. Artificial fences of palm leaves or plastic can be used initially, or fast growing plants such as *Sesbanea grandiflora* or sugar cane. *Sesbanea* is however prone to eelworm, which after two years may build up to levels which affect the propagated stock. Within 3–5 years fast growing trees will have established themselves as natural windbreaks, e.g. *Casuarina* species, *Tamarix* spp. Care should be taken that there is sufficient space for these windbreaks, whose canopies may get as much as 5 metres wide, and cast too much shade in the cooler months for plants to be raised beneath them. It is often useful to plant these trees along the nursery roads for this reason, leaving as much space as possible for raising plants. Different areas of land will be needed on the nursery for different methods of propagation, stages of growth and irrigation practices.

The lightly shaded areas are usually utilised for germinating seeds in pots. The plants are then moved to the more open sunlight when 50–100 mm high. For more delicate plants, cuttings and smaller seed sizes, a specially constructed germinating area is used. This is shaded with palm stalk slatting or plastic mesh usually supported at a sufficient height above ground to allow a man to walk under and tend the young seedlings. The beds are concrete-lined to conserve moisture, with drainage channels to drain excess water. Larger areas of land will be needed for plants

grown in pots rather than seed beds, as for agricultural vegetables. A hardening off area will also be needed when saline water and exposure to full light and wind can be experienced by the plants prior to travel to site.

Nursery buildings will include an office, an air-conditioned store for chemicals, a shaded potting area for soil mixing and potting and accommodation for staff. Roads and walkways should be designed so as to allow for maximum efficiency and minimum handling of pots from each area of the nursery and finally on to trucks for transport to site. In a hot climate, nurseries can be chiefly open-air, with shading to protect seedlings from bright sunlight at the germination stage.

Cuttings are to be established outside the normal cool season period of striking cuttings, desert coolers or air-conditioners may be needed if there is no part of the nursery that remains sufficiently cool. Heavy duty poly-thene houses installed with desert coolers have been successfully used for propagation as well as the raising of vegetables and high quality crops such as aubergines, cucumbers, tomatoes and peppers. Completely controlled environment houses have been set up in Abu Dhabi, Mexico and Arizona where waste heat from engine-driven electric generators desalts water which is used for irrigation and misters; the air temperature is cooled to a specific level and day length can also be controlled. Solar radiation and wind energy sources are also being utilised.

In areas where few resources are available for productive use, these recycling controlled-climate systems may be considered a useful extension of man's normal propagating and cropping methods. However, their use of expensive and high technology plastics, machinery and monitoring equipment will prohibit their use in any but the richest of nations.

Methods of propagation for different land uses
Different methods of propagation are used depending on the plants, the climate, the use of the plants and the scale of the project.

Agriculture
For agricultural projects, plants are usually sown from seed either *in situ* or in seed beds for planting when they are 50–100 mm high.

They may be drilled in rows to assist in weeding and later cultivations, or broadcast. Some seeding of range-land indigenous species has been carried out by helicopter in Australia. Where rainfall is predictable, sowing should take place just before the rains begin to take full advantage of the wet season. Where rainfall is unreliable, germination must rely upon regular irrigation until the seedlings are large enough to live on the soil moisture available from rainfall.

The major problem in agriculture at present is in selecting and breeding the varieties that are adapted to the adverse conditions regularly encountered in dry lands whilst retaining the productivity levels required. Perennial crops such as tree crops (rubber, for example) are grown in pots as for the forestry plants.

Forestry and horticulture
Plant propagation for forestry and productive and decorative horticulture includes raising plants from seed, cuttings, grafts, budding and layers. As these are chiefly perennial plants or trees, most are raised in pots until at least 6 months old before planting out.

Misters and foggers are particularly useful when cuttings are to be rooted. Cool temperatures must be maintained for rooting cuttings.

Cuttings will be inserted into boxes, hormone rooting powder being used for the more stubborn rooting species. These can be flood irrigated in the cool months, or will be taken under cover with mist irrigation and cooling conditions if taken at the hotter times of year. When rooted in the coarse, open soil mixture they can be potted on to larger pots (usually 112–125 mm diameter), maintained under cover and shade until established in the pots and then moved outside to the usual open beds, where the seed raised plants are also growing.

SOIL MIX Care should be taken that no large amounts of silt are included in the soil mix as, under irrigation, the soils will set like concrete, devoid of the air necessary for plant root respiration and hanging on to any salts accumulating from the irrigation water. Organic matter such as wood shavings, bark, saw-dust, vermiculite and peat, are no substitute for well-rotted manure for young plants. The buffering action offered by manure or seaweed fertilizers cannot be bettered. Young plants are more delicate, and as their roots are restricted in a small volume of soil in the pot, soil and water conditions must be better than on site conditions where plants are older, tougher and more able to grow away from adverse soil conditions.

POTS Pots may be of fibre, polythene, peat or, very rarely, earthenware. Small peat pots may be used for very small seeds and difficult-to-germinate species. The whole pot can then be transferred to a larger size with no disturbance to the plant roots.

Long pots, often 225 mm long, are needed for many of the indigenous species that have a fast growing tap root—the ones that survive on low water-tables. These species often react adversely to the root pruning which is necessary when growing trees and shrubs to half a metre height in the nursery. The tap root species are therefore often better planted at smaller sizes before the roots have grown too long and have been root pruned more than two or three times. Pots are sometimes arranged in sunken beds to protect pots and plants from the sun, keep the roots from overheating and to facilitate flood or other types of irrigation.

IRRIGATION Irrigation is often carried out by flooding from centrally placed hoses. Where water is of good quality and conservation is essential, misters and foggers can be used instead of flood, providing the soil has been thoroughly and completely wetted initially. With water quality of more than 1000 ppm, salts must be regularly leached from the pots. Salinities greater than 1500 ppm will kill off many young seedlings except the most tolerant.

FERTILISERS, PESTICIDES AND FUNGICIDES The manure in the initial soil mix will provide sufficient nutrients for the young plants. Where deficiency symptoms are seen, fertiliser can be added to the irrigation water or applied as a foliar spray for more rapid effects. Pesticides and fungicides can be sprayed when necessary. Incidence of attack is relatively low in arid areas. Nematocides must be flooded into the pot soil.

HARDENING OFF All plants must be hardened off before transporting to site, and, where saline irrigation water is to be used on site, plants should have up to four weeks acclimatization on increasing salinity irrigations. Plants which have not been forced into weak sappy growth on the nursery are 100% more likely to survive on exposed arid planting sites.

Maintenance and management
Regular maintenance in the harsh arid environment is essential to the survival of new planting schemes, as the ameliorating effect of vegetation on site conditions will not be achieved for several years after the plants have been planted.

The fast growth rate of many species, particularly when supplied with adequate irrigation, will however speed establishment and growth to maturity. A substantial shelter effect can be achieved by wind breaks only three years old. Gardens will show a great maturity of shade, cover and spatial effects within the same length of time, fruit trees can be cropped within three years and wood within ten where smaller timbers are needed.

Soil
Soil treatments of stabilisation, dune clearing, additions of organic matter and mulches will decrease as plants mature and leaf litter and plant residues add to the soil nutrients. Initially, sand clearance may be a large job after each sand blow. In farming and horticulture where crops are removed yearly, crop residues are ploughed back in order to maintain fertility, or livestock are grazed on the residues and supply manure to the soil. Yearly additions of organic

matter can greatly assist to maintain fertility and decrease soil erosion and compaction. However, it is not generally feasible to maintain high levels of organic matter in soils in very arid areas. Under such conditions organic matter is rapidly oxidised due to high prevailing temperatures.

Soil salinity must be regularly monitored in order to schedule leaching operations to prevent excessive build up of damaging salts.

Water

Irrigation systems require regular cleaning of canals and filters, flushing of pipes, replacing of worn parts, and leaching programmes to leach salts from the soil rooting zone. Soil wetting patterns and soil moisture tension should be regularly monitored to assess the amount of water to apply to the plants or crops. Soil tensiometers will assess this.

The salinity of irrigation water must be checked either by regular sampling or by continuous monitoring. The latter is essential where TSE is used. Breakdowns of effluent treatment plants can result in very rapid rises in salinity levels. Automatic shut-down facilities should be considered or preferably automatic switching to stand-by supplies of good quality water.

Periodic flushing of irrigation systems with chemicals to prevent build-up of algae and bacterial slime may also be necessary.

With open channel systems regular inspections and treatments to combat disease vectors such as the snail vector of bilharzia and to control mosquito breeding should be carried out.

Plants

Plant treatments will again decrease as the plants mature, except in the case of annuals and annual agricultural and horticultural crops. The operations that will need to be carried out include weeding, feeding, spraying against pests and diseases, brashing, pruning, adjusting tree guards, thinning and replacing trees and shrubs and oversowing grass.

In arid areas, weed growth is normally low. But in semi-arid areas and in irrigated areas a major labour input for agriculture is weeding, particularly after the wet season. Hoeing is generally the best method although herbicides are used on pernicious, spreading weeds.

Nitrogen fertilizers will initially need to be applied during spring and autumn growth flushes. Rank, soft growth should be avoided, particularly during the hottest time of the year, when young shoots can die due to desiccation. Soft growth also attracts pests and diseases.

Specific nutrient deficiencies such as iron can be corrected by foliar feed. Crops such as citrus are very salt sensitive and require constant monitoring for nutrient deficiencies. Phosphates can be applied to the soil if needed. However, after the initial three years, recycling of nutrients and build-up of organic matter should necessitate only spot application of occasional nutrient deficiencies.

The most usual pests and diseases include leaf miner, hopper, sucker, white ants, nematodes, mildew and rotting of young seedlings. Sprays, as the attack is noticed and before pests build up, keep easy control. Most arid areas are too dry for feeding locusts, although mosquitoes should be checked in irrigated areas. Standing water should always be covered.

Adjustment of tree guards and staking will continue until trees are strong enough and old enough to need no assistance. Some indigenous plants require little assistance in this manner e.g. *Acacia tortilis*, *Tamarix* spp. *Casuarina* spp.

For trees where a straight trunk is required, lower branches will be trimmed off close to the trunk (brashing)—where a particular canopy shape is required, or to encourage fruiting, pruning is carried out.

Pruning should take place in the cool season when transpiration is low. There is no real dormant season, although growth rate is very slow in the really hot summer months. Transpiration is then too excessive for maintenance operations other than sand clearing and weeding. All wounds should be dressed (e.g. with 'Arbrex') to avoid excessive transpiration and penetration by insects or disease.

Thinning of shelter belts and urban planting at close spacing for an initial 'immediate effect' will be necessary as plant canopies begin to foul each other. Unsuitable plants can be replaced and more decorative species substituted in urban areas as the microclimate improves. As grass areas deteriorate, overseeding may be required to provide new greenery. Food crops will follow a pattern of rotation to maintain soil fertility and prevent build up of pests and diseases. Routine tasks of weeding, hoeing to maintain soil aeration and water penetration, harvesting, packing for market and re-sowing will be carried out from year to year.

Management programmes can be devised scheduling operations, irrigations and staffing over the years. Budgets for buildings, equipment and chemicals can be derived from these programmes in relation to the treatments to soil, water and plants envisaged in the long term.

Estimates of labour requirements for weeding, hoeing pruning, *etc.*, operations can be made for future years. Irrigation scheduling will change as plants get larger and require more water or establish themselves on the natural water table. Requirements for water, chemicals, machinery and equipment can be calculated. Financial returns are analysed yearly and adaptations made as necessary and depending on market or public demand.

An efficient maintenance programme for a new site can change a mediocre area into a site of green splendour. Experiments with new species will increase the knowledge and understanding of the site so that its capabilities can be fully realized.

NOTES

1 Burchell and Lisotkin. *The Environmental Handbook*. Rutgers University Press: 1975
2 Department of the Environment. *Environmental Impact Analysis*. HMSO: London 1977

Appendix 1
general vegetation groups

NORTH AFRICAN–ASIAN DESERTS

Sahara Desert

Essentially a desert of herbs and small shrubs, with larger shrubs and trees where moisture levels are higher. Ephemerals are common in the north, halophytes in the saline areas. Succulent plants are uncommon. A large part of the central Sahara has virtually no vegetation. With rain vegetation increases in wadis, depressions and wherever run-off water augments rainfall.

The soils of the Sahara are composed of rock debris, desert detritus, and weakly developed soils. In the extremely arid parts of the Sahara the surface rocks and sediments have been little altered by either vegetation or climate.

CHARACTERISTIC SPECIES

Acacia albida	*Nerium oleander*
A. raddiana	*Olea europea*
A. seyal	*Panicum turgidum*
A. tortilis	*Phoenix dactylifera*
Achillea santolina	*Populus euphratica*
Anabasis aretoides	*Prosopis stephaniana*
Aristida coerulescens	*Retama raetam*
A. pungens	*Rhus oxyacantha*
Artemisia herba-alba	*Rottboellia hirsuta*
A. monosperma	*Salsola foetida*
Astragalus tribuloides	*S. inermis*
Atriplex halimus	*Salvadora persica*
Balanites aegyptiaca	*Stipa tortilis*
Calligonum comosum	*Suaeda fruticosa*
Calotropis procera	*S. vermiculata*
Cenchrus ciliaris	*Tamarix articulata*
Citrullus colocynthis	*Zilla spinosa*
Danthonia forskalii	*Zizyphus lotus*
Ephedra alata	*Z. spina-christi*
Euphorbia guyonianum	*Zygophyllum coccineum*
Haloxylon articulatum	*Z. decumbens*
Limoniastrum guyonianum	*Z. dumosum*
Maerua crassifolia	

Arabian deserts

The same general type of vegetation found in the Sahara stretches eastwards into Arabia, central Asia and India. The northern part of Arabia is part of the Irano–Turanian phytogeographical region, while the southern section is in the Sudano–Deccanian. The former belongs to the cooler desert regions and the latter to the tropical deserts. In the north *Zygophyllum dumosum* is the key plant, with a number of winter annuals and some succulent perennials, while in the south the vegetation is largely ephemeral and grows only after rain. Perennials include many halophytes growing in saline soils, but there are almost no true succulents even in the Rub 'al Kali.

CHARACTERISTIC SPECIES

Acacia albida	*Lasiurus hirsutus*
A. raddiana	*Launea spinosa*
A. tortilis	*Lycium arabicum*
Achillea santolina	*Maerua crassifolia*
Aerva tomentosa	*Moringa aptera*
Alhagi maurorum	*Nerium oleander*
Anabasis articulata	*Olea europea*
Aristida coerulescens	*Panicum turgidum*
A. plumosa	*Phlomis brachyodon*
Artemisia herba-alba	*Phoenix dactylifera*
A. monosperma	*Pistacia atlantica*
Astragalus spinosus	*Poa bulbosa*
A. tribuloides	*Populus euphratica*
Atriplex halimus	*Prosopis stephaniana*
Balanites aegyptiaca	*Reaumuria hirtilla*
Calligonum comosum	*Retama raetam*
Calotropis procera	*Rumex roseus*
Capparis decidua	*Salsola foetida*
Carex stenophylla	*S. inermis*
Cassia obovata	*Salvadora persica*
Citrullus colocynthis	*Salvia aegyptiaca*
Cleome droserifolia	*Stipa tortilis*
Cyperus conglomeratus	*Suaeda fruticosa*
Danthonia forskalii	*S. vermiculata*
Ephedra alata	*Tamarix articulata*
Eragrostis binnata	*T. ramosissima*
Erodium hirtum	*Urtica urens*
Frankenia hirsuta	*Zilla spinosa*
Gymnarrhenia macrantha	*Zizyphus lotus*
Halocnemon strobilaceum	*Z. spina-christi*
Haloxylon articulatum	*Zygophyllum album*
H. persicum	*Z. dumosum*
H. salicornicum	*Z. simplex*

Iranian deserts

Very little is known about the Iranian deserts but their flora are influenced by the Irano–Turanian and Saharo–Sindian regions. In the west they are influenced by the Mediterranean climate. There are stony deserts, grey desert soils, sierozems and saline soils. Nearly all the soils are calcareous at the surface or in the subsoil. Some soil development is seen in the sierozems and in depressions. Most upland soils have no development. Sand dunes are common. The best soils for irrigation are the alluvial soils in the floodplains. There are halomorphic soils along the Arabian and Persian Gulfs, the Gulf of Oman and the Arabian Sea. The other characteristics of the Iranian desert soils are: coarse-textured, except in depressions, calcareous throughout the profile, deep except in broken land, alkaline, very low in organic matter, saline in depressions and frequently covered with desert pavement.

CHARACTERISTIC SPECIES

Alhagi camelorum	Pennisetum dichotomum
A. maurorum	Phoenix dactylifera
Amygdalus scoparia	Pistacia atlantica
Aristida plumosa	Poa bulbosa
Artemisia herba-alba	Populus euphratica
Calligonum comosum	Prosopis spicigera
Carex stenophylla	P. stephaniana
Cenchrus ciliaris	Prunus amygdalus
Cyperus conglomeratus	Salsola foetida
Danthonia forskalii	S. inermis
Eragrostis binnata	Salvia aegyptiaca
Frankenia hirsuta	Siedlitzia rosmarinus
Glycyrrhiza glabra	Stipa tortilis
Gymnarrhena macrantha	Suaeda fruticosa
Haloxylon articulatum	Tamarindus indica
H. persicum	Tamarix articulata
Juniperus excelsa	T. stricta
Lycium arabicum	Zizyphus spina-christi
Noaea mucronata	Zygophyllum coccineum
Panicum turgidum	

Thar Desert
The vegetation can be divided into five plant communities: salt desert, clay desert, stone desert, sand desert and riverside thickets. The desert lies at the eastern end of the Saharo–Sindian region. The plant communities vary distinctly on sand, gravel and rock areas. There is a greater average density of trees and shrubs than normally appears in the Saharo–Sindian region. The four predominant soil types are: deep saline fine-textured alluvium; sand dunefields; sand dunes and sandy soils interspersed with medium-textured saline alluvium; and medium-textured, often silty, alluvium of recent origin.

CHARACTERISTIC SPECIES

Aerva tomentosa	Crotallaria burhia
Astragalus tribuloides	Cymbopogon schoenanthus
Boerhaavia diffusa	Dalbergia sisoo
Calligonum polygonoides	Euphorbia nereifolia
Calotropis procera	Farsetia aegyptiaca
Capparis decidua	Gymnocarpus fruticosum
Cassia obovata	Haloxylon persicum
Cenchrus ciliaris	Heliotropium dasycarpum
Citrullus colocynthis	Hyoscyamus muticus
Cleome papillosa	Indigofera argentea

Leptadenia aerva	Suaeda fruticosa
Lycium arabicum	Tamarindus indica
Prosopis spicigera	Tamarix articulata
Salsola foetida	Zizyphus rotundifolia
Salvadora persica	Zygophyllum coccineum
Salvia aegyptiaca	Z. simplex

Turkestan Desert
The vegetation varies with soil conditions. The driest habitat is the clay desert where Poa bulbosa is the dominant plant in spring. The stone deserts are scantily covered with small shrubs. The salt areas have shallow water-tables and support few halophytic shrubs. The desert is a very large expanse of alluvial plains, sand dunes and denuded plateaux. Stony and gravelly soils are confined to the foothills of the south and east mountains. Extensive soils are sand dunes, loessial and alluvial plains, fine-textured depressions, river terraces or flood plains. Silt is widespread. The parent rocks of the sierozems belong to the calcite-quartzite group and the soils are rich in bases and plant nutrients. The soils are mainly medium-textured sierozems, sand dunes, shallow plateau soils, and medium-to-fine-textured takyrs and solonchaks. Salinity is problematical in takyrs, solonchaks, river deltas, and the Caspian coastal plains.

CHARACTERISTIC SPECIES

Agriophyllum arenarium	H. persicum
Agropyron sibiricum	Halophyllum obtusifolium
Alhagi camelorum	Heliotropium dasycarpum
Anabasis aphyllum	H. sogdanianum
A. brevifolium	Iris ensata
Aristida karelini	Lycium turcomanicum
A. pennata	Nitraria schoberi
Artemisia arenaria	Noaea spinosissima
A. ordosica	Poa bulbosa
Astragalus tribuloides	Populus alba
Atraphaxis compacta	P. diversifolia
Calligonum aphyllum	P. euphratica
C. arborescens	Prosopis stephaniana
C. comosum	Prunus amygdalus
Capparis decidua	Psammochloa villosa
C. spinosa	Reaumuria fruticosa
Caragana microphyllum	Salix caspica
C. stenophylla	Salsola arbuscula
Carex stenophylla	S. collina
Danthonia forskalii	S. laricifolia
Eleagnus angustifolia	S. praecox
Elymus giganteus	Stellaria lessertii
Ephedra alata	Stipa tortilis
Frankenia hirsuta	Tamarix hispida
Glycyrrhiza glabra	T. juniperina
Halocnemon strobilaceum	T. laxa
Halostachys caspica	T. ramosissima
Haloxylon ammodendron	Thermopsis lanceolata
H. aphyllum	

Takla-makan Desert
The vegetation grows lushly along the streams but elsewhere it is sparse, herbaceous plants on low moisture soils, and scanty woody vegetation in the stabilised dunes.

Halophytes are found in old valleys, lake depressions and river deltas.

The central portion of the Takla-makan Desert is an enormous area of shifting sands, moving southwards. Several large rivers flow in from the Tien Shan and Kunlun Shan Mountains on the north, north-west and south-west borders. Soils are coarse-textured sand, and gravelly with surface stones in the foothills and on the slopes, sandy to medium-textured alluvial fans, fine alluvium in the flood-plains, and sand dunes in the centre. Soils generally are deep, except near the mountains and low in organic matter. Calcareous soils are probably found on the gravelly and medium-textured soils. Soil salinity is a widespread problem.

CHARACTERISTIC SPECIES

Agriophyllum arenarium	*Lycium turcomanicum*
Alhagi camelorum	*Nitraria schoberi*
Allium mongolicum	*N. sibirica*
A. polyrrhizum	*N. sphaerocephala*
Anabasis aphylla	*Noaea spinosissima*
A. brevifolia	*Populus diversifolia*
Artemisia caespitosa	*P. prunosa*
A. frigida	*Psammochloa villosa*
A. incana	*Salsola arbuscula*
Calligonum aphyllum	*S. collina*
C. mongolicum	*S. laricifolia*
Caragana bingei	*S. praecox*
C. pygmaea	*Stipa bungeana*
Carex stenophylla	*S. gobica*
Echinopsilon divaricatum	*Sympegma regellii*
Eleagnus angustifolia	*Tamarix chilensis*
Ephedra przewalskii	*T. hispida*
Halocnemon strobilaceum	*T. juniperina*
Halostachys caspica	*T. laxa*
Haloxylon ammodendron	*Tanacetum fruticosum*
H. persicum	*Ulmus pumila*
Horaninovia ulicina	*Zygophyllum kaschgaricum*
Kalidium caspicum	*Z. xanthoxylon*
K. cuspidatum	

Gobi Desert

The western floral affiliations dominate the eastern influences in the Gobi Desert. The plains have shrubs and semi-shrubs. Unstabilised dunes support grasses and widely-spaced shrubs, and where stabilised they support the best plant cover, provided there is a water-table which can be tapped. The desert is characterised by sequences of mountains, gravelly and stony foothills, plains and gentle slopes, and depressions. Sand dunes are extensive but less so than in the Takla-makan. Skeletal soils cover 25% of the Gobi Desert surface, brown gobi soils 40%, salt and sodium-affected soils 25%, and sand dunes 5%. The soils are loams, with gravel and stone, shallow with lime accumulations near the surface; non-saline, gypsiferous, coarse-textured deep and brown soils; solonchaks in enclosed depressions which are fine- to medium-textured; sodium saline takyrs without crusts in depressions; sodium-affected solonetz soils on slopes of large depressions and in the plains; and sandy soils and sand dunes on the plains, gentle slopes, rivers valleys and lake basins.

CHARACTERISTIC SPECIES

Agriophyllum arenarium	*Iris ensata*
Agropyron sibericum	*Lycium turcomanicum*
Amygdalus mongolica	*Morus alba*
Anabasis brevifolia	*Nitraria schoberi*
Aristida adscensionis	*N. sibirica*
Artemisia frigida	*N. sphaerocephala*
A. halodendron	*Peucedanum rigidum*
A. ordosica	*Populus diversifolia*
Calligonum arborescens	*Potaninia mongolica*
C. caput-medusae	*Potentilla mongolica*
C. mongolicum	*Reaumuria soongarica*
Caragana korshinskii	*Salix flavida*
C. microphylla	*S. mongolica*
C. tibetica	*Salsola arbuscula*
Carex physodes	*S. collina*
Caryopteris mongolica	*S. passera*
Eleagnus angustifolia	*S. praecox*
Ephedra distachya	*Stipa bungeana*
Euratia ceratoides	*S. gobica*
Haloxylon ammodendron	*Tamarix ramosissima*
H. aphyllum	*T. mongolica*
H. persicum	*Ulmus pumila*
Hedysarum scoparium	*Zygophyllum xanthoxylon*

Somali–Chalbi Desert

The vegetation resembles that of the southern Sahara and southern Arabia. Sparse vegetation is associated with rainfall of less than 100 mm, and widely-spaced herbs, grasses, sub-shrubs and dwarf trees are found in favourable locations. Scrub and tree savannahs are achieved when rainfall exceeds 200 mm. The soils are generally primitive, with some reddish soils on the Kenya–Somalia border. Deeper soils of clay pans are found in the uplands near rivers, and these are deeply calcareous, medium-to-fine-textured, moderately alkaline with some saline alluvium. In Djibouti, crystalline and calcareous soils are found, with some stony plains. Semi-arid soils are seen in the main plain and along the Indian Ocean coast. Somali soils are calcareous and gypsiferous, primitive, and often saline. Sand dunes are restricted to the coastal areas alongside the Indian Ocean. A large salt pan is found west of the Danakil mountains.

CHARACTERISTIC SPECIES

Acacia asak	*Atriplex halimus*
A. benadirensis	*A. farinosa*
A. etbaica	*Avicennia marina*
A. mellifera	*Balanites aegyptiaca*
A. nilotica	*B. racemosa*
A. seyal	*Barleria acanthoides*
Abutilon fruticosum	*Boscia minimifolia*
Acalypha fruticosa	*Boswellia freereana*
Adansonia digitata	*Brewia fastigiata*
Aerva tomentosa	*Cadaba mirabilis*
Albizzia amara	*Calotropis procera*
Aloe abyssinica	*Capparis aphylla*
A. somalense	*C. spinosa*
A. trichosantha	*Caralluma speciosa*
Aristida adscensionis	*Cassia obovata*
Arthrocnemum glaucum	*Cenchrus ciliaris*

Ceropegia subaphylla
Chloris virgata
Chrysopogon aucheri
   var. *quinqueplumis*
Cissus quadrangularis
Cleome scaposa
Coleus ignarius
Combretum collinum
Commiphora erithraea
Croton somalensis
Cymbopogon schoenanthus
Cynodon plechtostachyum
Dalbergia commiphoroides
Delonix elata
Enneapogon cenchroidoides
Eragrostis hararensis
Euphorbia luneata
Ficus sycomorus
Grewia tenax
Hyparrhenia hirta
Hypheane thebaica

Ipomoea pes-capre
Jatropha obdiadensis
Lasiurus hirsutus
Lavandula pubescens
Maerua crassifolia
Panicum turgidum
Pennisetum divisum
Peucedanum fraxinifolium
Phoenix dactylifera
Salsola foetida
Salvadora persica
Sporobolus longibrachiatus
Sterculia rivae
Suaeda fruticosa
Tamarindus indica
Terminalia brownei
Thespesia danis
Tribulus terrestris
Zizyphus spina-christi
Zygophyllum simplex

Sarcocaulon burmanii
Suaeda fruticosa
Tamarix articulata

Welwitschia mirabilis
Zygophyllum simplex
Z. stapfii

AUSTRALIAN DESERTS

The Australian deserts have no succulents, and very few spiny plants. The most common plants are the perennial evergreen spinifex (tussocky) grasses, small trees and shrubs (*Acacia* being the dominant genus). The *Chenopodiaceae* family are characteristic of the depression and saline soils. The soils are similar to other arid territories, except that sand dunes are limited in extent and are fixed by a fairly dense vegetation cover. The important soils are: coarse-textured and deep brown soils, red and brown hard pan soils, deep red earths of medium-to-fine texture, and sodium and saline soils. Extensive silcretions are found. There are calcareous soils on the less arid fringes and acidic soils in the interior. The stony tablelands, resembling regs and hamadas, are covered with broken silcrete or silified stones, and the soils are calcareous, gypsiferous or saline. The sand plains are extensive in central and northern Australia, occupying gently-sloping land, and contain fossil lateritic ironstone gravels. The sand dunes are found on the plains and are only problematical if disturbed. The coarse-textured brown soils are scattered over the semi-arid region in southern Australia and at higher elevations. The grey-brown fine-textured soils are found in the north-eastern and semi-arid zones, and in south-western Australia. Salt and sodium-affected soils are common.

SOUTH AFRICAN DESERTS

Kalahari–Namib

The vegetation of the Kalahari is dominated by Acacia species, both trees and large shrubs, and perennial and annual grasses in the north. In the south, there are low scattered shrubs, with a few Acacia species along any water courses and grass in the rainier years. The Namib has very little vegetation. The disposition and spacing of plants emphasises the use they make of condensed moisture, especially from the radiation fogs. In the inner Namib, a short grass grows, following the rainier summers. The Kalahari Desert is covered with coarse-textured materials with calcrete either exposed or covered with a thin layer of sand. In the north, ferruginous tropical soils are found and silcrete is widely seen. The soils are all weakly developed, and with the exception of the Great Western Escarpment, the entire region is a plain broken by shifting sand dunes in the south of the Namib. They are alkaline to slightly acid, lower in organic matter in the south than in the north. The textures are sand, sandy loam, gravelly sandy loam, clay or clay loam.

CHARACTERISTIC SPECIES

Acacia albida
A. karroo
Aizoon dinteri
Aloe dichotoma
Aristida brevifolia
Boscia albitrunca
Ceraria namaquensis
Citrullus vulgaris
Combretum primigenum
Cotyledon jasicularia
Cyperus conglomeratus
Distichlis scoparia
Eragrostis cyperoides
E. spinosa

Euclea pseudebenus
Euphorbia antisiphylitica
E. dregeana
E. echinus
E. mauritanica
Galenia africana
Lycium arenicolum
Mesembryanthemum spinosum
Nymania capensis
Pappea capensis
Pentzia incana
Phaeoptilum spinosum
Phragmites trichotomum
Salsola aphylla

CHARACTERISTIC SPECIES

Acacia brachystachya
A. cambagei
A. pendula
Aristida browniana
A. inaequiglumis
Astrebla elymoides
A. squarrosa
Atriplex nummularia
A. vesicaria
Boerhaavia diffusa
Calotis hispidula
Cassia eremophila
Casuarina cristata
C. lepidophloia
Chenopodium auricomum
Chloris acicularis
Dodonea viscosa
Enneapogon avenaceus
E. polyphyllus
Eragrostis eriopoda
E. setifolia

Eremophila maculata
Eucalyptus camaldulensis
E. microtheca
Eulalia fulvia
Grevillea striata
Hakea intermedia
Indigophera enneaphylla
Kochia aphylla
K. sedifolia
Myoporum platycarpum
Pittosporum phillyraeoides
Plechtrachne schinzii
Ptilotus polystachyus
Senecio gregorii
Stenopetalum nutans
Themeda australis
Tribulus terrestris
Triodia basedowii
T. pungens
Ventilago viminalis
Zygochloa paradoxa

NORTH AMERICAN DESERTS

There are two general types of vegetation: the sagebrush and the saltbush in the cooler portions, and mixed shrubs and succulents in the warmer. The saltbush are found at low elevations and on alkaline soils. The southern deserts are dominated by creosote bush. The community boundaries are determined by changes in soil conditions and the variable topography. The soils found most widely are the sierozems, lithosols, red desert soils, regosols and alluvial soils. Other soil groups include the red desert, grey desert, calcisol, solonchak, and solonetz soils. The semi-arid soils are brown, reddish-brown chestnut, and red chestnut. The sequence of soils is lithosols on mountains, medium- to coarse-textured red desert, desert or sierozems on alluvial fans and terraces, and alluvial solonchak, and solonetz in valleys. The red desert soils are found in the hottest parts of the arid region, sierozems in the cooler, grey desert soils in the transitional zones between them. The alluvial soils of recent history are found in California, and the sierozems in Sonora, Sinaloa and Baja California.

CHARACTERISTIC SPECIES

Acacia constricta	*J. spathulata*
A. greggii	*Kochia vestita*
A. paucispina	*Koeberlinia spinosa*
Agropyron spicatum	*Larrea divaricata*
Allenrolfia occidentalis	*Lemairocereus thurberi*
Aristida adscensionis	*Lophocereus schottii*
A. californica	*Lycium brevipes*
Artemisia tridentata	*Olneya tesota*
Atriplex canescens	*Opuntia cholla*
A. polycarpa	*O. fulgida*
Bouteloua simplex	*O. versicolor*
Bursera microphylla	*Pachycereus pringlei*
Celtis pallida	*Panicum obtusum*
Cercidium sonorae	*Parkinsonia aculeata*
Cereus giganteus	*Pinus monophylla*
Dalea scoparia	*Prosopis chilensis*
Dodonea viscosa	*Rhus microphylla*
Encelia farinosa	*Salicornia rubra*
Ephedra nevadensis	*Simmondsia californica*
Eschscholtzia mexicana	*Sporobolus airoides*
Euphorbia beaumierana	*S. chrysophylla*
Eurotia lanata	*Stipa speciosa*
Fouquieria splendens	*Tillandsia recurvata*
Franseria deltoidea	*Washingtonia filifera*
Hilaria jamesii	*Yucca brevifolia*
Ipomoea arborescens	*Y. elata*
Jatropha cordata	

SOUTH AMERICAN DESERTS

Monte–Patagonian Desert

Much of the Monte–Patgonian desert region is covered with resinous bushes with *Zygophyllaceae* dominating. Many species are wholly or partly leafless. Trees border rivers to form gallery forests, and perennial grasses are restricted to the moister locations. The vegetation of Patagonia is of widely-spaced xerophytic grasses and low cushion-like shrubs. The Monte desert region is found in the rain shadow of the Andes and the Patagonian, to the south, is composed of predominantly low table-lands. Soil development is weak, in the pampas and chaquene areas, shallow calcretions are common. Soil salinity is a problem, because high water-tables have developed from heavy irrigation. Mountain and hill soils are lithosols much

eroded, leaving a small amount of fine material and shallow stony soils. Footslopes grade from coarse-down to medium-texture, and soils of the red desert groups occur in the broad plains. Some sand dunes are found. Valley soils vary between sand and gravel and are alkaline, normally calcareous with concretions. Halomorphic soils are in enclosed basins and soils of salinas are deep, fine-textured calcareous and low in organic matter. The Patagonian plains have desert soils, or cemented gravels. They are medium-textured, moderately acidic, with a high organic matter content. Recent alluvial deposits are found along rivers and in depressions, and low soils tend to be marshy.

CHARACTERISTIC SPECIES

Acacia aroma	*L. divaricata*
A. furcatispina	*L. tridentata*
Adesmia campestris	*Lycium chilense*
A. hemisphaerica	*Muehlenbeckia cunninghamii*
Aphyllocladus spartioides	*Nassauvia maxillaris*
Aristida adscensionis	*Neosparton ephedroides*
A. humilis	*Opuntia glomerata*
Azorella compacta	*O. pampeana*
Begonia octopetalla	*Oxalis bryoides*
Berberis cuneata	*Panicum urvilleanum*
Bouteloua lophostachya	*Phacelia magellanica*
Bromus brevis	*Plectrocarpa tetracantha*
Calliguaya integerrima	*Poa ligularis*
Carex andina	*Portulaca rotundifolia*
Cassia aphylla	*Prosopidastrum globosum*
C. cassiramea	*Prosopis alba*
Cercidium australis	*P. alpataco*
Chuquiraga avellanedae	*P. argentina*
Condalia microphylla	*P. chilensis*
Danthonia picta	*P. torquata*
Elymus patagonica	*Pterocactus tuberosus*
Empetrum rubrum	*Salicornia ambigua*
Euphorbia portulacoides	*Salix humboldtiana*
Fabiana bryoides	*Schinus polygamus*
F. patagonica	*Sporobolus pyramidalis*
Festuca gracillima	*Stipa chrysophylla*
Geoffreya decorticans	*Suaeda divaricata*
Glycyrrhiza astragaline	*S. patagonica*
Halophytum ameghinoi	*Tillandsia xiphioides*
Hordeum comosum	*Verbena aphylla*
Hyalis argentea	*V. tridens*
Ipomoea minuta	*Zizyphus mistol*
Larrea ameghinoi	

Atacama–Peruvian Desert

The whole desert is virtually without vegetation, except along streams, or where the hill slopes are moistened by mist or drizzle in winter. The mist-covered lomas slopes occasionally support ephemerals. There are three significant soils: skeletal mountain and plain soils, recent river alluvial soils, and old lake soils. The sequence is: lithosols on the Andes, colluvial soils on the footslopes of gravel and rock debris, coarse-textured weakly developed soils on the central plains, and the regosols on the marine terraces which are coarse- to medium-textured. Saline soils are found in river valleys and sand dunes and alluvial fans are found at the mouths of the streams. Alluvial soils range in texture and depth from shallow coarse-textured soils near the mountains to deep fine-textured soils near the sea. They are neutral to alkaline, containing soluble salts, gypsum and calcium carbonate. Red desert soils are usually fine-textured, deep, moderately well-drained, and have lime concretions. The dark grey secondary soils are deep, plastic clays of high alkalinity and low permeability.

CHARACTERISTIC SPECIES

Acacia macrantha	*Muehlenbergia fastigiata*
Alstroemeria recumbens	*Opuntia ficus-indica*
Aristida adscensionis	*O. nigrispina*
Astragalus arequipensis	*Oreocereus trollii*
Azorella compacta	*Oxalis solarensis*
Bouteloua simplex	*Pennisetum chinense*
B. palmata	*Phacelia pinnatifida*
Caesalpinia tinctoria	*Plantago monticola*
Cercidium praecose	*Prosopis chilensis*
Cereus candelaris	*P. ferox*
C. macrostibas	*P. limensis*
Chenopodium guinoa	*Puya tuberosa*
Crassula cosmantha	*Salicornia pulvinata*
Cressa truxillensis	*Salix humboldtiana*
Dioscorea chancayensis	*Schinus molle*
Ephedra americana	*Solanum acaule*
E. multiflora	*Sporobolus virginicus*
Fabiana bryoides	*Stipa chrysophylla*
Festuca australis	*S. leptostachya*
Franseria fruticosa	*Trichocereus pasacana*
Geoffreya decorticans	*Tropaeolum minus*
Heliotropium curassavicum	*Urtica urens*

Note: The preceding plant lists are by no means exhaustive, and serve merely to indicate the *range* of plants to be found in each region. Also, there is no distinction of phytogeographical influences.

Abridged from *Deserts of the World* (University of Arizona Press, 1968) and *Plant Ecology* (Vol. VI, Arid Zone Research, © Unesco, 1955)

Appendix 2 plant selection

2.1 THE SELECTION OF PLANTS FOR CENTRAL SAUDI ARABIA

The purpose of the following lists of plants is to define a range of species, based on one phytogeographical region. A list of possible plant introductions is also given that might be considered provided soil conditions, climate and water availability are not limiting. Whenever a final plant list is compiled, it is essential that all the environmental factors and the restrictions they might impose are analysed beforehand.

Phytogeographical zone: Saharo–Sindian

INDIGENOUS TREES

Acacia albida	*Pistacia atlantica*
A. arabica	*Prosopis cinerea*
A. gerradii	*P. juliflora*
A. giraffae	*P. spicigera*
A. gummifera	*P. stephaniana*
A. mellifera	*Salvadora oleoides*
A. nilotica	*S. persica*
A. raddiana	*Schinus terebinthifolius*
A. senegal	*Tamarix aphylla*
A. seyal	*T. articulata*
A. tortilis	*T. gallica*
Albizzia julibrissim	*T. ramosissima*
A. lebbek	*T. passerinoides*
Eugenia jambolana	*T. stricta*
Eleagnus angustifolia	*Terminalia catappa*
Ficus bengalensis	*T. bellerica*
F. benjamina	*Thespesia populnea*
F. retusa nitida	*Vitex agnus-castus*
F. religiosa	*Zizyphus jujuba*
Maerua crassifolia	*Z. lotus*
Melia azedarach	*Z. mauretania*
Moringa aptera	*Z. spina-christi*
Phoenix dactylifera	

TREE INTRODUCTIONS

Acacia cyanophylla	*Casuarina cristata*
A. farnesiana	*C. cunninghamiana*
Albizzia chinensis	*C. equisetifolia*
Anona cherimifolia	*C. glauca*
Brachychiton acerifolia	*C. lehmanii*
B. gregorii	*C. stricta*
Callistemon citrinus	*C. torrulosa*
C. lanceolatus	*Cupressus arizonica*

Delonix regia	*E. redunea*
Duranta plumieri	*E. salubris*
Eucalyptus astringens	*E. sargentii*
E. brockwayi	*E. spathulata*
E. camaldulensis	*E. stricklandii*
E. campaspe	*E. transcontinentalis*
E. cladocalyx	*E. woodwardii*
E. coolabah	*Ficus carica*
E. forrestiana	*F. sycomorus*
E. gomphocephala	*Grevillea robusta*
E. intertexta	*Hypheane thebaica*
E. kruscana	*Jacaranda mimosaefolia*
E. landsdowneana	*Melaleuca pauperifolia*
E. largiflorens	*Parkinsonia aculeata*
E. longicornis	*Prosopis chilensis*
E. microtheca	*P. tamarugo*
E. patellaris	*Schinus molle*
E. pimpiniana	*Washingtonia filifera*
E. robusta	

INDIGENOUS SHRUBS AND GROUND COVER PLANTS

Achillea fragrantissima	*E. guyonianum*
A. santolina	*E. mauritanica*
Anabasis articulata	*E. nereifolia*
A. setifera	*Genista saharae*
Artemisia herba-alba	*Haloxylon aphyllum*
A. monosperma	*H. articulatum*
Atriplex halimus	*H. persicum*
Balanites aegyptiaca	*H. salicornicum*
Caesalpinia gilliesii	*Heliotropium dasycarpum*
C. pulcherrima	*Ipomoea pes-capre*
Calligonum arborescens	*Iris sisyrinchium*
C. comosum	*Lagerstroemia indica*
Calotropis procera	*Launea spinosa*
Capparis decidua	*Leptadenia pyrotechnica*
C. spinosa	*Limoniastrum guyonianum*
Carex physodes	*L. monopetalum*
Cassia lanceolata	*Lycium arabicum*
C. obovata	*L. persicum*
Clerodendrum inerme	*Monsonia nivea*
Coronilla juncea	*Nerium oleander*
Cyperus conglomeratus	*Phlomis brachyodon*
C. laevigatus	*Plumeria acutifolia*
Dodonea viscosa	*P. rubra*
Ephedra alata	*Punica granatum*
E. distachya	*Retama raetam*
Euphorbia ceratoides	*Rhanterium epapposum*

Rhus oxyacantha
Salsola tetrandra
Salvia aegyptiaca
S. lanigera
Sesbania aegyptiaca
Siedlitzia rosmarinus
Tecoma stans

Tecomaria capensis
Thevetia nereifolia
Zilla macroptera
Z. spinosa
Zygophyllum coccineum
Z. dumosum

SHRUB AND GROUND COVER PLANT INTRODUCTIONS

Allamanda cathartica
Aloe spp.
Arundo donax
Atriplex nummularia
Bougainvillea spectabilis
Carpobrotus acinaciformis
C. edulis
Hibiscus rosa-sinensis
H. syriacus
Iris spp.
Jasminum arabicum
Lantana camara

Lavandula spica
L. stoechas
Lippia citriodora
Myoporum spp.
Myrtus communis
Pistacia lentiscus
P. vera
Plumbago capensis
Polygonum capitatum
Rosa spp.
Santolina chamaecyparissus
Yucca gloriosa

2.2 THE SELECTION OF SUCCULENT PLANTS FOR CENTRAL SAUDI ARABIA

Reference: Herman Jacobsen: *Handbook of Succulent Plants*, Blandford Press, London 1960

Saharo–Sindian zone

Aeonium leucoblepharum
Aloe eru
A. inermis
A. pendens
A. rubroviolacea
A. sabacea
A. tomentosa
A. vacillans
Caralluma adensis
C. anemoniflora
C. arabica
C. chrysostephana
C. cicatricosa
C. commutata
C. flava
C. luntii
C. penicilliata
C. quadrangula
C. subulata
Ceropegia rupicola
Echidnopsis bentii
E. planiflora
E. scutellata
Euphorbia ammak
E. cactus
E. fruticosa
E. inarticulata
E. parciramulosa
Euphorbia tenuirama

E. tenuirama
Huernia macrocarpa var. arabica
Kalanchoe teretifolia
Opophytum forskhali
Rosularia haussknechtii
R. lineata
R. parviflora
R. persica
R. sempervivum
Sedum acre spp. neglectum
S. album
S. alpestre
S. bornmulleri
S. littoreum
S. lydium
S. microcarpum
S. obtusifolium
S. palaestinum
S. pilosum
S. sanguineum
S. tenuifolium
Sempervivum iranicum
Senecio anteuphorium var. odorus
S. pendulus
Suaeda fruticosa
Umbilicus intermedius
U. rupestris

Sudano–Deccanian Zone

Aloe perryi
A. tomentosa
A. vacillans
Caralluma adensis
C. anemoniflora
C. arabica
C. cicatricosa
C. penicilliata
C. quadrangula
C. socotrana
C. subulata
Cotyledon barleyi
Edithcolea sordida
Euphorbia arbuscula

E. fruticosa
E. inarticulata
E. parciramulosa
E. schimperi
E. spiralis
Kalanchoe abrupta
K. citrina
K. laciniata
K. robusta
K. rotundiflora
K. scapigera
Senecio anteuphorbium
S. pendulus

2.3 SELECTION OF PLANTS ACCORDING TO SALINITY TOLERANCE

Reference: R. Firmin *Afforestation*, Report to the Government of Kuwait, FAO, Rome 1971

Electrical conductivity in micromhos	Plant species
50,000+	*Avicennia marina, Nitraria retusa, Prosopis juliflora* (Kuwait strain), *Suaeda vermiculata, Zygophyllum coccineum*
40,000	*Casuarina glauca, Conocarpus lanciformis, Phoenix dactylifera, Tamarix maris-mortui, T. passerinoides*
35,000	*Atriplex nummularia, A. vesicaria, Juncus actutus, Prosopis stephaniana, P. tamarugo, Tamarix arvensis, T. deserti, T. dioica, T. florida, T. mannifera, T. meyeri, T. orientalis, T. pentandra*
30,000	*Acacia ligulata, Casuarina equisetifolia, Kochia indica, Phragmites communis, Prosopis juliflora, Tamarix aphylla, Zizyphus vulgaris*
25,000	*Acacia sowdenii, Tamarix nilotica,*
18,000	*Acacia pendula, A. salicina, Casuarina glauca, Eucalyptus camaldulensis, E. sargentii, E. spathulata, Nerium oleander, Parkinsonia aculeata*
16,000	*Acacia farnesiana, A. salicina, Callistemon lanceolatus, Casuarina cristata, C. stricta, Eucalyptus calcicultrix, E. camaldulensis* var. *obtusa, E. coolabah, E. microtheca, Prosopis chilensis, P. juliflora* var. *velutina*
14,000	*Acacia arabica, Albizzia chinensis, Casuarina lehmanii, Clerodendrum inerme, Eucalyptus pimpiniana, Haloxylon salicornicum, Sesbania grandiflora*
12,000	*Acacia stenophylla, Nassia latifolia, Callitris glauca, Dodonea viscosa, Eucalyptus kruscana, Melaleuca pauperifolia, Melia azederach, Punica granatum, Thevetia nereifolia*
10,000	*Albizzia lebbek, Butea monosperma, Eucalyptus annulata, E. brachycorys, E. cornuta, E. melliodora, E. occidentalis, E. stricklandi, Ficus carica, F. religiosa, Hakea laurina, Lagenaria pattersoni, Ricinus communis* var. *persicus, Salvadora oleoides, Thespesia populnea, Vitex agnus-castus*
8,500	*Caesalpinia gilliesii, Calligonum comosum, Casuarina cunninghamiana, Dalbergia sissoo, Dodonea attenuata, Eucalyptus cladocalyx, E. forestiana, E. grossa, E. lansdowneana, E.*

	largiflorens, E. Le Soueffi, E. robusta, E. salubris, E. spathulata, Inga dulcis, Terminalia arjuna
8,000	*Brachychiton gregorii, Eucalyptus brockwayi, E. dundasi, E. intertexta, E. woodwardii, Ficus bengalensis, Myrtus communis, Prosopis spicigera, Schinus molle, Terminalia catappa*
6,000	*Acacia deani, A. saligna, Agonis flexuosa, Balanites aegyptiaca, Cupressus arizonica, Euclayptus oleosa, E. torquata, Grevillea robusta, Olea europea, Pritchardii filifera, Tamarindus indica, Tecoma stans*
5,000	*Cordia myxa, Cupressus sempervirens* var. *stricta, Elaeagnus angustifolia, Eucalyptus astringens, E. campaspe, E. longicornis, E. redunea, E. transcontinentalis, Lantana aculeata, Populus euphratica, Terminalia belerica*
4,500	*Bombax malabaricum, Eucalyptus citriodora, Populus bolleana*
3,000	*Acacia tortilis, Albizzia julibrissim, Ficus sycomorus, Robinia pseudoacacia, Salix alba*
2,500	*Acacia cyanophylla, A. cyclopis, A. mellifera, A. raddiana, A. forestiana, A. gerradii*
2,000	*Eucalyptus tereticornis, Hypheane thebaica, Poinciana (Delonix) regia, Duranta plumieri, Populus oblega*
1,000	*Azalea* spp., *Bougainvillea* spp., *Populus euramerica, P. thevestina*

2.4 RELATIVE TOLERANCE OF CROP PLANTS TO SALT

Reference: *Saline and Alkali Soils*, U.S. Salinity Lab., 1969

High salt tolerance	Medium salt tolerance	Low salt tolerance
Fruit crops		
EC=12,000+	EC=12,000	EC=4,000
Date palm	Pomegranate	Pear
	Fig	Apple
	Olive	Orange
	Grape	Grapefruit
	Cantaloup	Prune
		Plum
		Almond
		Apricot
		Peach
		Strawberry
		Lemon
		Avocado
	EC=4,000	EC=2,000
Vegetable crops		
EC=12,000	EC=10,000	EC=4,000
Garden beets	Tomato	Radish
Kale	Broccoli	Celery
Asparagus	Cabbage	Green Beans
Spinach	Bell pepper	
	Cauliflower	
	Lettuce	
	Sweet Corn	
	Potatoes (white Rose)	
	Carrot	
	Onion	
	Peas	
	Squash	
	Cucumber	
EC=10,000	EC=4,000	EC=3,000

High salt tolerance	Medium salt tolerance	Low salt tolerance
Forage crops		
EC=18,000	EC=12,000	EC=4,000
Alkali sacaton	White sweetclover	White Dutch clover
Saltgrass	Yellow sweetclover	Meadow foxtail
Nuttall alkaligrass	Perennial ryegrass	Alsike clover
Bermuda grass	Mountain brome	Red clover
Rhodes grass	Strawberry clover	Ladino clover
Rescue grass	Dallis grass	Burnet
Canada wildrye	Sudan grass	
Western wheatgrass	Hubam clover	
Barley (hay)	Alfalfa (California Common)	
Birdsfoot trefoil	Tall fescue	
	Rye (hay)	
	Wheat (hay)	
	Oats (hay)	
	Orchardgrass	
	Blue grama	
	Meadow fescue	
	Reed canary	
	Big trefoil	
	Smooth brome	
	Tall meadow oatgrass	
	Cicer milkvetch	
	Sourclover	
	Sickle milkvetch	
EC=12,000	EC=4,000	EC=2,000
Field crops		
EC=16,000	EC=10,000	EC=4,000
Barley (grain)	Rye (grain)	Field beans
Sugar beet	Wheat (grain)	
Rape	Oats (grain)	
Cotton	Rice	
	Sorghum (grain)	
	Cord (field)	
	Flax	
	Sunflower	
	Castorbeans	
EC=10,000	EC=6,000	

The numbers following EC are the electrical conductivity values of the saturation extract in micromhos per centimetre at 25°C associated with 50% decrease in yield.

2.5 RELATIVE TOLERANCE OF PLANTS TO BORON

Reference: *Saline and Alkali Soils*, U.S. Salinity Lab., 1969

Tolerant	Semi-tolerant	Sensitive
Athel (*Tamarix Aphylla*)	Sunflower (Native)	Pecan
Asparagus	Potato	Black walnut
Palm (*Phoenix canariensis*)	Acala cotton	Persian (English) walnut
Date palm (*P. dactylifera*)	Pima cotton	Jerusalem artichoke
Sugar beet	Tomato	Navy bean
Mangel	Sweetpea	American elm
Garden beet	Radish	Plum
Alfalfa	Field pea	Pear
Gladiolus	Ragged Robin rose	Apple
Broadbean	Olive	Grape (Sultanina and Malaga)
Onion	Barley	Kadota fig
Turnip	Wheat	Persimmon
Cabbage	Corn	Cherry
Lettuce	Milo	Peach
Carrot	Oat	Apricot
	Zinnia	Thornless blackberry
	Pumpkin	Orange
	Bell pepper	Avacoado
	Sweet potato	Grapefruit
	Lima bean	Lemon

(In each group the plants first named are considered as being more tolerant and the last named more sensitive.)

2.6 TOLERANCE TO SALINE WATER

Salinity ppm.	
15,000	sheep on green grass
12,000	sheep on dry feed
10,000	septic systems, station cattle
8,000	non-working horses travelling cattle, man for short periods
6,000	working horses, dairy cattle
4,000	showers with salt water soap
3,000	man and poultry—limit for most agricultural crops
1,000	practically all plants

Appendix 3
plant species

3.1 'C₄' PLANTS

Reference: *Annual Reports of the Director of the Department of Plant Biology*, Carnegie Institute, Stanford, California, USA 1973–74, and 1974–75

Atriplex argentea
A. bunchanii
A. lentiformis
A. nummularia
A. patulata
A. polycarpa
A. rosea
A. sabulosa
A. sereneus
A. spongiosa
Cenchrus calyculatus
C. ciliaris
Chloris guyana
C. ventricosa
C. virgata
Cymbopogon refractus
Cynodon dactylon
Cyperus eragrostis
C. rotundus
C. ustulatus
Digitaria sanguinalis
Drosanthemum floribundum
Echinochloa crus-galli
E. frumentacea
Euphorbia atoto
E. atrococca
E. ciusiaefolia
E. celastroides
E. degeneri
E. forbesii
E. hillebrandtii
E. hookeri
E. multiformis
E. olowalauna
E. remyi
E. rockii
E. skottsbergii
E. taitensis
Eragrostis cilianensis
E. parviflora
Gomphrena globosa

Imperata chesemanii
I. cilindrica
Panicum coloratum
Paspalum dilatum
P. distichum
P. notatum
P. paspaloides
P. pumilum
P. vaginatum
Pennisetum clandestinum
P. maeruorum
Perotis rara
Poellnitzia rubrifolia
Portulaca grandiflora
P. oleracea
Saccharum italica
Sedum acre
Setaria italica
S. sphacelata
S. viridis
Sorghum halepensis
S. vulgare
Spinifex hirsutus
Sporobolus elongatus
Stenotaphrum secundatum
Suaeda inermis
S. taxifolia ssp. brevifolia
S. torreyana
Tridestromia oblongifolia
Theleophytum billardieri
Zea mays
Zoisya minima
Zygocactus truncatus

3.2 CAM PLANT SPECIES

Reference: Szarek and Tiṅg, 1977

AGAVACEAE
Agave americana
A. shawii
A. lurida
Yucca baccata
Y. filmentosa
Y. whipplei

AIZOACEAE
Aptenia cordifolia
Bergeranthus multiceps
Carpobrotus edulis
Conophytum flanum
Drossanthemum floribundum
Faucaria spp.
Lithops insularis
L. salicola
L venteri
Mesembryanthemum chilense
M. crystallinum
M. nodiflorum
Tetragonia fruticosa
Titanopsis calcarea
Trichodeadema barbatum

ASCLEPIADACEAE
Caralluma negevensis
Hoya carnosa
Stapelia nobilis
S. variegata
S. semota

ASTERACEAE
Aster tripolium
Kleinia articulata
K. radicans
K. repens
K. tomentosa
Notonia petraea
Senecio cephalopherus

S. gregori
S. herreianus

BROMELIACEAE
Acanthostachys strobilacea
Aechmea bromeliaefolia
A. distichantha
A marmorata
A nudicaulis
Aechmea pectinata
A. tillandsoides
Ananas ananassoides
A. comosus
A. sativus
Araeocassus flagellifolius
Billbergia amoena
B. nutans
Bromelia arenaria
B. humilis
Canistrum cyathiforme
Dyckia brevifolia
D. echoliroides
D. fosteriana
D. tuberosa
Guzmania monostachia
Hoplophytum grande
Neoregelia ampullacea
N. concentrica
N. cruenta
Nidalarium myendorfii
Orthophytum spp.
Puya alpestris
P. berteroniana
P. chilensis
P. copiapina
P. venusta
Quesnelia arvensis
Q. humilis
Q. testudo
Tillandsia aeranthos
T. albita

T. atroviridipetala
T. baileyi
T. balbisiana
T. circinnata
T. disticha
T. festucoides
T. funebris
T. gardneri
T. incarnata
T. ionantha
T. juncea
T. paleacea
T. polystachia
T. recurvata
T. straminea
T. streptocarna
T. tenufolia
T. tenuiloba
T. tricolor
T. usneoides
T. utriculata

CACTACEAE
Bergerocactus emoryi
Carnegiea gigantea
Cereus sp.
C. thurberii
C. peruvianus
Cephalocereus royenii
Chamaecereus sylvestris
Copiapoa cinerea
C. columna-alba
C. ferox
C. haseltoniana
C. lembekei
C. megarhiza
Echinocereus engelmanni
E. fendleri
E. ledigii
E. maritimus
E. triglochidiatus
Echinopsis eyriesii
Eulychnia acida
E. castanea
E. iquiquensis
E. saint-pilana
E. spinebarbis
Ferocactus acanthodes
F. gracilis
F. viridescens
Lobivia sp.
Lophocereus schottii
Machaerocereus gummosus
Mammillaria doica
M. louisea
M. rhodantha
M. tetrancistra
Melocactus intortus
Myrtillocactus cochal
Neochilena chilensis
Nopalea cochinellifera

Notocactus mammulosus
Opuntia acanthocarpa
O. basilaris
O. blakeana
O. bigelovii
O. cylindrica
O. discata
O. echinocarpa
O. ficus-indica
O. fulgida
O. inermis
O. humifusa
O. leptocaulis
O. megacantha
O. occidentalis
O. oricolor
O. ovata
O. phaeacantha
O. polyacantha
O. prolifera
Opuntia puberula
O. ramosissima
O. rubescens
O. strobiliformis
O. versicolor
Pachycereus pringlei
P. mammulosus
Phyllocactus pfersdorffii
Pilocopiapoe solaris
Trichocereus chiloensis
T. coquimbanus
Zygocactus truncatus

CRASSULACEAE
Aeonium haworthii
Bryophyllum calycinum
B. crenatum
B. daigremontiamum
B. fedtschenkoi
B. maculatum
B. pinnatum
B. tubiflorum
Cotyledon ladysmithiensis
C. peacockii
Crassula arborea
C. arborescens
C. argentea
C. lactea
C. macrowaniana
C. multicava
C. pallida
C. tomentosa
Dudleya attenuata
D. cultrata
D. farinosa
D. ingens Rose
D. lanceolata
D. pulverulenta
D. saxosa
Echeveria cilva
E. gibbiflora

E. glauca
E. kircheriana
E. pumila
E. secunda glauca
Kalanchoe beharensis
K. blossfeldiana
K. crenata
K. maculata
K. marmorata
K. verticillata
K. welwitschii
Nanathus malherbi
Rochea falcata
Sedum acre
S. aldofe
S. confusam
S. guatamalense
S. morganiamum
S. pachyphyllum
S. praealtum
S. pulchellum
S. purpurascens
S. purpureum
S. rubrotinctum
S. sexangulare
S. spectabile
S. spurium coccineum
S. tectorum
S. telephium
S. telephoides
Sempervivum arachnoideum
S. montanum
S. solboliferum
S. tectorum
S. wulfenii

CUCURBITACEAE
Xerosicyos perrieri
X. danguyii

DIDIEREACEAE
Alluaudia ascendens
A. humbertii
Didieria trolli

EUPHORBIACEAE
Euphorbia bubalina
E. caducifolia
E. drupifera
E. grandidens
E. nivulia
E. submammillaris
E. tirucalli
E. trigona
E. xylophylloides
Monadenium lugardae
Synadenium capulare

GERANIACEAE
Geranium pratense
Pelargonium crithmifolium

LABIATAE
Plectranthus prostatus

LILIACEAE
Aloe arborescens
A. aristata
A. broomii
A. cymbaefolia
A. globuligermia
A. juvenna
A. millotii
A. spinulosa
A. variegata (hybrid)
A. vera
Gasteria carinata (hybrid)
G. excelsa
G. verrucosa
X Gasterhaworthia tegeliana
X Gasterolea beguinii
Haworthia cuspidata
H. zantneriana
Sansevieria fasciata
S. liberica
S. trifasciata

ORCHIDACEAE
Arachnis spp.
Aranda spp.
Aranthera spp.
Ascocentrum ampullaceum
Brassovola perrini
X Brassolaeliocattleya
  'Maunalani'
Bulbophyllum gibbosum
Cattleya autumnalis
C. bicolor
C. forbesii
C. guttala
C. intermediae
C. labiata
C. loddigessi
C. mossiae
C. skinneri
C. trianaei
C. walkeriana
C. warnerii
Dendrobium taurinum
Encylia atropurpurea
E. flabellifera
E. odoratissima
Epidendrum alatum
E. ellipticum
E. floribundum
E. moseni
E. radicans
E. schomburgkii
Laelia cinnabarina
L. crispa
L. flava
L. milleri
L. perrini

L. purpurata
L. xanthina
Lanium avicula
Oncidium pumilum
Phalaenopsis schilleriana
Pleurothris ophiocephalus
Schomburgki crispa

Sophrontis cernua
Vanilla aromatica
V. fragrans

OXALIDACEAE
Oxalis carnosa

POLYPODIACEAE
Drymoglossum psiloselloides
Pyrrosia longifolia

PORTULACACEAE
Calandrinia grandiflora
C. maritima

Portulacaria afra

VITACEAE
Cissus hypoleuca
C. quadrangularis

WELWITSCHIACEAE
Welwitschia mirabilis

Appendix 4
plant uses

4.1 INDIGENOUS PLANTS USED FOR HUMAN NOURISHMENT

Reference: *Deserts of the World*, McGinnies, Goldman and Paylore, 1970

Genus and species U=Fruit E=Seeds O=Foliage		Deserts where found
Acanthosicyos horrida	U,O	Namib
Adamsonia digitata	U,O	African, Australian
Agriophyllum gobicum	O	Takla-makan
Alhagi maurorum	O	Iranian, Arabian, Sahara
Arjona patagonica	O	Monte–Patagonian
Arthrocnemum glaucum	O	Arabian, Sahara
A. indicum	O	Arabian, Sahara
Balanites aegyptiaca	O	Arabian, Sahara
Capparis spinosa	U,E	Turkestan, Sahara
Cereus giganteus	U	North American
Chenopodium guinoa	E	Atacama–Peruvian
Citrullus vulgaris	U	Sahara, Kalahari–Namib
Condalia microphylla	U	Monte-Patagonian
Eleagnus angustifolia	U	Gobi, Takla-makan, Turkestan, Arabian, Sahara
Erodium hirtum	E	Arabian, Sahara
Glycyrrhiza glabra	O	Turkestan, Iranian, Arabian, Sahara
G. glandulifera	O	Iranian
Hedysarum scoparium	E	Gobi, Turkestan
Hyalis argentea	U	Monte–Patagonian
Kalidium foliatum	O	Gobi
Lycium arabicum	O	Thar, Iranian, Arabian, Sahara
Neocracca heterantha	O	Monte–Patagonian
Nitraria schoberi	O	Gobi, Takla-makan, Thar
N. sibirica	O	Gobi, Takla-makan
Olea europea	U	Arabian, Sahara
Opuntia spp.	U	Mexican, North African
Panicum turgidum	E	Iranian, Arabian, Somali–Chalbi, Sahara
Phoenix dactylifera	U	Iranian, Arabian, Somali–Chalbi, Sahara
Pinus cembroides	E	North American
P. monophylla	E	North American
Pistacia atlantica	U	Arabian, Iranian, Sahara
Poliomintha incana	O	North American
Prosopis alba	U	Monte–Patagonian
Prunus amygdalus	U	Turkestan, Iranian, Arabian, Sahara
Pugionium cornutum	O	Gobi, Takla-makan
Quercus persica	U	Iranian
Ramorinoa girdae	O	Monte–Patagonian
Rumex roseus	O	Arabian, Sahara
Salvadora persica	O	Thar, Arabian, Somali–Chalbi, Sahara
Schinus molle	U	Atacama–Peruvian
Scorzonera judaica	roots	Arabian

Genus and species		Deserts where found
Simmondsia chinensis	E	North American
Solanum acaule	tubers	Atacama–Peruvian
S. verula	tuber	Atacama–Peruvian
Tamarindus indica	U	Thar, Iranian
Ulmus pumila	E	Gobi, Takla-makan
Urtica urens	O	Atacama–Peruvian, Arabian
Zizyphus lotus	U	Arabian, Sahara
Z. mistol	U	Monte–Patagonian
Z. spina-christi	U	Iranian, Arabian, Sahara

4.2 INDIGENOUS PLANTS USED FOR ANIMAL NOURISHMENT

Genus and species		Deserts where found
Acacia albida	O	Arabian, Sahara, Kalahari, Namib
A. aneura	O	Australian
A. aroma	U	Monte–Patagonian
A. brachystachya	O	Australian
A. georginae	O	Australian
A. giraffae	E	Kalahari–Namib
A. kempeana	O	Australian
A. macracantha	U	Atacama–Peruvian
A. pendula	O	Australian
A. sowdenii	O	Australian
Agriophyllum arenarium	O	Gobi, Takla-makan, Turkestan
A. gobicum	O	Takla-makan
Agropyron sibiricum	O	Gobi, Turkestan
A. spicatum	O	North American
Alhagi maurorum	O	Iranian, Arabian, Sahara
Allium mongolicum	O	Gobi, Takla-makan
Anabasis articulata	O	Arabian, Sahara
Argania spinosa	O,U	Sahara
Aristida adscensionis	O	North American, Atacama–Peruvian, Monte–Patagonian, Gobi, Sahara
A. browniana	O,E	Australian
A. californica (syn. *A. adscensionis*)	O	North American
A. contorta	O,E	Australian

Genus and species		Deserts where found
A. inaequiglumis	O,E	Australian
A. latifolia	O,E	Australian
A. pennata	O	Takla-makan, Turkestan
A. plumosa	O	Iranian, Arabian, Sahara
Artemisia frigida	O	North American, Gobi, Takla-makan
A. herba-alba	O	Iranian, Arabian, Sahara
A. tridentata	O	North American
Astrebla elymoides	O,E	Australian
A. lappacea	O,E	Australian
A. pectinata	O,E	Australian
A. squarrosa	O,E	Australian
Atalaya hemiglauca	O	Australian
Atraphaxis frutescens	O	Gobi
Atriplex canescens	O	North American
A. confertifolia	O	North American
A. halimus	O	Arabian, Sahara
A. nummularia	O	Australian
A. polycarpa	O	North American
A. vesicana	O	Australian
Bassia spp.	O	Australian
Bouteloua lophostachya	O	Monte–Patagonian
B. rothrockii	O	North American
B. simplex	O	North American, Monte–Patagonian
Bromus brevis	O	Monte–Patagonian
B. macranthes	O	Monte–Patagonian
Calandrinia balonensis	O	Australian
Calligonum comosum	O	Turkestan, Iranian, Arabian, Sahara
C. mongolicum	O	Gobi, Takla-makan
Caragana microphylla	O	Gobi, Takla-makan
C. stenophylla	O	Gobi, Takla-makan
C. tibetica	O	Gobi
Chenopodium auricomum	O	Australian
Chloris acicularis	O	Australian
Coleogyne ramosissima	O	North American
Condalia lycioides	O	North American
Convolvulus lanatus	O	Arabian, Sahara
Cornulaca monocantha	O	Sahara
Dactyloctenium radulans	O	Australian
Danthonia forskalii	O	Turkestan, Iranian, Arabian, Sahara
Deverra scoparia	O	Sahara
Dyeuxia fulva	O	Atacama–Peruvian
Dioscorea chancayensis	O	Atacama–Peruvian
Distichlis scoparia	O	Kalahari–Namib
D. spicata	O	North American
Eleagnus angustifolia	O	Gobi, Takla-makan, Turkestan, Arabian, Sahara
E. moorcroftii	O	Gobi
Elymus giganteus	O	Turkestan
E. patagonicus	O	Monte–Patagonian
Enneapogon arenaceus	O	Australian
E. polyphyllus	O	Australian
Ephedra nevadensis	O	North American
Eragrostis eriopoda	O	Australian
E. setifolia	O	Australian
Eremobium lineare	O	Arabian, Sahara
Eriachne aristidea	O	Australian
E. helmsii	O	Australian
Eriogonum wrightii	O	North American
Erodium hirtum	O	Arabian, Sahara
E. laciniatum	O	Arabian
Eulalia fulva	O	Australian

Genus and species		Deserts where found
Euphorbia beaumierana	O	North American
Eurotia ceratoides		Gobi, Takla-makan, Sahara
E. lanata	O	North American
Festuca pallescens	O	Monte–Patagonian,
Genista saharae	I	Sahara
Geoffroea decorticans	U	Monte–Patagonian, Atacama–Peruvian
Grayia spinosa		North American
Gymnocarpos przewalskii		Gobi, Takla-makan
Haloxylon ammodendron	O	Gobi, Takla-makan, Turkestan
H. aphyllum	O	Gobi, Turkestan
H. articulatum	O	Iranian Arabian, Sahara
H. persicum	O	Gobi, Takla-makan, Turkestan, Thar, Iranian, Arabian
H. salicornicum	O	Arabian
Hedysarum scopiarum		Gobi, Turkestan
Heterodendron oleifolium	O	Australian
Heteropogon contortus	O	North American
Hilaria jamesii	O	North American
H. mutica	O	North American
H. rigida	O	North American
Hordeum comosum	O	Monte–Patagonian
Indigofera enneaphylla (syn I. linnaei)	O	Australian
Iseilema vaginiflorum	O	Australian
Kalidium foliatum	O	Gobi
Kochia aphylla	O	Australian
K. planifolia	O	Australian
K. pyramidata	O	Australian
K. sedifolia	O	Australian
Lasiurus hirsutus	O	Arabian, Somali–Chalbi, Sahara
Lycium chilense	O	Monte–Patagonian
Muhlenbergia porteri	O	North American
Mulinum spinosum	O	Monte–Patagonian
Myoporum platycarpum	O	Australian
Nassauvia glomerulosa	O	Monte–Patagonian
Olea europea	O,U	Arabian, Sahara
Oxytropis aciphylla	E,O	Gobi
Panicum obtusum	O	North American
P. turgidum	O	Iranian, Arabian, Somali–Chalbi, Sahara
P. virgatum	O	North American
Pennisetum chinense	O	Atacama–Peruvian
Pentzia virgata	O	Kalahari–Namib
Peucedanum rigidum	O	Gobi
Phragmites communis	O	Kalahari–Namib
Pithuranthos tortuosus	O	Arabian, Sahara
Pittosporum phillyraeoides	O	Australian
Plantago ovata	O	Thar, Iranian, Arabian, Sahara
Plectrachne schinzii	O	Australian
Poa bulbosa	U	Turkestan, Iranian, Arabian
P. ligularis	O	Monte–Patagonian
Potaninia mongolica	O	Gobi, Takla-makan
Prosopidastrum globosum	O	Monte–Patagonian
Prosopis alba	E,O	Monte–Patagonian

Genus and species		Deserts where found
P. alpataco	U,O	Monte–Patagonian
P. algorobilla	U	Monte–Patagonian
P. chilensis	O	North American, Atacama–Peruvian, Monte–Patagonian
P. nigra	U	Monte–Patagonian
P. torquata	U	Monte–Patagonian
Psammochloa villosa	E,O	Gobi, Takla-makan, Turkestan
Pugionium cornutum	O	Gobi, Takla-makan
Purshia tridentata	O	North American
Quercus persica	U	Iranian
Rumex roseus	O	Arabian, Sahara
Salsola aphylla	O	Kalahari–Namib
S. collina	I	Gobi, Takla-makan, Turkestan
S. foetida	O	Thar, Iranian, Arabian, Somali–Chalbi, Sahara
S. richteri	O	Turkestan
S. zeyheri	O	Kalahari–Namib
Sarcobatus vermiculatus	O	North American
Schismus barbatus	O	Turkestan, Iranian, Arabian, Sahara
Simmondsia chinensis	E,O	North American
Sporobolus airoides	O	North American
S. cryptandrus	O	North American
Stipa glareosa	O	Gobi, Takla-makan
S. gobica	O	Gobi, Takla-makan
S. hypogona	O	Monte–Patagonian
S. ibari	O	Monte–Patagonian
S. tenacissima	O	Sahara
S. tortilis	O	Turkestan, Iranian, Arabian, Sahara
Suaeda fruticosa	O	Thar, Iranian, Arabian, Somali–Chalbi, Sahara, Kalahari–Namib
S. vermiculata	O	Arabian, Sahara
Themeda australis	O	Australian
Ulmus pumila	U	Gobi, Takla-makan
Ventilago viminalis	O	Australian
Verbena ligustrina	O	Monte–Patagonian
Zizyphus joazerio	U,O	Brazil
Zygophyllum simplex	O	Thar, Arabian, Somali-Chalbi, Kalahari–Namib

4.3 PLANT SPECIES AND MISCELLANEOUS USES

Use	Genus and species	Deserts where found
C=Construction material D=Dye F=Fibre W=Wax G=Gum		
T=Tannin S=Shade and shelter belts R=Rubber O=Oil		
G,T	*Acacia gummifera*	Sahara
C,O,D	*A. harpophylla*	Australian
C,O,S	*A. pendula*	Australian
T,G	*A. seyal*	Arabian, Sahar
F	*Apocynum hendersonii*	Gobi, Turkestan
F	*Agave aboriginum*	American
C	*Balanites aegyptica*	Arabian, Sahara
D	*Bromus brevis*	Monte–Patagonian
D	*B. macranthes*	Monte–Patagonian
C	*Callitris* spp.	Australian
F	*Calotropis procera*	Thar, Arabian, Somali-Chalbi, Sahara
F	*Cassia aphylla*	Monte–Patagonian
F	*C. crassiramea*	Monte–Patagonian
S,C	*Casuarina decaisneana*	Australian
G	*Cercidium australe*	Monte–Patagonian
G	*C. praecose*	Atacama–Peruvian
F	*Crotalaria burhia*	Thar
S	*Cupressus dupreziana*	Sahara
C	*Dalbergia sissoo*	Thar, Iranian
C	*Eleagnus angustifolia*	Gobi, Takla-makan, Turkestan, Arabian, Sahara
C	*E. moorcroftii*	Gobi
F	*Eragrostis binnata*	Iranian, Arabian, Sahara
S,C	*Eucalyptus camaldulensis*	Australian
S,C	*E. largiflorens*	Australian
C	*Euclea pseudebenus*	Kalahari–Namib
G,W	*Euphorbia antisiphylitica*	Kalahari–Namib
F	*Hypheane thebaica*	Arabian
C	*Juniperus excelsa*	Iranian
C	*Juniperus utahensis*	North American
C	*Olea europea*	Arabian, Sahara
C	*Olneya tesota*	North American
D	*Opuntia soehrensii*	Atacama–Peruvian
O	*Pappea capensis*	Kalahari–Namib
R	*Parthenium argentatum*	North American
O,T	*Peganum harmala*	Sahara
F	*Phoneix dactylifera*	Iranian, Arabian, Somali–Chalbi, Sahara
F	*Phragmites communis*	Kalahari–Namib
C	*Pistacia atlantica*	Iranian, Arabian, Sahara
S,C	*Populus alba*	Turkestan, Iranian, Arabian, Sahara
S,C	*Populus diversifolia*	Gobi, Takla-makan, Turkestan
S,C	*Populus euphratica*	Turkestan, Iranian, Arabian, Sahara
S,C	*Populus nigra*	Takla-makan, Turkestan
S,C	*P. simonii*	Gobi, Takla-makan
S,C	*Prosopis alba*	Monte–Patagonian
S,C	*Prosopis ferox*	Atacama–Peruvian
F	*Psammochloa villosa*	Gobi, Takla-makan, Turkestan
O	*Pugionium cornutum*	Gobi, Takla-makan
F	*Salix flavida*	Gobi
C,F	*S. humboldtiana*	Atacama–Peruvian, Monte–Patagonian
C	*Salvadora persica*	Thar, Arabian, Somali–Chalbi, Sahara
G	*Schinus molle*	Atacama–Peruvian
W	*Simmondsia chinensis*	North American
F	*Stipa tenacissima*	Sahara
C,T,S	*Tamarix articulata*	Thar, Iranian, Arabian, Somali–Chalbi, Sahara, Kalahari–Namib
C,S	*T. ramosissima*	Gobi, Takla-makan, Turkestan, Arabian
C	*Trichocereus pasacana*	Atacama–Peruvian
C	*T. terschechii*	Atacama–Peruvian
C	*Ulmus pumila*	Gobi, Takla-makan
F	*Yucca elata*	North American

4.4 PLANTS USED FOR SAND BINDING PURPOSES

Growth forms	Genus and species	Deserts where found
AN=Annual PR=Perennial GR=Grass SH=Shrub TR=Tree		
AN	Agriophyllum arenarium	Gobi, Takla-makan, Turkestan
AN	A. latifolium	Turkestan
PR	Allium polyrhizum	Gobi, Takla-makan
GR	Aristida karelini	Turkestan
GR	A. obtusa	Arabian, Sahara
GR	A. pennata	Takla-makan, Turkestan
SH	Artemisia arenaria	Turkestan
SH	A. filifolia	North American
HSH	A. halodendron	Gobi, Turkestan
PR,SH	A. monosperma	Arabian, Sahara
HSH	A. ordosica	Gobi, Turkestan
HSH	A. sphaerocephala	Turkestan, Kazakhstan
SH	Atraphaxis frutescens	Gobi
SH	Calligonum aphyllum	Takla-makan, Turkestan
SH	C. arborescens	Gobi, Turkestan
SH	C. caput-medusae	Gobi, Turkestan
SH	C. comosum	Turkestan, Iranian, Arabian, Sahara
SH	C. mongolicum	Takla-makan, Gobi
SH	C. zaidamense	Takla-makan
SH	Caragana korshinskii	Gobi, Turkestan
SH	C. microphylla	Gobi, Turkestan
SH	Caryopteris mongholica	Gobi
HSH	Convolvulus fruticosus	Gobi, Turkestan
TR	Eleagnus angustifolia	Takla-makan, Gobi, Turkestan, Arabian, Sahara
TR	E. moorcroftii	Gobi
GR	Elymus giganteus	Turkestan
SH	Ephedra przewalskii	Gobi, Takla-makan
HSH	Eurotia ceratoides	Gobi, Takla-makan, Sahara
SH,TR	Haloxylon ammodendron	Gobi, Takla-makan, Turkestan
SH	H. aphyllum	Gobi, Turkestan
SH,TR	H. persicum	Gobi, Takla-makan, Turkestan, Iranian, Thar, Arabian
SH	Hedysarum scoparium	Gobi, Turkestan
AN	Horaninovia ulicina	Takla-makan, Turkestan
PR	Iris ensata	Gobi, Turkestan
SH	Nitraria sibirica	Gobi, Takla-makan
SH	N. sphaerocarpa	Gobi Takla-makan
GR	Panicum urvilleanum	Monte–Patagonian
GR	Pennisetum chinense	Atacama–Peruvian
SH	Plectrocarpa tetracantha	Monte–Patagonian
SH	Poliomintha incana	North American
TR	Populus diversifolia	Gobi, Takla-makan, Turkestan
TR	P. nigra	Turkestan, Kazakhstan
TR	P. simonii	Gobi, Takla-makan
SH	Prosopis argentina	Monte–Patagonian
SH	P. strombulifera	Monte–Patagonian
GR	Psammochloa villosa	Gobi, Takla-makan, Turkestan
SH	Retama raetam	Arabian, Sahara
SH	Salix caspica	Turkestan
SH	S. flavida	Gobi
SH	S. mongolica	Gobi
SH	S. rubra	Turkestan
SH,TR	Salsola arbuscula	Gobi, Takla-makan, Turkestan
SH	S. collina	Gobi, Takla-makan, Turkestan
SH	S. laricifolia	Gobi, Takla-makan, Turkestan
SH	S. paletzkiana	Gobi, Takla-makan, Turkestan
SH	S. praecox	Gobi, Takla-makan, Turkestan
SH	S. richteri	Turkestan
SH	S. turcomanica	Turkestan
AN	Stilnolepis centiflora	Gobi, Takla-makan
GR	Stipa glareosa	Gobi, Takla-makan
GR	S. gobica	Gobi, Takla-makan
SH	Tamarix laxa	Takla-makan, Turkestan
SH	T. ramosissima	Gobi, Takla-makan, Turkestan, Arabian
SH	Tetraena mongolica	Gobi
TR	Ulmus pumila	Gobi, Takla-makan

4.5 INDIGENOUS PLANTS USED FOR FIREWOOD

Genus and species	Deserts where found
Acacia aneura	Australian
A. furcatispina	Monte–Patagonian
A. georginae	Australian
A. greggii	North American
A. harpophylla	Australian
Artemisia ordosica	Gobi, Turkestan
Caragana microphylla	Gobi, Turkestan
Cercidium floridum	North American
C. microphyllum	North American
C. sonorae	North American
Cupressus dupreziana	Sahara
Haloxylon ammodendron	Gobi, Takla-makan, Turkestan
H. aphyllum	Gobi, Turkestan
H. persicum	Gobi, Takla-makan, Turkestan, Thar, Iranian, Arabian
Hedysarum scoparium	Gobi, Turkestan
Juniperus utahensis	North American
Larrea divaricata	North American, Monte–Patagonian
Monttea aphylla	Monte–Patagonian
Olneya tesota	North American
Parkinsonia aculeata	North American
Pinus cembroides	North American
P. monophylla	North American
Pistacia atlantica	Iranian, Arabian, Sahara
Populus euphratica	Turkestan, Iranian, Arabian, Sahara
Prosopis chilensis	North American, Atacama–Peruvian, Monte–Patagonian
Tetraena mongolica	Gobi
Zizyphus lotus	Arabian, Sahara
Zygophyllum xanthoxylon	Gobi, Takla-makan

4.6 INDIGENOUS PLANTS WITH MEDICINAL USES

Genus and species	Deserts where found
Achillea santolina	Arabian, Sahara
Aerva topmentosa (syn A. javanica)	Thar, Arabian, Somali–Chalbi, Sahara
Alhagi camelorum	Takla-makan, Turkestan, Iranian, Arabian
Aloe dichotoma	Namib
Anabasis articulata	Arabian, Sahara
Artemisia herba-alba	Iranian, Arabian, Sahara
Calotropis procera	Thar, Arabian, Somali–Chalbi, Sahara
Cassia obovata	Thar, Arabian, Somali–Chalbi, Sahara
Citrullus colocynthis	Thar, Iranian, Arabian, Sahara
Cleome chrysantha	Arabian, Sahara
Cymbopogon schoenanthus	Thar, Iranian, Arabian, Somali–Chalbi, Sahara
Dodonaea viscosa	North American, Australian
Ephedra americana	Atacama–Peruvian
E. breana	Atacama–Peruvian
E. multiflora	Atacama–Peruvian
E. nevadensis	North American
E. przewalskii	Gobi, Takla-makan
Euphorbia nereifolia	Thar
Flourensia cernua	North American
Glycyrrhiza glandulifera	Iranian
Hyoscyamus muticus	Thar, Arabian, Sahara
Krameria illuca	Monte–Patagonian
Melianthus comosus	Kalahari-Namib
Nerium oleander	Arabian, Sahara
Opuntia soehrensii	Atacama–Peruvian
Peganum harmala	Sahara
Pithuranthos tortuosus	Arabian, Sahara
Plantago ovata	Thar, Iranian, Arabian, Sahara
Prosopis strombulifera	Monte–Patagonian
Salvadora persica	Thar, Arabian, Somali–Chalbi, Sahara
Schinus molle	Atacama–Peruvian
Tamarindus indica	Thar, Iranian
Tamarix articulata	Thar, Iranian, Arabian, Sahara, Somali–Chalbi
Tanacetum achilleoides	Takla-makan
Urtica urens	Atacama–Peruvian, Arabian
Zygophyllum album	Arabian, Sahara

4.7 PLANTS KNOWN TO BE SIGNIFICANT INDICATORS OF SALINE CONDITIONS

Genus and species	Deserts where found
Allenrolfea occidentalis	North American
Aponcynum hendersonii	Gobi, Turkestan
Arthrocnemum glaucum	Arabian, Sahara
Distichlis spicata	North American
Ephedra przewalskii	Gobi, Takla-makan
Halocnemon strobilaceum	Takla-makan, Turkestan, Arabian, Sahara
Lycium intricatum	Sahara
Nitraria sphaerocarpa	Gobi, Takla-makan
Populus diversifolia	Gobi, Takla-makan, Turkestan
Sarcobatus vermiculatus	North American
Suaeda fruticosa	Thar, Iranian, Arabian, Somali–Chabli, Sahara, Kalahari–Namib
Tamarix ramosissima	Gobi, Takla-makan, Turkestan Arabian

4.8 PLANTS KNOWN TO BE SIGNIFICANT INDICATORS OF PHREATOPHYTIC CONDITIONS

Genus and species	Deserts where found
Alhagi maurorum	Iranian, Arabian, Sahara
Artemisia ordosica	Gobi, Turkestan
A. sphaerocephala	Gobi, Turkestan
Calligonum monogolicum	Gobi, Takla-makan
Calotropis procera	Thar, Arabian, Somali–Chabli, Sahara
Caragana microphylla	Gobi, Turkestan
Eleagnus angustifolia	Gobi, Turkestan, Takla-makan, Arabian, Sahara
Eragrostis binnata	Iranian, Arabian, Sahara
Eucalyptus camaldulensis	Australian
E. largiflorens	Australian
Haloxylon ammodendron	Gobi, Takla-makan, Turkestan
H. aphyllum	Gobi, Turkestan
H. persicum	Gobi, Takla-makan, Turkestan, Thar, Iranian, Arabian
Hedysarum scoparium	Gobi, Turkestan
Hypheane thebaica	Arabian
Iris ensata	Gobi, turkestan
Nitraria schoberi	Gobi, Takla-makan, Turkestan
Phoenix dactylifera	Iranian, Arabian, Somali–Chabli, Sahara
Phragmites communis	Kalahari–Namib
Populus simonii	Gobi, Takla-makan
Prosopis stephaniana	Turkestan, Iranian, Arabian, Sahara
Psammochloa villosa	Gobi, Takla-makan, Turkestan
Salix flavida	Gobi
Sarcobatus vermiculatus	North American
Tamarix articulata	Thar, Iranian, Arabian, Somali–Chalbi, Sahara, Kalahari–Namib
T. ramosissima	Gobi, Takla-makan, Turkestan, Arabian
Thermopsis lanceolata	Gobi, Turkestan

4.9 PLANTS INDICATING OVERGRAZING DISTURBANCE

Genus and species	Deserts where found
Apolopappus fruticosus	North American
Boerhaavia diffusa	Australian, Thar, Sahara
Chenopodium pellidicaule	Atacama–Peruvian
Chenopodium guinoa	Atacama–Peruvian
Dactyloctenium radulans	Australian

ENVIRONMENTAL CONSIDERATIONS FOR AGRICULTURAL DEVELOPMENT

Reference: 'Environmental Health and Human Ecologic Considerations in Economic Development', World Bank, 1974

Ecology

Is the planned development to fall within a climax ecosystem, or within one which is in a state of flux? Has the area undergone man-induced ecological changes? Are the major constituents of the ecosystem known, and how will the project affect them?

Will the project so alter the environment as to preclude its use for other activities, including agricultural uses?

What provisions will be made for restoring borrow pits and other scarred sections of the construction area, by filling, grading, re-seeding or planting to prevent erosion? What are the erosion problems?

Water

If new water sources are to be tapped, what is known of their extent and replenishment?

Will water-logging and soil salinity become a problem, and how will they be handled?

Will the diversion of water to cultivated areas seriously degrade the capabilities of the original water system to support valuable biological species?

What long-range changes, which may be undesirable in the environment, may accompany the irrigation system development?

Social and health considerations

Will changes in the population and/or lifestyle brought about by the project be likely to create environmental, health or social problems?

Will the project be monitored to gauge its effects on the environment, human health and social welfare?

Will food wastes and water cycles aggravate sanitation and disease problems? Has adequate provision been made for sanitation?

Will stored products be the target of insect and rodent pests? Will pesticides and fertilisers be employed? If so, what steps will be taken to minimise their undesirable effects?

Design and planning

Does the design and construction of the project incorporate all the necessary measures to protect environment and health?

Will the project provide for training in the techniques of erosion control, water management, forestry and range management? Will those involved in continuing management and supervision be on the alert for environmental problems?

Does the consolidated development plan take the ecological factors into consideration?

Are such items as road patterns, land excavations, fill sites, refuse disposal activities, *etc.*, planned to minimise damage to the natural environment?

What provisions have been made for monitoring the effects of the development on the environment, and what long-range changes might be expected?

Selected Bibliography

Adams, R. and M. *Making the Desert Bloom. The Architectural Review*, Vol. 161, No. 964: London June 1977

Adams, R. and M. *Technical Considerations on Salinity*, Technical Note No. 24, *Landscape Design* (Journal of the Landscape Institute) No. 114: London May 1976

Arnon, I. *Crop Production in Dry Regions*, Vols. I & II. Barnes and Noble: 1972

Billings, E. *Plants and the Ecosystem*. MacMillan & Co Ltd: 1964

Cloudsley-Thompson, J. L. *Man and the Biology of Arid Zones*. Edward Arnold: 1977

Dalby, D. and Harrison-Church, R. *Drought in Africa*. Centre for African Studies, University of London, 1973

el Khatib, A. B. *Seven Green Spikes*, FAO TF 17, 1973. Ministry of Agriculture, Saudi Arabia

Encyclopaedia Britannica (15th Edition). Encyclopaedia Britannica Inc: Chicago 1974

Environmental Services Division, New South Wales, Australia *Environmental Impact Study of Gold Mining Project in the Great Sandy Desert* (Report). New South Wales 1975

Evanari, M., Shanan, L. and Tadmor, N. *The Negev—The Challenge of the Desert*. Harvard University Press: Cambridge, Mass. 1971

FAO *Crop Water Requirements*, Irrigation & Drainage Paper 24. FAO: 1977 (rev)

FAO *Effective Rainfall*, Irrigation & Drainage Paper 25: 1974

FAO/Unesco *Irrigation, Drainage and Salinity : A sourcebook*. Hutchinson: 1973

FAO *Irrigation Practice and Water Management*, Irrigation & Drainage Paper 1: 1971

FAO *Sandy Soils*, Soils Bulletin 25: 1975

Firmin, R. *Afforestation* (Report to the Government of Kuwait). FAO: Rome 1971

Forestry and Timber Bureau *The Use and Misuse of Trees and Shrubs in the Dry Country of Australia*. Australian Government Publications: Canberra 1972

Geiger, D. *An Approach to Responsible Nutritional and Agricultural Development*. Strategies for Responsible Development: Dayton, Ohio 1976

Grove, A. T. *Africa South of the Sahara*. Oxford University Press: Oxford 1967

Hagan, R. M., Haise, H. R. and Edminster, T. *Irrigation of Agricultural Lands* (No. 11). American Society of Agronomy: Madison, Wisconsin 1967

Heiman, H. *Salt Water Farming, New Scientist*, No. 222: London 1961

Hodge, C., and Duisberg, P. *Aridity and Man*. American Society for the Advancement of Science: Washington, D.C. 1963

Hudson, N. W. *Field Engineering for Agricultural Development*. Clarendon Press: Oxford 1975

Hutchinson, J. *A Botanist in South Africa*. P. R. Gawthorn, London, 1946

Imperial Agriculture Bureau *The Use and Misuse of Shrubs and Trees as Fodder*. Aberystwyth, Wales 1947

Israelson and Hanson *Irrigation Principles and Practices*. Wiley: 1950

Jellicoe, G. & S. *The Landscape of Man*. Thames and Hudson: London 1975

Kelly, K. and Schnadelbach, R. T. *Landscaping the Saudi Arabian Desert*. Delancey Press: Philadelphia 1976

Kendrew, W. G. *The Climate of the Continents*. Oxford University Press: Oxford 1961

Malcolm, C. V. *Plant Collection for Pasture Improvement in Saline Arid Environments*. Western Australia Department of Agriculture: 1969

Malcolm, C. V. and Clarke, A. J. *Plant Collection for Saltland Revegetation and Soil Conservation*. Western Australia Department of Agriculture: 1973

Menshing, H. *Piedmont Plains and Sand Formations in Arid and Humid Tropics and Sub-Tropic Regions*, Zeitschrift für Geomorphologie No. 10. Gebruder Borntraeger: Berlin 1970

Meteorological Office, London:

Meteorological Office Manuscripts

Arabia, 1957 FGZA

Chile, 64445

French North Africa, 1942 36562

Libya, 1973 0114079

North East Africa (63609) 5

North West Africa, 1959 0098886

South Africa, 1975 119385

General Climatic Information

al Kulaib, A. M. *Weather and Climate of Kuwait*. Directorate General of Civil Aviation, Kuwait

Arctic Desert Tropic Information Centre. *Climate and Weather in the Central Gobi of Mongolia* (No. D-101). Air University, Maxwell Air Force Base: Alabama 1951

Arroyo, E. A. *Pluviometrica de las Zonas del Desierto y las Estepas Calidas de Chile*. Universitaria S.A. Santiago (MO 54811)

Flohn, H. *Investigations on the Climate Conditions of the Advancement of the Tunisian Sahara.* World Meteorological Organization: Geneva 1971

Jefferson, M. *The Rainfall of Chile* (Geographical Society No. 7). Oxford University Press: New York 1921

Landsberg, H. E. *World Survey of Climatology.* Elsevier Scientific Pub. Co: New York, 1974

World Meteorological Organization. *Meteorology as related to the Human Environment, No. 2.* Bulletin 312, 1971

Monod, T. *Pastoralism in Tropical Africa.* Oxford University Press (for IAI): 1975

Monyo, Ker and Campbell *Intercropping in Semi Arid Lands,* Symposium at Faculty of Agriculture, Forestry and Vetinary Science, University of Dar es Salaam. IDRC: 1976

National Academy of Sciences, Washington, D.C. *More Water for Arid Lands*: 1974
Underexploited Tropical Plants with Promising Economic Value: 1975

National Institute of Sciences Bulletin *Proceedings of the Symposium of the Rajputana Desert.* India, 1952

Olgay, V. *Design with Climate.* Princeton University Press: New Jersey 1969

Oliver, J. *Evaporation Losses and Rainfall Regime in the Central and Northern Sudan. Weather,* Vol. 20, No. 2, 1965
Proceedings of the Second International Drip Irrigation Conference. San Diego 1974
Proceedings of the Symposium of the Rajpuntana Desert. Bulletin of the National Institute of Sciences: Indiana 1952
Proceedings of the Water Harvesting Symposium, Phoenix, Arizona. U.S. Department of Agriculture: 1974

Russell, E. W. *Soil Conditions and Plant Growth,* 10th edition. Longman: London 1973

Ruthenberg, H. *Farming Systems in the Tropics.* Clarendon Press: Oxford 1971

Second International Drip Irrigation Conference *Proceedings.* San Diego, 1974

Stamp, D. *Asia.* Methuen and Co: London, 1967.

Stoddart, L. A., Smith A. D., Box, T. W. *Range Management,* 3rd edition. McGraw Hill: 1975

Thomas, M. F. and Whittington, G. W. *Environment and Lands Use in Africa.* Methuen and Co: London 1969

Thomas, W. L. (Jnr.) *Man's Role in Changing the Face of the Earth.* University of Chicago Press: 1967

Thorne & Peterson *Irrigated Soils.* McGraw Hill: 1954

Till, M. R. 'Salinity Damage Symptoms', *South Australian Journal of Agriculture,* 1965

United Nations: *Plan of Action to Combat Desertification.* 1977

Unesco *Arid Zone Research : Hydrology.* © Unesco: Paris, 1953 and 1959

U.S. Department of Agriculture *Proceedings of the Water Harvesting Symposium.* Phoenix, Arizona: 1974

U.S. Salinity Laboratory *Saline and Alkaline Soils.* 1954

Van Everdingen, R. O. *The Deeper Groundwater in Libya.* Bulletin of the International Association of Scientific Hydrology, Vol. 8, No. 3, 1962

Willens, A. F. and G. A. 'An Investigation into the Potential Uses of Trickle Irrigation for Desert Reclamation and Fodder Production in the Emirate of Abu Dhabi', *Proc. 2nd Int. Drip Irrigation Congress.* 1974

Willens, A. F., Willens, G. A., Wood P. J. 'An Irrigated Plantation Project in Abu Dhabi' *Commonwealth Forestry Institute Review* 54,2

Willens, G. A. 'Planting in Hot Arid Climates'—Chapter 12 from *Design with Plants* (ed. B. Clouston). Wm. Heinemann: London 1977

Withers and Vipond *Irrigation Design and Practice.* Batsford: 1974

Wyman, D. *Shrubs and Vines for American Gardens.* The Macmillan Company: London 1949

Glossary

Adventitious (buds, shoots, roots): buds, shoots or roots which develop out of order with the normal development of such structures

Aeolian: wind-borne

Aesticladous: having summer leaves

Alluvial: water-borne

Anti-cyclone: a system of winds rotating outwards from a centre of high barometric pressure

Articulate: distinctly-jointed

Basiphyllous: leaves developing at the base of a shoot

Brachyblastic: short-stemmed or with short shoots

C_3 plant: a normal plant which grows and respires according to the standard exhalation of carbon dioxide during the day for photosynthesis, and oxygen during the night for respiration

C_4 plant: a plant that has the ability to close its stomata during the day, thus limiting water loss from its inner tissues. It fixes carbon dioxide at night as malic acid when the stomata are open, and re-forms carbon dioxide in the daytime within the cell for photosynthesis in daylight

Calcrete: deposition of calcium carbonate in crystalline form after the evaporation of moisture in the soil

CAM plants: plants that can select the C_3 or C_4 mode of life according to the prevailing conditions

Carboxylase: the carbon-oxygen reaction in the plant's tissues, whereby carbon dioxide is stored for later use

Chasmophyte: a plant whose roots are capable of penetrating into rock fissures, e.g. *Thymus capitatus*

Chernozem: a black humus-rich soil developed in sub-humid, semi-arid climates and often under grass-covered prairies

Chlorophyll: the green pigment in plants that catalyses foods from sunlight energy, carbon dioxide and water during the process of photosynthesis

Climax: the last stage in plant community development where a state of equilibrium is reached

Coastal upwellings: an upward movement of air when air moves over the sea towards the land

Cretaceous: geological period between 65 and 35 million years ago

Cyclone: a system of winds rotating inwards towards a centre of low barometric pressure

Datum soils: soils selected as standards for reference

Dimorphic: the ability of a plant to generate differently-sized shoots or leaves

Ecosystem: a system of interacting organisms in a particular habitat

Edaphic factors: the controls exerted by the character of the soil

Epidermal cells: external cells

Erosion: the gradual disintegration of the soil surface by chemical or physical weathering

Evapotranspiration: the sum of water loss from both plants and soil measured over a specific area

Field capacity: the moisture content of a soil following ample irrigation or heavy rain after initial free drainage has occurred

Flume: a section of a channel constructed narrower than the main channel, either to control or to measure water flow

Flocculation: the aggregation of soil particles

Frutescent: shrub-like

Geomorphology: the study and interpretation of land-forms

Gypsophyte: a plant that grows on gypsum soils

Halophyte: a plant that grows on saline soils

Hydromorphic soils: soils formed under the influence of water

Hydrology: the study of water in the surface and sub-surface of the Earth

Hydrogeology: the study of the deep reservoirs of water within the Earth's crust and beyond the influence of the hydrological cycle

Hypodermal cells: cells under the external epidermal cells

Insolation: the differential expansion of rock when strongly heated by the sun, causing thin sheets of the rock to split off

Interxylary: the zone between the xylem cells

Isohyet: a line drawn on a map connecting points with equal rainfall

'k' factor: the coefficient of advection measuring the heat transfer by a horizontal flow of air

Lamella: a thin film between cells

Levée: an embankment to prevent river floods

Lignin: a number of waxy substances formed by a plant and deposited on its outer surface collectively known as 'lignin'

Littoral: coastal

Loess: the accumulation of wind-blown dust originally derived from desert areas

Mesophytic plants: plants with no special protection against excessive transpiration growing under average conditions of water supply, intermediate between hydrophytes (water-loving) and xerophytes (drought-tolerant)

Microclimate: the climate of a specific small area close to the soil surface (usually within 2 metres) which often differs from the main climatic pattern

Nematocide: a pesticide developed for use against eel-worms which attack the plant through its roots

Orogeny: a process of major disturbance to the Earth's crust during which mountains are formed

Palaeoalluvial: ancient water-borne material

Palaeoclimatology: the study of ancient climates

Palisade layer: a layer of green plant tissue below the epidermal cells where carbon dioxide fixation during photosynthesis mainly occurs

Petrophyte: a plant able to grow on rocks

Phanerophyte: a flowering plant

Photosynthesis: the process by which plants are able to use the energy of sunlight to create food from carbon dioxide and moisture vapour extracted from the air

Plant ecology: the study of the habitats and life of plants in relation to their environment

Phreatophyte: a plant that indicates the presence of sub-surface water

Pleistocene: geological period 2 million years ago; part of the Quaternary Period

Psammophyte: a plant that grows on sand

Psychroxerophyte: a drought-resistant plant growing in cold territories

Quaternary: the latest geological period, which started 2 million years ago

Rendzina: a thin organic soil having few diagnostic horizons whose main characteristics are dominated by the influence of immediately-underlying calcareous material

Respiration: the process whereby the sugars built up during photosynthesis are broken down by oxidation to produce energy, carbon dioxide and water

Rhizophagolithophyte: a plant that actively dissolves rock by the agency of acids secreted from their roots, enabling subsequent root extension to take place

Salinity: the measure of impregnation of soil or water by chemical salts

Sclerophyllous: hard-leaved (plants), usually evergreen

Sierozem: the driest, light coloured soils of arid regions that have a clear profile differentiation. Their texture is heavily dependent on parent material and is frequently sandy. Silt content commonly exceeds clay, calcium accretions occur at 300–500 mm and gypsum may occur at a depth of 1 metre

Silcrete: the deposition of silica compounds on stones within the soil profile

Solarised soils: sun-affected soils

Solonetz: a solonchak soil which has been leached (washed out) and its calcium salts replaced by very alkaline sodium and magnesium salts. The clay and organic matter particles deflocculate (break down) and are also washed down the soil profile and form hard 'pans' (layers)

Solonchak: intensely saline soils usually formed on calcareous soils where the water table is high or drainage is impeded

Stomata: minute pores in the epidermis, usually of leaves, through which gaseous exchange of moisture, carbon dioxide and oxygen takes place. Changes in turgidity of the two guard cells surrounding each pore, open and close it, so regulating the exchange

Suffrutescent: sub- or under-shrubs

Takyr: a saline lake-bed soil with a slippery surface crust

Tertiary: a geological period 7 to 65 million years ago

Thermophyllous: leaves of plants that are sensitive to heat.

Transpiration: the loss of water vapour from land plants through their stomata

Xerophytism: the ability of a plant to withstand dry conditions

Xylem: thickened cells that transport water and mineral salts to tissues inside the plant, and support the plant

Index